From Theology to Social Theory

American University Studies

Series VII
Theology and Religion

Vol. 73

PETER LANG
New York • Bern • Frankfurt am Main • Paris

Marsha Aileen Hewitt

From Theology to Social Theory

Juan Luis Segundo and the Theology of Liberation

PETER LANG
New York • Bern • Frankfurt am Main • Paris

Library of Congress Cataloging-in-Publication Data

Hewitt, Marsha
    From theology to social theory : Juan Luis Segundo
and the theology of liberation / Marsha A. Hewitt.
        p. cm. — (American university studies. Series VII,
Theology and religion ; vol. 73)
        Includes bibliographical references.
        1. Liberation theology—History of doctrines.
2. Segundo, Juan Luis—Contributions in liberation
theology.   I. Title   II. Series: American university
studies. Series VII, Theology and religion ; v. 73.
BT83.57.H47   1990   230'.2'092—dc20   89-28143
ISBN 0-8204-1258-9   CIP
ISSN 0740-0446

CIP-Titelaufnahme der Deutschen Bibliothek

Hewitt, Marsha Aileen:
From theology to social theory : Juan Luis
Segundo and the theology of liberation / Marsha
Aileen Hewitt. — New York; Bern; Frankfurt
am Main; Paris: Lang, 1990.
    (American University Studies: Ser. 7, Theology
    and Religion; Vol. 73)
    ISBN 0-8204-1258-9

NE: American University Studies / 07

Printed by Weihert-Druck GmbH, Darmstadt, West Germany

". . . non-conforming thought and action are crying needs in Christendom today; . . . in this context we must not be afraid of pursuing what may turn out to be détours or even false trails. Freedom cannot be defended without risk and experiment."

—Ernst Käsemann

Table of Contents

Preface

Perhaps the most compelling aspect of the theology of Juan Luis Segundo lies in his extensive and sustained dialogue with some of the major cultural and political thinkers of the nineteenth and twentieth centuries. Especially since the publication of his book, *The Liberation of Theology* in the mid-nineteen seventies, his main intellectual interlocutors are not primarily theologians, but rather figures such as Gregory Bateson, Sigmund Freud, Max Weber, Vladimir Lenin, George Luckács, and most importantly, Karl Marx. Segundo's intellectual curiosity has taken him into many areas of general political and cultural theory, which he draws upon by way of re-thinking the role of Christianity and its potential contribution to the liberation of the Latin American people.

This re-thinking has led Segundo to a critical evaluation of not only Christianity, but of religion in general, as an ideological and cultural formation which possesses its own contradictory social potential. Segundo confronted that contradictory potential and as a result re-defined Christianity and religion as ideology, which has taken him into a further consideration of their political nature, and how they may function in support or negation of the *status quo*. In this respect Segundo's work is a contribution to the study of religion itself, as well as to Christianity in the Latin American context, with its potential for social and political transformation.

The goal of this book is to offer a critical assessment of Segundo's dialogue with those non-theological intellectual traditions that have been important influences on his thought. My intention is to analyze the meaning and implications of these influences on Segundo's theology. Both Segundo and liberation theology have been touched by some of the main currents of our time whose primary interest is the emancipation of human beings from all forms of alienation and oppression. I have also tried to identify some of the more serious contradictions and problems Segundo opens in his effort to transform theology into a practical force for social change partly as a way of assessing how adequate any theology is to this task.

Despite the enormous problems Segundo runs into in his dialogue with his chosen interlocutors, the questions he raises confront Christian theology with an unavoidable and necessary challenge, which has not yet been fully met: the historical project of making the world a better place. In this sense

Segundo is participating in the general effort to transform theology from within that is also demonstrated by liberation theology in all its variations, such as feminist liberation theology, Black liberation theology or *Minjung* theology. All these theological enterprises share a common goal: the realization of human freedom. Just how adequate theology is to this struggle remains to be seen, as it also remains to be seen what impact this process will have on theology itself. Juan Luis Segundo is one of the few theologians — if not the only one — who has implicitly addressed the issue of what happens to theology when it makes a serious attempt to become itself a practical, emancipatory social theory and practice. Part of the purpose of this book is to clarify and analyze this problem by exploring some of the inner directions and logic of Segundo's thought.

There are always many people who, in a variety of ways, participate in the making of a book. In particular, I wish to thank Charles Davis, one of the most humane and encouraging people I have ever known. Our many hours spent in discussion of this work were immensely valuable in helping me to develop my ideas in an atmosphere that was always supportive, and never intrusive. I also thank Fred Bird for his many helpful suggestions; Donald Wiebe, for reading the manuscript carefully and his general support of it; Victoria Pinnington, who patiently and expertly typed, re-typed and did all the computer work necessary for a presentable text. I am grateful to her and to Katherine McCallum, who have both been a steady source of support. Slobodan Drakulic, my husband, discussed almost every aspect of the book with me and pushed me to clarify and sharpen the argument.

This book is dedicated to Justin Nicholas, whose birth occurred while the last pages of the text were about to be completed.

Toronto, Canada
August, 1989.

My sincere thanks to Vanier College, Montreal, for its support in making the publication of this book possible.

INTRODUCTION

... there must be made available to all men everything necessary for leading a life truly human, such as food, clothing, and shelter; the right to choose a state of life freely and to found a family, the right to education, to employment, to a good reputation, to respect, to appropriate information, to activity in accord with the upright norm of one's own conscience, to protection of privacy and to rightful freedom in matters religious too.

Hence, the social order and its development must unceasingly work to the benefit of the human person if the disposition of affairs is to be subordinate to the personal realm and not contrariwise, as the Lord indicated when He said that the Sabbath was made for man, and not man for the Sabbath.

This social order requires constant improvement. It must be founded on truth, built on justice, and animated by love; in freedom it should grow every day toward a more humane balance. An improvement in attitudes and widespread changes in society will have to take place if these objectives are to be gained.

—*Pastoral Constitution on the Church in the Modern World*
(Gaudium et Spes), n. 26.

There are several points of view about the actual genesis of Latin American liberation theology, and the conditions and influences out of which it developed. However, most of the exponents and critics of liberation theology identify Vatican II, with its spirit of openness to the modern world and its orientation to "the whole of humanity" (*Gaudium et Spes*, n. 2) as exerting the single, most pervasive impact on the emergence of the theology of liberation. The Council's statements of concern with the extreme social and economic problems facing millions of human beings in the world, and its recognition of the need for profound changes in society was particularly important for those Latin American theologians and lay Christians who were involved in active efforts to improve the steadily deteriorating material conditions affecting most of Latin America. Gustavo Gutierrez, the Peruvian theologian who wrote the first systematic account of the theology of liberation, explains in that book that: "It [liberation theology] is a theological reflection born of the experience of shared efforts to abolish the current unjust situation and to build a different society, freer and more humane." [1]

The various initial steps toward the creation of what came to be known as liberation theology in Latin America converged in the Second General Conference of the Latin American Episcopal Council (CELAM II) assembled at Medellin, Columbia, in 1968. The most significant result of the

Medellin conference was that the concept of liberation was adopted as a practical, political goal for Latin American society. Medellin also established the language of liberation as a permanent feature of theological discourse in Latin America. Furthermore, the theme of liberation and theology is now widely debated, from different perspectives, in many countries throughout the world. The Medellin conference was understood as giving concrete form and application to the direction taken at Vatican II, within the Latin American context, along with a clear commitment to liberation.[2] The second Vatican Council, and in particular its document *Gaudium et Spes*, was a motivating force in the struggle for social change for many priests, bishops and theologians in Latin America even prior to Medellin. The movement of "Priests for the Third World," founded in 1965-66, for example, was directly inspired by *Gaudium et Spes*, which was interpreted as an articulation of the theme of liberation.[3] But it was at Medellin where the theology of liberation, with its self-conscious practical commitment to the historical liberation of Latin America, actually emerged. Medellin in part provided the vehicle whereby Latin American theologians radicalized and sharpened the themes of social justice articulated at Vatican II, and yet were able to develop a theology that was not heterodox. The liberation theologians of Latin America, while perhaps going much farther in their interpretations of Vatican II than the Council itself ever intended, claim their theology rests solidly within the tradition of Vatican II. Thus Medellin became, as it were, the radicalizing force of Vatican II through the application of Council statements to the specific conditions of Latin America:

> The documents approved by the bishops at Medellin had an extraordinary impact. The reason is that, although they assume the stance already laid out by the Council's Pastoral Constitution of the Church in the Modern World . . . they transform it in the direction of more radical and more explicit criticism of the injustices of Latin American society and politics. . . . The impression created by Medellin was of a church suddenly awake to its moral responsibilities, now preparing to mobilize its considerable resources for the pursuit of social justice and peace.[4]

It was in this general context of the shift within the Catholic church produced by Vatican II, along with the growing sense of urgency felt by many Christians about the economic immiseration affecting the majority of Latin Americans as well as the increased political repression[5] that was spreading throughout most Latin American countries, that the theology of liberation was born.

However, it is not my intention to examine in detail the historical conditions which gave rise to the theology of liberation. My interest is rather to probe a more fundamental question: what *is* the theology of liberation? In my view, liberation theology is not yet fully understood, neither by its sympathizers nor its opponents. Most accounts of liberation theology, especially by authors outside Latin America, describe its main features, explain its basic suppositions and themes and how they relate to the basic doctrines of Christian belief. While this kind of exposition is necessary, is has by now become somewhat repetitive. Most North Americans who are interested in liberation theology and are to some extent informed about it are quite familiar with its 'preferential option for the poor', the central place of the Exodus narrative, its use of the Old Testament prophets to underline God's commitment to justice, and its reading of the synoptic gospels as evidence of the solidarity of Jesus with the victims of oppression and suffering. Most approaches to liberation theology are faith-oriented and theological.

However, the meaning of the theology of liberation goes much farther than a basic commitment to social justice and holds more profound implications that have not yet been explored. This is understandable to some extent, since liberation theology is not a finished, internally consistent theory. It has not yet fully developed its own methodology, but more importantly, it has not yet come to grips with its own internal contradictions. One of these contradictions has to do with the fact that as a theology that attempts to have a concrete impact on history and society, it must thoroughly situate itself theoretically *in* history and society. It must, and does, adopt historical, social, political and economic categories of analysis in order to understand the complex problems that exist, and which oppress the majority of human beings on this planet.

What a theology of liberation must do, and cannot avoid, is to open itself to the insights of human experience gained from the social sciences, and in particular, from social theory. In short, this theology must, and indeed does to some extent, embrace secular thought and discourse in order to construct an adequate analysis of reality which is the first step toward concrete change. And the question is, how can theology be adequate to this enormous task, and yet remain theology? By theology, I mean theology in its classical definition, whose staring point is the conscious, methodical explanation of divine revelation, received and grasped in faith. In this sense, theology is understood as the science of faith. Liberation theology's first concern is not with developing theology in this way, but rather with constructing a "science" of society, history, politics, and economics. If this is so, how can a theology, however critical or progressive, seek to become a practical, emancipatory force in the historical process without transforming itself utterly into a theory that is not theology in its classical definition? This is an urgent question that most liberation theologians do not raise, and in not doing so, fail to confront one of the deepest contradictions inherent in liberation theology. If this theoretical contradiction remains hidden and unexplored, the danger is that liberation theology will self-destruct from within, and become relegated to the status of a geographically and culturally limited form of theology that missed its historical opportunity: to transform all of Christian theology and bring it into history as a progressive, emancipatory force.

There is a notable exception to this, however, and that is Juan Luis Segundo, a Uruguayan Jesuit priest whose later works begin to identify, and to some extent develop the broader and more radical implications of liberation theology. More than any other liberation theologian, it is Segundo who confronts the major secular thought of the nineteenth and twentieth centuries, and in particular, the thought of Karl Marx. In this book, I will look closely at his debate with Marx, which is crucial to Segundo's thinking, and develop a critical analysis of the impact of Marx on his work. This kind of study has not been done on any liberation theologian, and is long overdue. Segundo recognizes clearly, along with Clodovis Boff, that *"since Marx, it is no longer permissable to theologize as before with regard to social problems.* And to the extent that theology continues to ignore an etiological approach to these problems, this critique will be justified . . . The touchstone of the authentic response of theology to this critique will be whether it will be able to accept the truth it contains without losing out entirely."[6]

With this statement, Boff identifies the crux of the problem facing contemporary theology. But it is Juan Luis Segundo who attempts to explore this problem directly through a transformation of the methodological, theoretical structure of theology itself. In doing this, Segundo draws liberation theology much closer to a critical social theory and away from theology *per se*. Indeed, Gustavo Gutierrez declares that liberation theology self-consciously aspires to be a "critical theory" insofar as it is a "critical reflection" that is "indissolubly linked to historical praxis."[7] As far as Gutierrez is concerned, the statement by the Peruvian socialist Jose Carlos Mariatequi, that, "The ability to think history and the ability to make it become one,"[8] is perfectly valid for a critical theology.

For the theology of liberation, what is ultimately important is the making of history, rather than its interpretation.[9] When Marx asserted in his famous thesis eleven on Feuerbach that philosophers have only interpreted the world, whereas the real point of human activity is to change it, he was also announcing the end of classical and idealist philosophy. When liberation theology makes an identical claim for itself (since making history *is* to change the world), it also announces the end of theology in its traditional, classical form. Whether liberation theology is explicitly conscious of this or not, is beside the point. Part of the reason for this book, is to render this implication explicit.

The notion of theory as a practical, effective force with the potential of producing concrete historical and social change, is a basic presupposition of critical theory, an inclusive term for a whole range of intellectual pursuits associated with the Frankfurt Institute of Social Research,[10] founded in 1923. The 'Frankfurt School', as it came to be known, was made up of philosophers, literary critics, sociologists, psychologists, economists and political scientists such as Max Horkheimer, Theodor Adorno, Walter Benjamin, Herbert Marcuse, Erich Fromm, and others, who were influenced by the philosophical and anthropological views of the early Marx, which they developed further into a critical theory of culture and society that was based upon an explicit emancipatory interest. I refer to the Frankfurt School insofar as it provides a theoretical reference point for analyzing the critical methodology of Juan Luis Segundo, which shares both explicitly and implicitly, certain general basic traits with critical theory. I will go even further, concurring with Dennis McCann, that Juan Luis Segundo is "more of a social theorist"[11] than a theologian. In order to explain what I mean by the preceding statement, I will quote briefly from an essay by Max Horkheimer, whose definition of critical theory is relevant for understanding the theological method of Segundo. If Segundo's methodological writings are read in the light of critical theory Segundo's work becomes more intelligible. According to Horkheimer, the "real" task of theory is to expose the contradictions within society, not simply for the purpose of describing the concrete historical situation, but in order that theory should act itself as a "force . . . to stimulate change."[12] Critical theory embodies a consciously critical attitude toward society that struggles to change the course of history: "Every part of the theory presupposes the critique of the existing order and the struggle against it along lines determined by the theory itself."[13] Thus critical social theory is understood as a practical, transformative activity with an emancipatory intent. Liberation theology aspires, in an equally self-conscious way, to the same goal: to act as a practical activity oriented toward liberation. Both critical theory and liberation theology utilize a similar methodology in relation to the question of history, social change, and human emancipation.

Segundo reiterates a basic principle of critical theory when he writes that,

> The most progressive theology in Latin American is more interested in *being liberative* than in *talking about liberation*. In other words, liberation deals not so much with content as with the method used to theologize in the face of our real-life situation.[14]

And further: "I maintain that not one single dogma can be studied with any other final criterion than its impact upon praxis."[15]

Statements such as these show that Juan Luis Segundo is attempting to construct a critical theological method, which is close to a critical social theory, and although is intended to apply specifically to the particular conditions of Latin America, in fact has a universal dimension possessing implications for the whole of theology. Segundo's methodological approach situates theology within the flux and relativity of the historical process, so that theology occupies a place which is dialectically related to the demands and conditions of each historical period. The result is a theory that is partial, open-ended and provisional. Furthermore, any truth claims put forward from the perspective of such a theory are in like fashion, partial, open-ended and provisional. Segundo claims that this approach to theology and its relationship to history is in line with Jesus' own theological perspective which Segundo sees as illustrated in Jesus' dispute with the Pharisees about the meaning and importance of 'signs from heaven' or 'signs of the times'.

> It is here that we begin to glimpse the different understanding of signs that underlies the two different theologies. The theology that requires 'signs from heaven' is interested in knowing whether the concrete happenings in question, the very same ones to which Jesus alludes, proceed from God without any doubt at all or could possibly proceed from the devil. Jesus' theology of signs replies with a boldness that scientific Christian theology has lost completely. For all practical purposes it says that the sign in itself is so clear-cut that even if it is the devil who is liberating these people from their afflictions, it is because the kingdom of heaven has already arrived and is in your midst. Thus Jesus' theology completely rules out applying any theological criterion to history *except the direct and present evaluation of happenings here and now.*[16]

At this point, I wish to draw to the reader's attention that I do not focus upon Segundo's earlier five-volume series, *A Theology for the Artisans of a New Humanity,* since it is more practical and pastoral in its orientation and intent, and reflects a rather traditionalist methodology in relating

Christianity to the concerns of daily life. His later work, generally from 1976 on, reflects a critical sharpness and more profound theoretical approach which more systematically develops the methodology of liberation theology. Segundo addressed the "Artisans" volumes to "mature" Christians who are "looking for a theology which is equally adult."[17] *A Theology for the Artisans of a New Humanity* originated as a series of lectures designed for seminar courses for adult education, which took place over three-to-four-day periods, structured in a lecture/discussion format. The purpose of these courses was to reach the "busy layman," who was probably a middle-class urban dweller experiencing a crisis of faith insofar as he/she did not feel his/her Christian faith to be relevant to daily life concerns. With the publication of *The Liberation of Theology*, however, Segundo's writing and the audience for whom it is intended shifts quite noticeably. Here, Segundo begins to define liberation theology and its methodology and his audience is clearly not restricted to Latin Americans: Segundo is writing for North Atlantic readers with some degree of higher education, but also, for academic theologians. In *The Liberation of Theology*, a much more intellectually ambitious book, Segundo enters into critical dialogue with a wide range of groups and individual thinkers, such as the European political theologians, Christian Democrats, "academic" theology, Black liberation theology, Max Weber, Karl Marx, and many others too numerous to cite here. Segundo discusses these groups and writers with varying degrees of critical force, all the while defining liberation theology and giving it a particular direction, making an important contribution to the development of this theology. With *The Liberation of Theology*, Segundo shifts his focus from pastoral concerns, to a methodological development of a critical theology of liberation the implications of which are relevant far beyond Latin America and the third world. I would argue that *The Liberation of Theology* marks a kind of turning point in Segundo's career, wherein he attempts to bring not only liberation theology but *Christianity itself* to the level of a critical theory of society that can act as a force for social change. I do not think it would be excessive to say further, that Segundo implicitly goes through and beyond a theology of liberation to expose the possibility of Christianity becoming a dynamic force in the historical process of social change. In so far as Segundo opens up these questions and gives some indication of their implications, he stands as one of the most significant Latin American theologians writing today. This aspect of Segundo's thought does not really appear with critical force until *The Liberation of Theology*.

One striking aspect of the appearance of *The Liberation of Theology* was that it was published just four years after Gustavo Gutierrez's *Teologia de la liberacion, Perspectivas*, or *A Theology of Liberation*, the first major effort by a Latin American theologian to define liberation theology. There, Gutierrez stated the purpose of his book in this way:

> Let us ourselves be judged by the Word of the Lord, to think through our faith, to strengthen our love, and to give reason for our hope from within a commitment which seeks to become more radical, total, and efficacious. It is to reconsider the great themes of the Christian life within this radically changed perspective and with regard to the new questions posed by this commitment. This is the goal of the so-called *theology of liberation*.[18]

With *A Theology of Liberation*, Gutierrez gave shape to the theoretical and methodological parameters of Latin American liberation theology. It is regarded as a classic statement and definition of liberation theology to the present time; however, it is not the last word by any means. Nor do I think Gutierrez intended it as such.

Segundo's *The Liberation of Theology* represents in part an implicit critique of Gutierrez, a fact which is manifested in its very title, which reverses the title of Gutierrez's *A Theology of Liberation*. The title of Gutierrez's book could be understood to imply a theology whose central concern is with the *theme* of liberation. The formulation, "a theology of liberation" can refer to a new or separate branch of theological study about the meaning of human liberation within history that could perhaps coexist with other theological disciplines. I want to be perfectly clear that in writing this, I intend to make no definitive critical statements about Gutierrez. My interest is in Segundo, and the critique of Gutierrez he implied when he wrote *The Liberation of Theology*. Segundo elaborated upon this critique of Gutierrez in a lecture delivered at Regis College, Toronto:

> We were not interested at all in creating a new kind of branch of theology that *spoke of liberation*, or in making liberation the explicit center of the whole of theology, instead of any other theological theme. In this sense, the title this theological trend received after Gustavo Gutierrez's famous book *A Theology of Liberation* made us perhaps quite fashionable, but helped also to distort to some extent our aim. . . .[19]

Segundo's intention is not to write or theorize *about* liberation; he instead seeks to liberate theology, and construct a theology that is by its very nature *liberative*. The obvious question, is, however, from what must theology be liberated? In my view, Juan Luis Segundo seeks to liberate theology *from* the strictly metaphysical, *to* the thoroughly historical and political realm of human experience. In other words, Segundo seeks to liberate theology from itself, in the sense of breaking down the distinctions between the meta-physical and historical planes of reality, with the result that all reality and human experience is situated within the historical and social realm of existence. It is Segundo's overriding concern with the "real-life questions"[20] of the contemporary historical period which leads him to dismiss excessive preoccupations with theological orthodoxy as relating to the "magical." For him, praxis must be prior to theory, or theory is in itself useless: "Any orthodoxy that does not essentially point toward orthopraxy is magical."[21] He understands "orthopraxy" to represent a dynamic interaction of theory and praxis, which is understood as a practical, transformative activity with the goal of liberation. Theology is relegated to a secondary status because by its nature *as* theology, it can only function as a reflection upon praxis.

Segundo's understanding of the theology/practice relationship closely parallels the understanding of the connection between theory and practice in critical theory, as I have already argued. The methodological principles of critical theory provide a means of locating Segundo within a theoretical context that allows a fuller understanding of what he is attempting to achieve in the area of theology. In similar fashion to the critical theorists of the Frankfurt School, Segundo is engaged in constructing a critical theology/theory of society, which itself aspires to be a dynamic, practical activity with an emancipatory goal, within history. But can Segundo achieve this without inevitably dissolving theological categories into those of critical social theory?

The central focus of any theology is God, or Transcendence, whether it be with God's relationship to humanity and human history, nonetheless it is God. Segundo's methodology presupposes a shift in focus, from Transcend-ence to history, society and politics. Consequently, Segundo's thought moves into different categories of analysis and concepts, and thus inevitably passes over to a different order of truth. Herbert Marcuse's description of the transition from Hegel's philosophy to Marx's social theory provides an apt and pertinent analogy for what Segundo is attempting in the area of theology: "His [Hegel's] system brought philosophy to the threshold of its negation and thus constituted the sole link between the old and the new form of critical theory, between philosophy and social theory."[22] In other words, the theology of liberation as Segundo develops it, may well represent a transitional phase or process within theology itself, from the "old" or classical theology to a "new" kind of Christianity as a transformative, emancipatory force within history. And herein lies the deeper meaning of liberation theology—its promise to both expose and release the liberative power of Christianity as a negative force of the existent state of affairs in history and society. Segundo is able to move liberation theology in this direction partly as a result of the profound impact of Marx on his thinking. In fact, Segundo's critical methodology owes a great deal to the theory of Marx and is particularly influenced by Marx's eleventh thesis on Feuerbach which I will now quote in full: "The philosophers have only interpreted the world, in various ways; the point, however, is to change it." It is precisely in the key of the eleventh thesis on Feuerbach, for example, that Segundo interprets Jesus' theological dispute with the Pharisees in which Jesus counters their demand for a sign from heaven, with his own insistence on discerning the signs of the times. In fact, the eleventh thesis on Feuerbach permeates the methodological approach of Segundo's theology.

I must admit that in writing this book, I have not always been completely comfortable referring to Segundo's later work as theology, nor even in classifying Segundo as a liberation theologian, although it is in this latter category that he most precisely fits. To call Segundo a "liberation theologian" could be misleading, giving the impression that Segundo, like many others, theologizes *about* liberation. It is clear by now that Segundo does not see himself in this way; perhaps it would be more accurate to refer to Segundo as a "liberatory theologian," that is, a theologian whose immediate emancipatory interest is to liberate theology from the metaphysical to the historical and political realm of human existence, as I indicated earlier. Nonetheless, the question remains, whether Segundo can still be called a *theologian* as such, since in the works under study here, his preoccupation is not with God, nor religious concepts, but with humanity and society, and the historical project of liberation.

One of the ways in which Segundo approaches these themes involves an analysis of the meaning of values and their relationship to human action. Segundo's interest in values is concerned with their motivating power in history, whereby people act to change their concrete situation and achieve freedom. For Segundo, faith in particular *human* values motivates people to devise ideologies whereby those values may be rendered effective in the historical process of liberation. It is the historical process that moves toward human liberation through social change that is the urgent concern of Segundo, and is (to use his own terminology) the "key" in which he approaches theology. His approach to Jesus of Nazareth, for example, is almost entirely in this key. The meaning of Jesus' actions and words, for Segundo, is to be found almost exclusively in those human values he represented and acted upon. Segundo emphasizes that Jesus was a man of his times, and was interested in the concrete needs of human beings in their particular situation. In his view, Jesus' assertion that the Sabbath was made for man is an example of Jesus' concern with the primacy of human welfare over religious concerns and demands. It is Jesus' life, words and deeds, which interest Segundo much more than his substantive relationship to God. Segundo's preoccupation with social change leads him to focus much more on Jesus the man, than Jesus as Christ. Segundo marginalizes the significance of those strictly theological aspects of Jesus in order to emphasize the human, historical Jesus and the values he represented. The following passage from *The Historical Jesus of the Synoptics* is a clear statement of Segundo's approach to "christology", or what he prefers to call "antichristology".

> Jesus was an ordinary human being. He had no religious title whatsoever. He was just another layman in the religiously structured society of Israel, a common craftsman (to specify his social status). At a certain point in his life his words and deeds began to attract attention, then adherence or rejection. As a result of the adherence or rejection, both his partisans and his detractors reached conclusions about *what* he was. It would be not only anachronistic but terribly wrongheaded, however, to fashion a discourse about *who or what* Jesus is for people today who, in the ordinary course of their existence, would have no interest whatsoever in him. By that I mean people who, if the exact same events were to recur again today, would pass them by as a curious happening that held no interest for them.
>
> The basic, noteworthy fact is that we have nothing *directly* from Jesus of Nazareth. He *always* reaches us already *interpreted* by persons or groups *interested* in him. That means that we have no access to him except through *those interests* in one way or another.
>
> Time and again academic christology assumes that interest in Jesus is aroused when people, in some more or less confused and inchoate way, recognize him to be God or, at least, an envoy close to God. The presupposition of the *antichristology* I propose to offer here is exactly the opposite. If people came face to face with a specific, limited human being, ambiguous as everything involved in history is, and came to see him as God or a divine revelation, it was because that human being was of interest, and humanly significant. And if people today arrive at the same final vision of him today, it will only be because the latter fact is verified again: that is, because he is of interest and humanly significant to them.[23]

This quotation is a striking example of Segundo's methodology and its implications when applied to christology. The result is Segundo's claim that he is constructing an "antichristology." Perhaps, then, and in all seriousness, Segundo's theology might be referred to as "antitheology." However it is, Segundo divests the ministry of Jesus of theological meaning, and instead offers an interpretation of Jesus that focuses upon the political and also ethical dimension of his life. Segundo focuses on those human values that Jesus embodied and expressed ideologically, which is to say, in a language which always took account of, and was relevant to, his own historical context. Jesus' stress upon the love of the neighbour,and his interventions in people's lives in order to alleviate their human distress, illustrates the ethical dimension of Jesus' actions. This aspect of Jesus' ministry is important for Segundo, who is also concerned with the ethics of social change, as well as the change itself. Social change must always be directed toward the well-being of human beings, and exactly in their material circumstances. For Segundo, the theme of liberation is both a political and ethical category, political because social change can only occur through human effort, and ethical because praxis must always express values relating to human welfare. The ethics and the praxis of human beings involved in the process of realizing their own liberation must be expressed, for Segundo, through historically relevant ideologies.

Ideology is a key concept in Segundo's methodology, and in this respect he is unique among liberation theologians. He is convinced that a popular ideology must emerge in Latin America whereby those values which are oriented toward human welfare and freedom in history may be effectively realized. For Segundo ideology is not simply a theory or world view but necessarily implies a dynamic, practical activity through which human beings produce concrete changes within their society. Segundo knows, however, that ideologies can work the other way, to support and maintain those social and political structures of domination and exploitation. He also knows that in the Latin American context, Christianity continues to be the prevailing popular ideology accepted by the majority of Latin Americans. Segundo, along with other Latin American theologians, acknowledges the fact that certain sectors of the church, for whatever motive, have historically sided with the ruling elites of Latin America, with the effect of working against the interests of the Latin American people.[24] In this sense, Christianity can function as ideology in the pejorative sense, as a form of false consciousness that justifies the status quo of an unjust and exploitative social order. On the other hand, Segundo claims that Christianity, under certain conditions, may be transformed into ideology which is a progressive and emancipatory force for human liberation. Segundo can only make this argument on the premise that religion per se, of course, including Christianity, is ideology, a claim that no other Christian theologian would easily make. This premise allows Segundo to use ideology against ideology, in much the same fashion, for example, that Lenin advocated socialist ideology over against bourgeois ideology. Liberation theology thus attempts to become an ideology-critique of Christianity, exposing its regressive elements as part of the process of its self-transformation into a liberative theology. Such a theology cannot exist as another theological discipline "dominated by scholarly experts."[25] This theology must inevitably seek to abolish the existent theology and replace it entirely.

For Segundo, ideology – that is, the correct ideology – is essential to the historical project for human liberation. By correct ideology, I do not mean that Segundo proposes a closed, rigid orthodoxy, worked out to the last detail, and which demands slavish support from its own advocates. Segundo is aware that in order to be effective, ideologies must be flexible enough to adapt to the particular demands and conditions of a given historical situation. The only absolute feature of ideologies must be a permanent commitment to liberation. Thus the content of ideologies must reflect the particular demands of the context in which they exist, and strive to actualize the absolute values pertaining to human freedom. In my view, what Segundo would propose as an appropriate ideology for bringing change to Latin America would involve a practical Christian ethics of the love of the neighbour directed toward the liberation of human beings from all forms of alienation.

Furthermore, what Segundo envisions as a more humane society in Latin America does not necessarily involve a revolutionary struggle, but a change in the existing socio-political structures which would resemble a kind of social democracy or state capitalism, which is what Segundo means by "socialism": "By 'socialism' . . . I simply mean a political regime in which the ownership of the means of production is taken away from individuals and handed over to higher institutions whose main concern is the common good."[26] Here he proposes a definition of socialism that is implicitly reminiscent of Lenin's view of the state as the mechanism whereby socialism is achieved. Perhaps the similarity between Segundo and Lenin on the role of the state in bringing about socialism derives in part from the fact that both Lenin and Segundo write within the context of poor, industrially underdeveloped countries.

Segundo's theology is radical in its implications because his methodology goes to the very root of fundamental theological principles, and reverses them, *radically*. At the centre of Segundo's theology are notions that stress the primacy of human praxis in the historical process of liberation, over all theological concepts, which become necessarily subordinate to praxis. Theological reflection can only be secondary to the concrete demands of each historical epoch. The result is that Segundo thoroughly politicizes and historicizes Christian theology, including the gospels, to the point that their specific theological (not religious) dimension all but disappears. What remains approximates a critical social theory with a strong Christian ethical substrate, which in turn rests upon the gospel imperative to love the neighbour.[27]

It can be reasonably argued, that in Segundo's hands, liberation theology reveals itself as containing the seeds of its own negation *as theology*, which is inevitable when politics becomes an ontological category, and when history is posited as the sole locus of human freedom. What Segundo does in his later methodological work, whether he intends it or not, is to expose those seeds of theological self-negation within liberation theology and push them very near to their logical conclusion. I will stress once more that the "antichristology" of Segundo's treatment of the historical, human Jesus is an illustration of Segundo's methodology applied to the gospels. In my view, it logically follows that if religious faith as such has any place in the historical project for social change, it can only be as an inspirational force within each individual's own beliefs. If Christianity is to be a force for changing society, then it is in the form of a critical, public ideology that offers a credible alternative to the existing ideological constructs already present in Latin America. It is my view that these are the logical conclusions implicit in Segundo's later work. Segundo openly states that a strictly formal, inactive faith in God or Christ is ultimately irrelevant in itself, for the project at hand: liberation of humanity from all forms of alienation.

For Segundo, "a human societal life liberated as much as possible from all alienation constitutes the *absolute* value" of human praxis with the result that "all religious institutions, dogmas, sacraments, and ecclesiastical authorities have only a *relative* (i.e., functional) value."[28] One is left wondering if, with Segundo, theology *qua* theology has come to its historical conclusion. What possible place *sui generis*, can theological concepts have in a world where the meaning of all human purpose and activity is understood in the light of the ultimate goal of human liberation in history? Finally, Segundo tells us that unless religious faith is politicized and translated into ideologies, it is meaningless because it can have no efficacy in history and no impact upon society. In itself, faith can do nothing toward achieving social justice and human freedom.

It is no easy task to write about the thought of Juan Luis Segundo. His thinking and writing is often eclectic and selective. This is especially true when Segundo enters into a dialogue with other authors, because Segundo's main interest is to appropriate selected ideas from those authors into his own theory. There are times when Segundo cites quotations from other writers out of context, and he often makes no effort to present the general line of thought of those authors. There are also instances when Segundo goes to such lengths to appropriate the ideas of others, that he alters the meaning of their thought. This is particularly true when Segundo dialogues with Marx, as I demonstrate in Chapter IV. At certain points, Marx's thought is quite unrecognizable, but again, it seems that Segundo is interested more in what Marx says for his own theory, than in what Marx actually writes. Segundo also tends to roam through various disciplines, drawing here and there upon selected ideas that he finds useful for his own purpose: for example, he draws upon certain insights from cybernetics, systems theory and even thermodynamics to explain and find support for his own views. One must probe Segundo's thought carefully through a close critical analysis of his texts, which is what I have tried to do here. I have tried to clarify his meaning partly by referring to other writers with whom Segundo seems to have theoretical affinities as a means of drawing out the implications of his thought. This is the case, for example, in Chapter 1. There I survey the field of the current work on the highly controversial subject of ideology, in order to try and situate Segundo within that area, since ideology is so crucial to his theory. Since Segundo himself makes no reference to the body of literature which exists on the subject of ideology, it might appear that the definition of ideology he formulates is somewhat idiosyncratic. In presenting some of the various theories of ideology, I demonstrate that Segundo's conception of ideology represents an approach that has its own proper place within the ongoing debate about ideology. There is little point to situate Segundo within the theological controversy surrounding the term ideology. Even most of the liberation theologians who use the term do so very loosely, and make no serious effort to define it, whether they hold a sympathetic view of ideology or not. It is outside the field of theology that the debate on ideology takes place, and where sustained and systematic effort is being made to define it. Before beginning an analysis of what ideology means for Segundo, there must be some general sense of the contours of the debate, and what definitions of ideology have emerged as a result. Otherwise, there will remain a solid core of confusion within the discussion of ideology, which will reproduce itself, and not make an analysis of Segundo's concept any easier. And I must emphasize that without an as clear as possible comprehension of what Segundo means by ideology, one cannot properly understand what he is doing in theology.

One of the interesting ironies of Segundo's conception of ideology is that in spite of the deep influence of Marx, Segundo adopts a view of ideology which is directly opposed to Marx's analysis. While Segundo is somewhat aware of this difference between himself and Marx, he nonetheless works on Marx's concept of ideology to the point that he neutralizes Marx's critique, bringing Marx much closer to his own view than is in fact warranted. Segundo's appropriation of certain of Marx's ideas is one of the most problematic aspects of Segundo's thought, and leads him into highly contradictory positions. The main point of difficulty between Marx and Segundo is that Marx's understanding of humanity and history is explicitly and irrevocably anti-theological, as it were, and Marx makes this point more than once, especially in his numerous critiques of Hegel. Segundo tries to argue that Marx's theory is not necessarily antithetical to certain basic theological assumptions, i.e., belief in God. In doing this, Segundo finds himself in an impossible contradiction. The way in which Segundo develops his critical methodological approach to history and social change which is explicitly indebted to Marx, strongly suggests that he cannot logically sustain a purely theological dimension within his own theory. Segundo's own methodology forbids it. All Segundo can do is stress a (Christian) ethics of love of the neighbour as an absolute feature of any ideology whose goal is human liberation and social change. However, any ethics that places human welfare above all other values would be equally acceptable to Segundo. Thus Segundo is forced to restrict the meaning of Jesus' ministry to the historical and political level, which is entirely consistent within his own methodological framework.

What I have written about Segundo is entirely my own interpretation. I hope this book will make a contribution to a critical understanding of Segundo's work since 1976, which is important since his later work manifests a progressive maturity of his development of methodology. Where Segundo is unclear, I have tried to bring out his meaning; where he is contradictory, I have tried to account for the contradictions. Finally, I will stress once more that Latin American liberation theology cannot be properly grasped without studying Segundo, who first raises and then confronts, in a very direct way, extremely difficult issues for contemporary Christianity. Whatever are the problems of his thought, Segundo develops the implications of liberation theology in an uncompromising fashion, so that theology is brought to the brink of its traditional historical role. It is there that Juan Luis Segundo is perhaps the most significant Latin American theologian writing today.

17

NOTES

1. Gustavo Gutierrez, *A Theology of Liberation*, translated by Sister Caridad Inda and John Eagleson (Maryknoll, N.Y.: Orbis Books, 1979), p. ix.

2. Enrique Dussel, *A History of the Church in Latin America: Colonialism to Liberation (1492-1979)*, translated by Alan Neely (Grand Rapids, Michigan: William B. Eerdmans Publishing Company, 1981), p. 143.

3. See, for example, *Gaudium et Spes, The Documents of Vatican II*. All Sixteen Official Texts Promulgated by the Ecumenical Council, 1963-1965, Walter M. Abbott, S.J., General Editor, Very Rev, Msgr. Joseph Gallagher, Translation Editor (New York/Cleveland: Corpus Books, 1966), n.9: ". . . the conviction grows not only that humanity can and should increasingly consolidate its control over creation, but even more, that it devolves on humanity to establish a political, social and economic order which will to an ever better extent serve man and help individuals as well as groups to affirm and develop the dignity proper to them. . . .

    People hounded by hunger call upon those better off. . . . Now, for the first time in human history, all people are convinced that the benefits of culture ought to be and actually can be extended to everyone.

    Still, beneath all these demands lies a deeper and more widespread longing. Persons and societies thirst for a full and free life worthy of man — one in which they can subject to their own welfare all that the modern world can offer them so abundantly. . . ." Although this section of *Gaudium et Spes* does not speak of liberation, it is not difficult to understand that liberation theologians and other Christian social activists could read the theme of liberation into this part of the document. This quotation articulates, in a general fashion, a commitment to social justice; if this commitment is read not in ahistorical terms of moral principles, but in the light of the specific, material conditions that generate extreme forms of social injustice in Latin America, then parts of Gaudium et Spes could be interpreted as a call to liberation, *no matter what the authors of the document intended.*

4. Dennis McCann, *Christian Realism and Liberation Theology: Practical Theologies in Creative Conflict* (Maryknoll, N.Y.: Orbis Books, 1981), pp. 131-132.

5. According to Penny Lernoux, all but three countries (Colombia, Venezuela, and Guyana) in South America were governed by military dictatorships by 1978, with Central America following in the same political direction. *Cry of the People: United States Involvement in the Rise of Fascism, Torture, and Murder and the Persecution of the Catholic Church in Latin America* (Garden City, N.Y.: Doubleday and Company, Inc., 1980), p.10.

6. Clodovis Boff, *Theology and Praxis*, translated by Robert R. Barr, (Maryknoll, N.Y.: Orbis Books, 1987), pp. 13-14.

7. Gustavo Gutierrez, *A Theology of Liberation*, p. 11.

8. Ibid, p. 18, n. 36.

9. Clodovis Boff, *Theology and Praxis*, p. 48.

10. For a full discussion of the Institute and its members, see Martin Jay, *The Dialectical Imagination: A History of the Frankfurt School and the Institute of Social Research 1923-1950* (Boston: Little, Brown & Company, 1973).

11. Dennis McCann, *Christian Realism and Liberation Theology*, p. 143.

12. Max Horkheimer, "Tradition and Critical Theory," in *Critical Theory: Selected Essays* (New York: Herder & Herder, 1972), p. 215.

13. Ibid, p. 229.

14. Juan Luis Segundo, *The Liberation of Theology*, translated by John Drury (Maryknoll, N.Y.: Orbis Books, 1976), p. 9.

15. Juan Luis Segundo, "Capitalism Versus Socialism: Crux Theologia," in *Frontiers of Theology in Latin America*, pp. 240-259, edited by Rosino Gibellini, translated by John Drury (Maryknoll, N.Y.: Orbis Books, 1979), p. 255.

16. Ibid, pp. 253-254.

17. Juan Luis Segundo, *A Theology for the Artisans of a New Humanity*, Vol. I, *The Community Called Church*, translated by John Drury (Maryknoll, N.Y.: Orbis Books, 1973), p. xi.

18. Gustavo Gutierrez, *A Theology of Liberation*, p. ix.

19. Juan Luis Segundo, S.J., *The Shift Within Latin American Theology*, Lecture given at Regis College, Toronto, printed offset by Regis College Press, March 22, 1983, p. 6.

20. Juan Luis Segundo, *The Community Called Church*, p. ix.

21. Ibid, p. 64.

22. Herbert Marcuse, *Reason and Revolution: Hegel and the Rise of Social Theory*, (Boston: Beacon Press, 1969), pp. 252-253.

23. Juan Luis Segundo, *The Historical Jesus of the Synoptics*, Vol. II, *Jesus of Nazareth Yesterday and Today*, translated by John Drury (Maryknoll, N.Y.: Orbis Books, 1985), p. 17.

24. Juan Luis Segundo, *The Liberation of Theology*, p. 13. The historical role of the Catholic Church in Latin America is extremely complex, and by no means monolithic in its relationship to the indigenous people or the ruling groups. For example, Jose Comblin writes: "One key to understanding the Catholic Church in Latin America is the realization that is has had a basic ideological split from the earliest days of Western colonization. This split was an example of the eternal division in the church — legitimizing the establishment of supporting justice for the people — but it was particularly specific and important in Latin America. . . . The present church is also a divided church. The roots of each of its divisions have never changed: the action of those who are fighting for social change is based on the same reasons as were used in the past; the agreement of the others with the aristocratic elites is also based on the same theory as in the past. The latter firmly believe that the Latin American people are not yet prepared to receive a democratic life." *The Church and the National Security State* (Maryknoll, N.Y.: Orbis Books, 1979), pp. 50-52.

19

The Catholic Church in Latin America has been and continues to be both a progressive and regressive force in Latin American society. See also "Visions of the Kingdom: The Latin American Church in Conflict," in "NACLA: Report on the Americas," Volume XIX, Number 5, September/October, 1985, pp. 14-45; Enrique Dussel, *A History of the Church in Latin America.*

25. Juan Luis Segundo, *The Community Called Church*, p. vii.

26. Juan Luis Segundo, "Capitalism Versus Socialism: Crux Theologica," p. 249.

27. In this sense, Segundo is close to Max Horkheimer, who recognized the inevitable connection between theology and a politics not defined as calculative instrumentality, when he said, "a politics which, even when highly unreflected, does not preserve a theological moment in itself is . . . mere business." Quoted in Charles Davis, *Theology and Political Society*, (Cambridge: Cambridge University Press, 1980), p. 133.

28. "Capitalism Versus Socialism", p. 243.

Chapter I

TOWARD A DEFINITION OF IDEOLOGY

Ideology is the object of the most problematic and controversial polemics, which is all the more surprising when one considers that its theoretical content is often vaguely understood or ill-defined. It is one of those terms which, both on the level of popular and academic discourse, bears more weight than it should properly sustain. Ideology is used in a variety of sometimes contradictory ways and is applied to any number of attitudes and ideas, more often than not in a pejorative manner, by interlocutors whose aim is to discredit a contrary, or perhaps simply different, point of view.

The theological approach to ideology is no less fraught with problems, and tends to reflect and reproduce the general confusion and lack of precision that accompanies the term; consequently, ideology as a concept loses much of its critical capacity. One of the most common and repeated accusations brought against liberation theology, is that it "ideologizes" Christian faith, or reduces it to the level of a legitimating veneer for an atheistic, left-wing politics, usually understood as "Marxist." Such accusations, however, tend to lack theoretical substance because ideology is used primarily as a rhetorical device rather than as an analytic concept. Such is the case, for example, with the document, "Instruction on Certain Aspects of the 'Theology of Liberation'", issued by the Sacred Congregation for the Doctrine of the Faith, which I examine in detail later. This document assumes an equation between ideology, Marxism, and falsehood.

On the other hand, it is common for liberation theologians to accuse classical, traditional theology of possessing an "ideological" function (however unconsciously or not) that supports the political and social *status quo*. Liberation theology maintains that traditional theology falls into this function by virtue of its ahistorical and abstract character, which renders such theology incapable of any effective capacity to address the human suffering that results from exploitative and unjust social structures. From the point of view of liberation theology, an ahistorical, apolitical theology is actually a contradiction in terms, since it does have a hidden political function: under the guise of protecting the integrity of the Christian faith, theology may in fact legitimate the existing socio-political order. This brief summary fairly encapsulates what are, I think, the basic features of the use of ideology within contemporary theology. What these different positions on ideology share however, is a mistrust and aversion to ideology, and certainly they would all disagree that their approach to theology is ideological. There seems to be a common understanding in theology that ideology implies untruth.

What then can be said about a theologian such as Juan Luis Segundo, who not only flatly asserts that Christianity, like all religions, is indeed ideology, and further, that religious faith without an accompanying ideology is in itself empty and meaningless?[1] This is a rather startling claim for a *theologian*; for Segundo, ideology is a central and crucial concept in his analysis of faith. One weakness, however, in Segundo's treatment of ideology is his tendency to focus upon what it *does* in relation to faith, rather than what it *is*. Therefore, before embarking upon a detailed discussion of Segundo's use of ideology, it is necessary to offer an analysis of the concept of ideology. The most fruitful way to do this it to look at some representative analyses and interpretations of ideology as a means of both theoretically contextualizing and illuminating Segundo's argument.

Segundo himself does not engage in this background theoretical work, which leaves the impression that his use of ideology is highly voluntaristic and even arbitrary. While this is not exactly true, it remains to present a kind of overview of some of the arguments and problems associated with efforts to define ideology. Such a discussion will facilitate a clearer comprehension of what Segundo means by ideology, and why he insists that to be effective and meaningful religious faith is contingent upon ideologies.

We should not ignore the fact that the study of ideology, which is taking place outside theology, is a highly controversial and conflict-laden pursuit about which there is no agreement. Nonetheless, it is still possible to present some sense of the scope of the debate, and a delineation of its essential features. This field of study has become highly sophisticated and specialized in recent years, bordering on several disciplines that include discourse analysis, hermeneutics and communication theory. The range of literature is as varied as it is enormous, and it is by no means my intention to summarize it completely. My interest is in *Segundo's* theory of ideology, but since he makes little effort to contextualize his own thinking, and thus locate himself within the larger field of intellectual debate, this will be the task of the following pages. I will present some of the main themes connected with the study of ideology to establish its conceptual parameters and open the way toward a critical analysis of Segundo's theory of ideology, which is all the more necessary given that Segundo claims the right to work out his own definition of ideology as an inclusive term for "all systems of means" which is "used to attain some end or goal."[2]   What remains to be seen is whether or not this is a valid approach to ideology.

Ideology and Domination: The Marxist Approach

   The controversy surrounding the concept of ideology can be formulated into two basic and opposed definitions: 1) ideology as a system of illusory and deliberately misleading beliefs, since Marx and Engels generally known as "false consciousness"; 2) ideology as a system or systems of "interacting symbols, as patterns of interworking meanings"[3] which are part of the process of the production of social meaning and ideas. Ideologies may also refer to "popular ideas and sentiments,"[4] or a developed system of ideas or beliefs of a particular people or social group, whose primary purpose is to persuade, and whose secondary purpose is to prescribe.[5]   This aspect of ideology can be included in the second definition, as a further elaboration upon it.   The definitions above are deliberately schematic in order to differentiate between those conceptions of ideology which focus exclusively on its distorting function, as in the first definition, and those which, while recognizing the distorting aspects of ideology, allow for an understanding of ideology which is also a progressive, creative force within human experience.
   The first definition of ideology is essentially the view of those writers, Marxist and non-Marxist alike, who have attempted to elaborate upon the concept of ideology put forward by Marx and Engels in *The German Ideology*.   Here, Marx and Engels challenged the claims of German philosophy, which conceived of truth as an independent, ideal realm that transcended the socio-historical world of contingency and particularity. It was a concept of truth that was essentially ahistorical and abstract, in the view of Marx and Engels. They wrote: "In direct contrast to German philosophy which descends from heaven to earth, here we ascend from earth to heaven."[6] This sentence is a direct critique of the Hegelian concept of an Absolute Mind, or Spirit, that works itself out in history through the individual consciousness of men:

> The Germans move in the realm of the 'pure spirit', and make religious illusion the driving force of history. The Hegelian philosophy of history is the last consequence, reduced to its 'finest expression' . . . for which it is not a question of real, or even of

political, interests, but of pure thoughts . . . that devour one another and are finally swallowed up in 'self-consciousness'.[7]

Marx insisted that human consciousness was materially based, rooted in the "productive forces" of the society, and that the "sum of productive forces, capital funds and social forms of existence . . . is the real basis of what the philosophers have conceived as 'substance' and 'essence of man'."[8] Thoughts and ideas of individual men were "bound to material premises,"[9] so that "Morality, religion, metaphysics, all the rest of ideology and their corresponding forms of consciousness, thus no longer retain the semblance of independence."[10] The point of this insistence upon the material basis of human consciousness was to show how ideas and beliefs – in other words, ideology – function as a mechanism in the process of exploitation and domination. If ideas were understood as independent forces, then values systems and religious beliefs could function to obscure the material reality of human existence.

If morality and religion are perceived as detached from their material context, and thus possess their own autonomy and power, mystification sets in which obscures and conceals the facts of the true nature of class society with all its inequality and injustice, which is the consequence of the forces of production and the relations of production they create in a capitalist society. It is first and foremost in the economic and political self-interest of the ruling class of any historical epoch to mask the concrete, material mechanism of exploitation through an appeal to the independent validity of beliefs and values, the universal credibility of which actually functions to legitimate the prevailing social order.

> For each new class which puts itself in the place of one ruling before it, is compelled, merely in order to carry through its aim, to represent its interest as the common interest of all the members of society, that is, expressed in ideal form: it has to give its ideas the form of universality, and represent them as the only rational, universally valid one.[11]

Thus the social relationships within a given society may be understood and legitimated in terms of "the concept of man," or the "essence of man," or human nature abstracted from its material condition.

Thus, this severing of ideas, or ideology from its material base as an attempt to conceal the real nature of class society, was understood by Marx as a powerful factor in maintaining domination, the economic and political hegemony of one particular class over another. This point is precisely what some Marxists and non-Marxists have taken up from *The German Ideology* and elaborated upon, that is, the ways in which ideology functions as a mechanism of domination. This preoccupation with the relationship between ideology and domination, has unleashed an enormous volume of literature with nearly as many varying interpretations and has taken the concept of ideology far away from the original focus of Marx. This has been possible because, in the words of Claude Lefort,

> Strictly speaking, there is no theory of ideologies in Marx's work; his analyses are ambiguous and to make use of his work, one must interpret it. . . . In addition, returning to Marx's undertaking can retrace his procedure only at a distance. . . .[12]

Whether Lefort is correct in this assessment of Marx's concept of ideology or not, in making this statement he opens the discussion about Marx's theory of ideology that allows for great expansion and interpretation of Marx's own concept, while attempting to preserve Marx's original insight into the connection between ideology and domination. Lefort, along with those writers who stress the relationship between ideology and power are drawing upon a "theoretical and political tradition which is strongly indebted to Marx"[13] and it is this emphasis upon the links between ideology and domination which is understood as the necessary critical force of any conception of ideology. However, the connection with Marx which sustains the link between ideology and domination is more a formal than substantive connection, because the terrain of what constitutes domination – in Marx, class society – shifts to a different locale.

Since Marx, there has emerged a theory of ideology which no longer strictly focuses upon domination in terms of the legitimation of a particular concrete class interest at the expense of a subordinate class, but shifts to an analysis of ideology and domination in terms of philosophy of language and communication. An example of this particular development of ideology is found in the work of Anthony Giddens, who formulates four basic points, or "theses" on ideology which attempt to refine the relationship between ideology and domination in terms of "signification" and "representation." Firstly, Giddens argues that it is fruitless to understand or criticize ideology in terms of an unfavourable comparison with the achievements of science, which means an evaluation of ideology in terms of its "specific content" or "truth claims."[14] Secondly, he argues that ideology must be understood in "relation to a theory of *power* and *domination* – to the modes in which systems of signification enter into the existence of sectional forms of domination,"[15] with the result that sectional interests are represented as universal interests. For Giddens, this is the "basic mode in which forms of signification are incorporated within systems of domination in class societies."[16] Thirdly, he argues that an overemphasis on the importance of "propositional belief claims" of ideologies itself obscures the real relationship between ideology and domination, which is embedded in the mechanisms ("modes of signification") which produce a daily world in which, for example, economic life and political life are perceived to be separate realities. "The insulation of the economic from the political I take to be one of the major mechanisms of class domination."[17]

An illustration of what Giddens means by dividing the content of ideology from the "modes of signification" which are operative in the most subtle and concrete aspects of daily existence and consciousness can be very simply indicated by the following example: a worker who is a self-conscious trade unionist, and who believes that his exploitation as a worker lay in the fact that he is underpaid for his labour and who may even develop a whole theory about what constitutes a fair wage, which he does not have, is still blind to the deeper awareness that his exploitation is embedded not so much in his low wages as in the very existence of the wage system as such. Giddens' final conclusion, which emerges from the above three points, is to diminish the importance of the actual content of ideologies by denying the necessity of a common value system as a prerequisite condition for the maintenance of a social order.[18] Giddens questions the claim that legitimation is a "fundamental mode in which the coherence of class-dominated societies is secured."[19] He does not concur with the idea that "crises of legitimation are the main sources of tension which threaten the stability of Western capitalist societies."[20] The problem with a theory of legitimation crisis as a destabilizing force, capable of undermining the given social and political order, is that it denies pluralism as an accepted characteristic of contemporary, industrial societies. In fact, pluralism is widely acknowledged to be a progressive, creative feature of liberal democracies, and it is largely associated with 'freedom' and 'tolerance', which are in turn understood as the mainstays of democratic societies. Giddens rejects the "emphasis on the significance of a common value system as a coordinating mechanism of order."[21] In his view, it is not the content of ideologies which is so important a factor in maintaining domination, but the epistemological structure of consciousness itself, which is in turn mediated by the concrete conditions of human experience. The epistemological structure of human consciousness does not exist as an entity apart from the complex terrain of the totality of social interaction and human experience, and is inextricably interwoven with it. What is of interest to Giddens is the modes or mechanisms of ordinary human thought which lead people to construct and

accept certain beliefs about reality more than what the beliefs are themselves.

In de-emphasizing (although not completely negating) the importance of
the propositional content of ideologies, Giddens then raises the question of
the relationship between epistemology and domination, that is, how and in
what ways the very structure of thought can foreclose on or undermine the
emancipatory interests of individuals and social groups. Giddens proposes
a concept of ideology that centres upon the workings of everyday consciousness, which inevitably takes him into the field of psychoanalysis and theories
of structuration.[22]   It serves no purpose in this discussion to explore his
argument further, but it is useful to indicate the direction in the thinking on
ideology of writers like Giddens to illustrate just how complex the field of
study of ideology has become since Marx.   Giddens makes this close
connection between ideology and daily consciousness because of his interest
in the relationship between language as praxis and the impact of ideology on
action. Thus Giddens raises the critique of ideology to another plane, which
is to approach ideology more through a philosophy of language on the
assumption that language occupies a large and crucial part of daily life praxis
in which the mechanisms of domination are embedded in a myriad of subtle
ways. This brief outline of the parameters and conceptualizations involved
in Giddens' approach to ideology is one indication of the possibilities
inherent in an analysis of ideology which helps to construct a theoretical
framework within which to examine the concept of ideology, and to
demonstrate something of the complexity and problems inherent in the study
of ideology.

Although no discussion of ideology can take place without some
reference to Marx's definition of the term, it cannot be said that those
writers who address the concept and problem of ideology are necessarily
Marxist. This applies not only to Giddens, but many other writers as well,
some of whom will be covered here. The only connecting link between
Marx's concept of ideology and the various conceptions of ideology
examined here, is the recognition of the relationship between ideology and
domination that is certainly one of its constitutive elements, although not at
the expense of other important features and possibilities. Marx's concept
of ideology continues to exercise a powerful influence on the study of
ideology, and most of the major works on ideology "attempt to continue the
tradition initiated by the Marxian concept of ideology."[23]   Yet one of the
reasons why the study of ideology is so loaded with controversy is because,
according to György Márkus, "Both Marxist and non-Marxist interpretations

of the Marxian concept of ideology seem to disagree about even the most elementary questions concerning its meaning."[24]

However open to debate and disagreement Marx's concept of ideology may be, I am in agreement with Márkus that in Marx's view, the material realm constitutes the basis of his exclusive identification between ideology and domination. Márkus stresses that Marx always emphasized that the distortions and mystifications produced by ideology were primarily rooted in concrete, material life conditions, and that "fetishistic modes of thought 'arise from the relations of production themselves'."[25] Márkus uses this point to further elaborate upon Marx's concept of ideology in terms of a discussion of "false consciousness":

> The Marxian theory is concerned with those specific social-historical conditions which make it impossible for thinking to recognize self-reflexively its own historical constitution and which thereby lock this thinking into a system of categories or images that both justifies and attempts to perpetuate its very historical limitations.[26]

Thus Márkus argues that Marx conceived of ideology primarily and most importantly as a closed, and thus rationally limited phenomenon, rooted in and determined by material conditions, with a concrete class or interest-legitimating function, and that whatever he said or implied about ideology was consistent with this view. But even more important than the question of Marx's consistency or even clarity, is the question, can ideology ever be understood in any other terms? If, in the tradition of Marx, ideology is always understood only in relation to questions of mystification, power and domination, then it seems that ideology can never be linked to emancipatory interests. But this view can only be defended if ideology is understood as produced by, and confined to, the material conditions which produce and reproduce class society. In this sense, ideology cannot pass so easily over into the analysis of the epistemology of daily consciousness as the key factor in the operation of domination. When ideology is analyzed in terms of epistemology, language and communication, representation and signification, then the possibility arises that ideology is not only and exclusively a mode of domination, since its links with material class interests as Marx saw them, are broken. This is a conceptualization of ideology in terms of an "ahistoric rationality,"[27] which is contrary to Marx. Márkus argues that:

> Marx's polemics against the hidden interests constituting and determining the systems of ideology . . . are conducted in the name of historically defined, concrete and 'limited' needs and sufferings which are produced and induced by the same social interests.[28]

However Marx conceived of ideology, the possible justifiability of other approaches cannot be ignored. What is questionable, however, is the insistence in other approaches to ideology upon the exclusive identification of ideology and domination. John B. Thompson is an example of another theorist who situates ideology within a theory of language and communication while also insisting upon the exclusive connection between ideology and domination. Thompson differentiates the "two uses" of ideology in "the history of the concept": one is the "neutral conception" of ideology, which poses ideology as a "system of thought" or beliefs which pertain to social action and political projects. The other concept of ideology views it as integral to the general process of "sustaining asymmetrical relations of power," or the maintenance of domination.

Thompson's analysis leads him into discussions of discourse analysis and hermeneutics, which need not be reproduced here, through which he attempts to develop his thesis on language and ideology, which he claims must be studied in an "integrated approach."[29] One of his main points is to critically examine and reject the "neutral conception" of ideology, which he sees represented in the work of writers such as Alvin Gouldner, Martin Seliger, and to a lesser extent, Clifford Geertz. He charges that these approaches to ideology dissolve the connection between ideology and the critique of domination, which he insists must be preserved. Thompson is an example of those theorists of ideology who remain influenced by Marx (although not necessarily himself a Marxist) to the extent that he continues to assert the necessary link between ideology and domination, while himself abandoning the notion of ideas as "sublimates" of the material realm.

Thompson labels Seliger's concept of ideology as "inclusive" because it "mixes together" those factual descriptions, situation analyses, moral and technical prescriptions that are features of ideologies.[30] The basis of Thompson's critique against this approach to ideology is that it "breaks down" every link between ideology and the critique of domination, since it applies the term to any political or social belief system, thus "stripping the concept of its critical edge." Such a concept of ideology cannot, in his view, relate adequately to the institutional and structural features of society and to an analysis of power.[31]

What Thompson seems to overlook is that an "inclusive" conception of ideology can as well accept that while ideology functions in the service of domination, it can also have a progressive social function; one feature does not necessarily annihilate the other. Thompson does not seem to see, or at least accept this possibility. Thus he rejects Gouldner's concept of ideology, on the same grounds as Seliger, charging Gouldner with dislocating ideology from its critical component, the critique of domination. Gouldner's concept of ideology is unsatisfactory for Thompson primarily because it "dissolves the connection between ideology and domination" and thus the "concept is stripped of its . . . negative force, which it had in the writings of Marx." [32]

Thompson attempts to elaborate upon his repeated conviction that "*to study ideology is to study the ways in which meaning (signification) serves to sustain relations of domination*"[33] by offering an outline of the "basic modalities" of the interconnection between ideology and domination. These modalities are: 1) ideology as legitimation of a particular system of domination; 2) ideology as dissimulation, or deliberate distortion, which follows from legitimation; and 3) ideology as reification, or the representation of a transitory, historical state of affairs as if it were natural, or permanent and atemporal.[34]

This threefold definition of the modalities of ideology can be more fully understood through a definition from Claude Lefort who has attempted to deepen the link between representation and domination, and Marx:

> Marx implies (in The German Ideology) that a society cannot continue to exist as a human society unless it creates a representation of its unity. . . . Thus, even though social division is not determined in the universal division of class (that of the bourgeois and the proletariat), the existence of 'limited social relations' implies the projection of an imaginary community under cover of which 'real distinctions' are determined as 'natural', the particular is disguised under the traits of the universal, the historical erased under the atemporality of essence.[35]

Lefort is interested in the symbolic dimension of the social domain, and he opens the issue of how patterns and structures of representation operate in terms of domination, which helps to illuminate the approach to ideology adopted by Thompson, who also seeks to uncover ways in which ideology embodies and produces those "relations of force" which bind individuals, and underlie their "utterances."[36] Thus, the analysis of ideology in terms of language, representation, signification and even dissimulation inevitably raises the question of ideology and symbolic interaction which forms a cultural matrix within which and through which human beings organize social and psychological processes. When ideology is conceived of in relation to this level of human experience, then it cannot be seen as a strictly or exclusively negative social, psychological or cultural force. Then ideology is loosened from its moorings in the narrow, and pejorative sense of Marx, opening up the possibility of ideology understood as a potentially liberative force, which is of great importance for Segundo. I caution to add that I am not arguing in advance that ideology *is* a progressive, emancipatory force; I am trying to show that there are writers on the subject who make this argument, and forcefully. They seek to demonstrate that ideology must be dislocated from its restricted function as a "sublimate" of the material forces of class society.

An over-emphasis upon ideology as strictly serving the relations of domination, is in danger of producing a concept that is itself one-sided and distorted. It is an interest-theory of ideology in the sense that the conclusion precedes the argument in such a way as to foreclose upon any other conclusion. While it is useful to show how ideology functions negatively in the most subtle, complex and minute interactions and understandings of ordinary, daily life, it is not the only valid approach. Symbols, representations and forms of signification for all their ambiguity, are also capable of generating a progressive and constructive force in social life. They can be either repressive or emancipatory, and theorists like Paul Ricoeur and Clifford Geertz attempt to analyze this aspect of ideology. When others, such as Thompson discuss ideology in terms of language and signification, they broach upon a theory of social symbolic interaction. What Thompson has in common with those he opposes, such as Ricoeur, is that he allows the possibility that ideology and ideas possess an independence in a way Marx refused.

Marx understood that ideas, beliefs and values are determined by the material realm of human existence, generating systems of thought which function to maintain the given social order:

> The ideas of the ruling class are in every epoch the ruling ideas: i.e., the class which is the ruling *material* force of society, is at the same time its ruling *intellectual* force. The class which has the means of material production at its disposal, has control at the same time over the means of mental production, so that thereby, generally speaking, the ideas of those who lack the means of mental production are subject to it. The ruling ideas are nothing more than the ideal expression of the dominant material relationships, the dominant material relationships grasped as ideas; hence of the relationships which make the one class the ruling, therefore, the ideas of its dominance.[37]

In passages such as this, which abound in *The German Ideology*, Marx closes the possibility that ideology could have any progressive function in society, and that the task around ideology demands the unmasking of its dissimulating characteristics in order to reveal the true class nature of society, and its causes.

Not even Lenin followed Marx in this strict delineation of ideology, asserting rather the power of ideology – the correct ideology – as a necessary and positive force in the socialist project of the reconstruction of society.

He insisted that "Without revolutionary theory there can be no revolutionary movement,"[38] realizing that the revolutionary struggle was also taking place on the level of ideology: "the *only* choice is — either bourgeois or socialist ideology," and, "Hence, to belittle the socialist ideology *in any way, to turn aside from it in the slightest degree*, means to strengthen the bourgeois ideology. . . ."[39] What Lenin recognized was the power of ideas to motivate human beings to engage in political projects with the aim of social transformation. He understood that ideology could function as both a dominating, repressive force ("bourgeois ideology") or function as an emancipatory force ("socialist ideology"). Thus Lenin advocated a certain degree of autonomy to ideology as a necessary motive force in building and spreading the revolution, although it must not be forgotten, under the careful guidance and control of the vanguard party.

If the concept and analysis of ideology is restricted to no more than a regressive function, if ideology is studied only in terms of power and domination, then such an analysis is itself divested of critical capacity and is thus open to distortion. It is uncritical if it refuses to seriously consider a broader understanding of the concept. Ideology cannot be fully studied or evaluated as long as it remains fixed within the parameters of the original Marxist definition. Writers who insist upon formulating concepts of ideology within the theoretical limits put forward by Marx, risk burying their own theories "under the rubble of Marxism,"[40] which is further complicated by the fact (if we accept it) that, according to Lefort, "strictly speaking, there is no theory of ideologies in Marx's work."[41]

Ideology as a Progressive Cultural Force

Paul Ricoeur offers an interpretation of ideology in terms of the symbolic constitution of the social-historical world that moves away from the thesis that ideology's main function is to sustain domination. He too is aware of the "several snares" inherent in the attempt to define ideology, which he also traces to the "deep influences of Marxism."[42] Ricoeur asserts that the problem with working out definitions of ideology strictly in terms of its relation to social classes in a capitalist society, is to engage in a "sterile polemic" with Marxism.[43]

> It is necessary, it seems to me, to escape from the fascination exercised by the problem of domination, in order to consider the broader phenomenon of social integration, of which domination is a dimension but not the unique and essential condition. If it is taken for granted that ideology is a function of domination, then it is assumed

uncritically that ideology is an essentially negative phenomenon, the cousin of error and falsehood, the brother of illusion.[44]

What Ricoeur sets out to do is to show that "the phenomenon of ideology is susceptible of a relatively positive assessment."[45] Ricoeur offers a multi-faceted analysis of ideology which conceives of it in terms of the "meaningful, mutually oriented and socially integrated character of action." [46] Ideology functions to integrate the social memory of a group from an inaugural event which gave rise to that group, and which must be sustained and infused into the present, as a way of injecting creative meaning into the self- understanding or representation of that group.[47] "A founding act can be revived and reactualized only in an interpretation which models it retroactively, through a representation of itself."[48] Ideology thus assumes a justifactory function which allows a group to understand itself and its place in the world, its reason for being, thus bestowing it with a specific identity. Ideology in this sense of justification is different from ideology in the sense of legitimation, since legitimation implies support of domination, whereas justification is not necessarily connected to domination, since even the most dominated, oppressed social group can "justify" itself and its existence, especially in religious terms. Poor Christians in the third world, for instance, may be able to find a sense of meaning for themselves in the eyes of God, as is described in Jesus' Sermon on the Mount. This sense of justification in no way implies a *legitimation* of poverty as an either desirable or necessary condition, however. Rather, in picturing themselves as closer to God, who desires their liberation from poverty, the poor find hope in the possibility that material poverty may be overcome.

Another aspect of ideology mentioned by Ricoeur is its "dynamism," its function as the motive form of social praxis. Ideology as social motivation implies both justification and action: "For it's mediating role remains irreplaceable, as attested to by the fact that ideology is always more than a *reflection*, it is always also a *justification and project*. This 'generative' character of ideology . . . "allows then, for social action and thus social change, which carries with it the belief in the "just and necessary" character of the action.[49]

However, it is the justificatory aspect of ideology which transforms the ideas it conveys into "opinions," where thought becomes mutated into beliefs "in order to enhance its social efficacy"[50] so that anything can become ideological, including "ethics, religion, philosophy." Here, it seems, Ricoeur is close to Marx. Because ideology, through symbolic representation, attempts to construct "an overall view, not only of the group, but also of history, and ultimately, the world,"[51] ideology assumes a codified, schematic character, operating as a grid or code through which events are meaningfully rendered and made coherent.   This line of argument compels Ricoeur to consider another level of ideology, its "epistemological" status, which is that of "the moment of rationalization," [52]   which is what he means by opinion. Yet Ricoeur is quick to caution against a simple condemnation of ideology because of this: "schematization, idealization and rhetoric are the prices to be paid for the social efficacy of ideas."[53]

Ricoeur fully understands how these features of ideology can render it uncritical – "ideology is operative . . . we think from it rather than about it"[54] – and thus lead to the possibilities of distortion, dissimulation and mystification which in turn help to service those conditions capable of sustaining social relations of domination. Yet in stressing that the integrative and mediating function of ideology can lead to supporting and sustaining domination, ideology cannot be so simply reduced to this negative aspect. No matter what the negative aspects and functions of ideology may be, and Ricoeur outlines them in detail, they cannot obscure the fact that "ideology is an unsurpassable phenomenon of social existence, insofar as social reality always has a symbolic constitution and incorporates an interpretation, in images and representations, of the social bond itself."[55]

Ricouer's discussion of ideology as mediating and integrative, leads him inevitably to a discussion of the relationship between ideology and knowledge, where he concludes that there is no such thing as completely objective, or total knowledge: there is no such thing as a "mind totally clarified from the sociological point of view."[56] This is due to the essential human existential condition of "belonging," which is defined by position in society, social class, cultural and historical conditions "upon which we can never entirely reflect."[57]   Belonging is essential to the human condition because it is *a priori* to any capacity or activity of reflection. This fact of belonging within a particular context precedes, but does not preclude, the possibility of critical distance and self-reflexivity, which are the requirements of critical thinking.   If we acknowledge this fact of belonging as an ontological condition which excludes the possibility only of complete reflection, then it follows that knowledge is inevitably mediated through ideology. "In accepting this belonging which precedes and supports us, we accept the very first role of ideology, that which we have described as the mediating function of the image, the self- representation."[58]

If we accept that all knowledge is partial, socially, historically embedded, and mediated by ideology, where is the possibility of an ideology critique? Are we condemned to never see our own ideological disposition, but only that of the other? In answer to this problem, Ricoeur raises the notion of "distanciation" which is made possible within a hermeneutics of the text, which contains "crucial indications for a just reception of the critique of ideology." [59] According to Ricoeur, distanciation is an integral part of the hermeneutics of the text, wherein "distancing is intimately part of any reading whereby the matter of the text is rendered near only in and through as distance."[60] Thus Ricoeur takes the technique of distanciation, as a means of understanding a text, and applies it to the interpretation of ideology, and in this way poses the possibility of an ideology critique that is self-reflective, even though only partially and incompletely.

> Thus the critique of ideology can be and must be assumed in a work of self-under-standing, a work which organically implies a critique of the illusions of the subject . . . distanciation, dialectically opposed to belonging, is the condition of possibility of the critique of ideology, not outside or against hermeneutics, but within hermeneutics.[61]

Ricoeur attempts to formulate a critical theory of ideology in relation to a theory of knowledge since like ideology, knowledge is necessarily partial, incomplete and fragmented, never free of ideological colouring. What ideology reveals is that all knowledge is conditioned by an "interest", and that even a "critical theory of ideology is itself supported by an interest in emancipation."[62] This is because the precondition of all self-understanding, of all knowledge and ideological reflection is belonging, and for Ricoeur, this fact is "insurmountable." Thus any ideology critique is itself supported by a specific interest, since, as is the case with all forms of knowing, ideology can never sever its "links to the basis of belonging. To forget this primordial tie is to enter into the illusion of a critical theory elevated to the rank of absolute knowledge."[63]

Ricoeur's conclusion about the relationship between ideology and knowledge, then, is that knowledge can never cut its ties to ideology, since "ideology is always the grid, the code of interpretation" through which we strive for knowledge. Nonetheless, the ideological mediation and conditioning of understanding does not preclude the possibility of critique and deeper forms of understanding. Ideology does not necessarily imply legitimation of domination, and thus epistemological closure and irrationality. It does function in this manner if it is divested of independence in the realm of human motivation and action. Ricoeur's approach to ideology opens up the possibility of understanding ideology as a progressive social force, with a capacity to generate concrete action and critical reflection. It can be further explored in terms of a creative link between theory and praxis, possibilities which are very far away from the views of Marx.

These considerations point in the direction that all knowledge is ideological, including science. This is what Karl Mannheim discovered in his study of ideology, and his attempt to develop a sociology of knowledge. Mannheim realized that "what is intelligible in history can be formulated only with reference to problems and conceptual constructions which themselves arise in the flux of historical experience."[64] There is no norm or formal criteria that can claim a universal, abstract status beyond its historically changing content, since the meaning which constitutes our understanding of the world is "historically determined in a continuously developing situation."[65] Since there is no such thing as 'value-free' knowledge, what is required is:

> A clear and explicit avowal of the implicit metaphysical presuppositions which underlie and make possible empirical knowledge (which) will do more for the clarification and advancement of research than a verbal denial of the existence of the presuppositions accompanied by their surreptitious advancement through the backdoor.[66]

Whatever the negative implications of Mannheim's concept of ideology, one of his most important insights is that the problem of truth and knowledge cannot be broached in isolation from the whole complex web of concrete social and historical existence. Thought is thus a process *within* human experience which is mediated by social forces. Thus we arrive at the conclusion of Paul Ricoeur: "My question — the troubling question — is this: from what place does the investigator speak in a generalized theory of ideology? It must be admitted that this place does not exist."[67]

If it can be said that all thought is ideological, what are the implications for rationality, critical reflexive thought, and their connection with concrete social praxis? Does this drive us back to the position that the main tendencies of ideologies are dissimulation and legitimation, with the purpose of duping human beings to accommodate themselves to an unjust reality? Can we justifiably defend the possibility that ideologies can function as emancipatory influences on the level of thought and practice? It is important to repeat this question in an attempt to come to grips with a reasonable definition of ideology, since the question itself remains unresolved and still open to debate. Alvin Gouldner is another writer on ideology who attempts to answer this question on the basis of a similar promise as raised by Ricoeur, which is that ideology also has progressive value, even if limited. He is also close to Thompson in that he too approaches the study of ideology in terms of discourse, as a "culture of critical speech."[68]

According to Gouldner, ideologies emerged with the Enlightenment, as an alternative means of grounding truth claims as opposed to explanations and knowledge based on religious beliefs and tradition. As systems of belief shifted from being grounded in religion, to philosophy and then science, these systems of belief began to assume the claim of self-validation. The decline in the credibility of religion occurred because the "political authority with which it was linked was no longer taken seriously."[69] For Gouldner, ideology develops as a "modern symbol system" based upon the "detraditionalization" of society: with the genesis of ideology in the Enlightenment, traditional authority structures are questioned by new modes of interpretation of social life which introduce the possibility of self-validating, "rationally grounded" projects of social change. Ideologies replace "religious thought systems"[70] delineating a transition from religious authority as the basis of understanding and action to "secular thought systems" whose foundation of truth is contained within itself.

Thus ideology, as a "post-traditional, modern symbol system"[71] operates as a "shared language," a "shared grammar of rationality," or "culture of critical discourse" with the capacity to question the "validity of truth claims" in the sense of "proposals and counterproposals" which take place within a dialogical community.[72] Thus ideologies, as the "self-consciousness of ordinary language"[73] constitute a critical "metalanguage." To continue with Gouldner's concept of ideology, it is a "rational mode of discourse" which attempts to justify its assertions through a reasoned argument; ideology is the response to the modern "problematic nature of social reality" in post-traditional society.[74] One of the essential social functions of ideology is to "expose the lie that science is self-sufficient and self-grounded"[75] — in other words, that there is no such phenomenon as pure, objective knowledge.

Gouldner recognizes that ideology is also cognitively deficient, and rationally limited in the sense of the absence of critical self-reflexivity, so that as a mode of critical, public discourse that calls into question the accepted truth claims of a society or social group, and thus other ideologies, ideology fails to be aware of its own self-interest. This is the main thrust of Gouldner's critique of Marxism as itself an ideology which contains "a specific communication pathology," that is, its claim to scientific objectivity that refuses to see itself as also limited and conditioned by specific historical contexts.[76]

What is needed then is the development of an ideology-critique, or more important, a self-reflexive critical theory that can push beyond the limits of rationality contained in ideologies. This is especially important since Gouldner also recognizes that ideology as a system of symbolic interaction in the social domain serves to "justify and mobilize public projects of social reconstruction."[77] What this implies is the necessity of a dialectical relationship between theory and praxis, infused with a conscious emancipatory interest.

Again, we are some distance from Marx's sharper but more limited notion of ideology. Gouldner, too, recognizes that ideology is a limited phenomenon in terms of rational deficiencies defined by the absence of critical self-reflexivity, and thus points to the negative aspect of ideology. But one of the most important points in Gouldner's analysis is that of ideology as a rational, symbolic discourse with the generative power to mobilize social action, something also recognized by Ricoeur. In the following chapter, I will show how important this particular point is for Segundo's conception of ideology as a mobilizing force for social change in Latin America. Before beginning that discussion, it remains to further examine ideology as "process of symbolic formulation" because it is this aspect of ideology which is the "connecting element" between the theory and practice of ideology and is especially important in any analysis of the relation between ideologies and religion.

Clifford Geertz approaches the concept of ideology in terms of attempting to construct a theory of public, symbolic interaction, which will focus upon the power of ideology to "grasp, formulate, and communicate social realities that elude the tempered language of science," and its capacity to mediate complex meanings of social-cultural life that cannot be literally grasped. "For all mental processes," writes Ernst Cassirer, for example, "fail to grasp reality itself, and in order to represent it, to hold it all, they are driven to the use of symbols."[78] This is a perspective Geertz certainly would agree with. For him, the relationship between ideology and symbol arises in the social realm of public discourse, where metaphor, analogy and various forms of rhetoric interact to create a mode, or "vehicle of conception" that mediates and transmits meaning. Ideology is the embodiment through a symbolic interaction of various beliefs which contain a "multiplicity of referential connections between it and social reality"[79] whereby people can understand that reality and their place in it. Although ideology tends to schematize and simplify the complex nature of social reality, it is, nonetheless, able to convey the significance and meaning of reality in a way that cannot be publicly grasped otherwise.

The implication here is that reality cannot be directly and objectively understood in its entirety; there always remains a space or disjunction between understanding and reality, so that ideology provides a means which mediates reality and consciousness in an attempt to integrate them, as Ricoeur also argued. According to Geertz: "Thinking, conceptualization, formulation, comprehension, understanding . . . consists . . . of a matching of the states and processes of symbolic models against the states and processes of the wider world."[80] Human beings need to construct ideologies in order to be able to understand and act in the social world, and action in the social realm implies politics: "it is through the construction of ideologies, schematic images of social order, that man makes himself for better or worse a political animal."[81]

This statement pinpoints the relationship between values and action that attempt to realize those values, or more simply, the relationship between means and ends. Ideologies enable human beings to orient themselves within their world in order to be able to act within it – in order to actualize themselves as political agents with a conscious political purpose. Like Gouldner, Geertz identifies ideology as a modern phenomenon when he locates the genesis of ideology,

> At the point at which a political system begins to free itself from the immediate governance of received tradition, from the direct and detailed guidance of religious or philosophical canons, on the one hand, and from the unreflective precepts of conventional morality on the other.[82]

This is the same point made by Gouldner. When tradition is no longer a credible authority referent, when those social and political institutions that were based upon and legitimated by the authority of tradition begin to crumble, then ideology becomes the key factor in and chief source of sociopolitical and cultural meaning.

Ideology, by use of symbol, metaphor, irony, hyperbole, or whatever other rhetorical devices – "extends" the range and capacity of language to render the world meaningful, and as such, provides a map of "problematic social reality" and a matrix for "the creation of a collective conscience."[83] Geertz contends that ideologies are most prominent, and probably necessary in the third world, including Latin America, where "the initial steps away from a traditional politics of piety and proverb are just now being taken."[84] The social and political instability that exists in many parts of Latin America which is still in the throes of revolutionary struggles, the violence of government - initiated counterinsurgency measures, the struggle against poverty and illiteracy, the strife and insecurity produced by factional conflicts within the government and ruling elites, the interference of the United

States in political and economic affairs, and the virtual absence of any form of civil society in most Latin American countries has generated the "search for a new symbolic framework in terms of which to formulate, think about and react to political problems" that may include anything from various brands of Marxism to a "reconstructed traditionalism."

In other words, it can be argued that Latin America is now in the process of developing an ideology which can emerge as the main motive force for a social reformation. This effort is reflected in the work of Segundo, who it seems to me is attempting to formulate a mélange of essentially traditional, but reconstituted Christianity and Marxist theory in order to respond to and participate in the particular changes taking place in Latin America now. His work also reflects an attempt to give these changes some ideological direction and coherence that will stand as a credible alternative to the prevailing National Security ideology that exists in many parts of Latin America, on the one hand, and the so-called Marxist-Leninist brand of guerrilla, revolutionary ideology on the other. This becomes apparent if we interpret his approach to ideology by way of writers like Geertz, Ricoeur and Gouldner. Segundo's efforts in the area of ideology and Christianity is a partial response, at least, to the crumbling foundations of traditional authority structures on both the political and ecclesial level, that has prevailed in Latin America for over 400 years. Segundo is trying to construct a viable and effective (that is, publicly credible) politico-religious ideology that both accounts for and provides a solution to the contemporary problems of Latin America.

This is comprehensible if ideology is allowed the capacity to "name" the given situation and also to inspire a consequent commitment that will lead to social action. Thus ideology concerns itself with establishing beliefs and values and the means whereby these values may become operative in society. This aspect of ideology Geertz identifies as the proper *locus* of the study of ideology, and not an evaluation of its substantive content, although this is not unimportant.

> No more than scientific studies of religion ought to begin with unnecessary questions about the legitimacy of the substantive claims of their subject matter ought scientific studies of ideology to begin with such questions.[85]

The propositional content of a particular ideology cannot be the main focus of working out a concept of ideology because the truthfulness or rightness of a specific ideology is necessarily defined by and contingent upon the concrete situation to which it applies. It may be both appropriate and necessary to adopt a revolutionary ideology in the context of Latin America, while this particular ideology may be completely absurd in North America or Western Europe. Thus a careful theoretical approach toward ideology must "circumvent" the question of ideological content, rather focusing on such issues as the origin of ideologies, under what conditions they emerge, its function and its potential as either repressive or progressive, and its power to motivate social action.

Although Segundo's approach to ideology shares several elements in common with Ricoeur, Gouldner and Geertz, these are not the writers with whom Segundo engages in serious dialogue. It might be said that Segundo's interest in ideology stresses a methodological approach, more than an analysis or evaluation of the substantive content of ideology. This particular emphasis on methodology as the means for explaining the nature of the meaning of ideology for faith and religion has extremely important implications for Segundo's theology, as will be shown later. However, in working out his own particular conception of ideology, Segundo only seriously debates with Marx, and his definition of ideology. The advantage of Marx's perspective on ideology is that it is sharp and precise; he is able to show with a high degree of clarity the relationship between the material conditions of human existence and the ideas and concepts by which human beings understand their social reality. The potential danger with theories of ideology put forward by writers such as Ricoeur, Gouldner and even Geertz is that they are susceptible to producing concepts of ideology that are vague. Their approach to ideology also implies a blurring of the distinction between ideology and critical social theory, thus hindering the latter's ability to formulate a general ideology-critique, which is an important function of any critical social theory.

These above-mentioned problems become particularly relevant to an analysis of Segundo's understanding of ideology and its meaning in relation to faith and to religion, specifically the Christian religion. Although Segundo accepts Marx's view of ideology as a valid approach, he also insists on the potentially progressive and constructive possibilities of ideology on both the level of thought and action. His main interest in ideology, however, is practical and concrete, i.e., in the role and power of ideology in the process of effecting concrete social change, and social reconstruction, and in this sense, he espouses Lenin's view of ideology. Segundo does not attempt to explain his conception of ideology with reference to the large body of literature that exists on the subject, and thus he does not attempt to account for the development of his own theory of ideology or situate it in the context of what others have written about ideology. At times, it is not always clear just what Segundo does mean by ideology in regard to its connection with faith. This topic will be the focus of discussion in the subsequent chapters.

NOTES

1. Juan Luis Segundo, S.J., *The Liberation of Theology*, p. 121.

2. Juan Luis Segundo, "Jesus of Nazareth Yesterday and Today," *Faith and Ideologies*, Vol. I, translated by John Drury (Maryknoll, N.Y.: Orbis Books, 1984), p. 16.

3. Clifford Geertz, "Ideology as a Cultural System," *The Interpretation of Cultures* (New York: Basic Books, 1973), p. 207.

4. John Petrov Plamenatz, *Ideology* (London: Macmillan, 1971), p. 23.

5. Ibid., p. 75.

6. Karl Marx, *The German Ideology, The Marx-Engels Reader*, edited by Robert C. Tucker, Second edition (New York: W.W. Norton & Company, Inc., 1978), p. 154.

7. Ibid., p. 166.

8. Ibid., p. 165.

9. Ibid., p. 154.

10. Ibid., p. 155.

11. Ibid., p. 174.

12. Claude Lefort, "On the Genesis of Ideology in Modern Societies," *Canadian Journal of Political and Social Theory, Ideology/Power* (Hiver/Printemps, 1983), Vol. VIII, Numbers 1-2, pp. 44-45.

13. John Keane, "Democracy and the Theory of Ideology," *Canadian Journal of Political and Social Theory, Ideology/Power* (Hiver/Printemps, 1983), Vol. VIII, Numbers 1-2, p. 5.

14. Anthony Giddens, "Four Theses on Ideology," *Canadian Journal of Political and Social Theory, Ideology/Power* (Hiver/Printemps, 1983), Vol. VIII, Numbers 1-2, pp. 18-19.

15. Ibid., p. 19.

16. Ibid., p. 19.

17. Ibid., p. 20.

18. Ibid., p. 20.

19. Ibid., p. 21.

20. Ibid., p. 21.

21. Ibid., p. 20.

22. A more developed outline of this aspect of Giddens' work can be found in a recent book by John B. Thompson, *Studies in the Theory of Ideology* (Cambridge: Polity Press, 1984).

23. György Márkus, "Concepts of Ideology in Marx," *Canadian Journal of Political and Social Theory, Ideology/Power* (Hiver/Printemps, 1983), Vol. VIII, Numbers 1-2, p. 84.

24. Ibid., p. 84.

25. Ibid., p. 88.

26. Ibid., p. 99.

27. Ibid., p. 87.

28. Ibid., pp. 86-87.

29. John B. Thompson, *Studies in the Theory of Ideology*, p. 74.

30. Ibid., p. 78.

31. Ibid., p. 82.

32. Ibid., p. 88.

33. Ibid., p. 130.

34. Ibid., p. 131.

35. Claude Lefort, "On the Genesis of Ideology in Modern Societies," p. 50.

36. John B. Thompson, *Studies in the Theory of Ideology*, p. 173.

37. Robert C. Tucker (Ed.), *The German Ideology*, pp. 172-173.

38. Vladimir Il'ich Lenin, *What is to Be Done? Selected Works*, Vol. I (Moscow: Progress Publishers, 1970), p. 138.

39. Ibid., p. 151.

40. Claude Lefort, "On the Genesis of Ideology in Modern Societies," p. 43.

41. Ibid., p. 45.

42. Paul Ricoeur, *Hermeneutics and the human sciences: Essays on language, action, and interpretation*, edited, translated and introduced by John B. Thompson (Cambridge: Cambridge University Press, 1981), p. 223.

43. Ibid., p. 223.

44. Ibid., p. 223.

45. Ibid., p. 222.

46. Ibid., p. 225.

47. Ibid., p. 225.

48. Ibid., p. 225.

49. Ibid., p. 226.

50. Ibid., p. 226.

51. Ibid., p. 226.

52. Ibid., p. 226.

53. Ibid., p. 227.

54. Ibid., p. 227.

55. Ibid., p. 231.

56. Ibid., p. 242.

57. Ibid., p. 243.

58. Ibid., p. 243.

59. Ibid., p. 224.

60. Ibid., p. 244.

61. Ibid., p. 244.

62. Ibid., p. 245.

63. Ibid., p. 245.

64. Karl Mannheim, *Ideology and Utopia*, translated from German by Louis Wirth and Edward Shils (New York: Harcourt, Brace, 1959), p. 71.

65. Ibid., p. 76.

66. Ibid., p. 80.

67. Paul Ricoeur, *Hermeneutics and the human sciences*, p. 240.

68. Alvin W. Gouldner, *The Dialectic of Ideology and Technology* (New York: Seabury Press, 1976), p. 2.

69. Ibid., p. 6.

70. Ibid., p. 25.

71. Ibid., p. 17.

72. Ibid., p. 20.

73. Ibid., p. 24.

74. Ibid., p. 135.

75. Ibid., p. 36.

76. Ibid., p. 45.

77. Ibid., p. 54.

78. Ernst Cassirer, *Language and Myth*, translated by Susanne K. Langer (New York: Dover Publications Inc., 1953), p. 7.

79. Clifford Geertz, "Ideology as a Cultural System," p. 213.

80. Ibid., p. 214.

81. Ibid., p. 218.

82. Ibid., p. 219.

83. Ibid., p. 220.

84. Ibid., p. 221.

85. Ibid., p. 230.

Chapter II

THE MEANING OF FAITH

Having explored some of the varying interpretations of ideology, we may conclude, with Segundo, that it is theoretically possible to attribute to ideology a function other than the legitimation of domination. We have seen that within the ongoing controversy around definitions and concepts of ideology, there are those writers who oppose Marx's view of ideology, and argue that ideology may also be understood as a progressive, necessary and even emancipatory social force. This view emphasizes the socially functional purpose of ideology, because it assumes that human beings need schematic codes of interpretation whereby to understand their own particular world, and meaning and place in that world. Because of their schematic, codified nature, ideologies are more easily comprehensible than complex, critical social theories and are thus more accessible to large social groups. The most important feature of ideologies for writers like Ricoeur, Geertz and especially Segundo is their function for motivating people to concrete action that is directed to social change and reconstruction. Thus ideologies allow people to act politically, in the sense of participating in fashioning a social order that corresponds to a particular image of what that order ought to be, with its concomitant distribution of power. These two aspects of ideology, as the image or standard of the ought-to-be as well as the means for realizing it, are crucial for Segundo's concept of ideology. Since Segundo approaches the issue of ideology from the point of view of Christian theology, for him the main focus concerning ideology is formulated in terms of the relationship between faith and ideology. But this is not entirely true, since Segundo understands faith in much broader terms than religious faith. Segundo analyzes faith as an essential *a priori* component of all ideologies, which can include religion, but not necessarily. Religious faith is one form of faith. As far as he is concerned, there is no ideology that is not preceded by some form of faith, and no faith that is not embodied in ideologies.[1] Although Segundo separates faith and ideology, he does so for analytical purposes in order to clearly define the elements, which are otherwise "inextricably mingled,"[2] yet distinct. Here it is necessary to identify a latent contradiction in Segundo's analysis of the relationship between faith and ideology. For the most part, he maintains a distinction which he characterizes as "radical" and "fundamental" between the two, since faith is the underpinning of values, while ideology is the means whereby those values are carried out in human praxis. However, there are times when Segundo makes statements like ideology is a "logical system of interconnected values," which includes both the values, or meaning-structure that orients a human life, along with means whereby those values are realized in concrete historical existence. He also says, at one point, that:

> Faith starts off by teaching us which value is the one to which we can 'entrust' our whole life, but then we also have to structure the rest of it. . . . This brings us to the whole problem-complex dealing with means. We see that faith gradually shifts from what we might call questions of 'conscience' to what we might call questions of 'method'.[3]

Statements such as these threaten to erupt in a confusion that arises when the boundaries distinguishing faith, values and ideology become blurred. Perhaps this confusion in reading Segundo can be avoided somewhat if it is borne in mind that, throughout Segundo's work the relationship between faith, values and ideology is structured in terms of a dialectical interaction and interpretation, so that he is perfectly consistent when he says, repeatedly, that faith, values and ideology are "inextricably mingled" but separate. Unfortunately, Segundo never explicitly describes the dialectical nature of this relationship, but dialectical it is, and it does help to avoid possible later confusions in reading Segundo if it is always borne in mind. Thus it becomes clear that faith and ideology each conditions and modifies the other within the context of historical contingency and change. Finally, in Segundo's view, faith cannot be conceived apart from ideology as ideology cannot stand apart from faith. If this occurs, both faith and ideology become distorted.

Prior to its connection with ideology, faith must first be understood in terms of its relationship to values or meaning-structure, and it is a relationship that is so close that at times faith and values seem to merge in Segundo's work. Faith relates to values-structure as its grounding, or as its hope in itself, in the sense that "In the end it will be seen that it was better to act" in accordance with a particular values-structure.[4] The commandment of Jesus to love one another (John 13:34-5) can illustrate this point. If one believes that the commandment to love one another is divinely inspired, i.e., comes from God, and that love is *in itself* a value that ought to motivate and guide a human life, then love is the meaning-structure or basic value to which a person adheres. For Segundo, however, the commandment to love one another can only be made meaningful in and through ideologies, that is, that system of means whereby values are actualized or rendered effective in praxis.

Thus a distinctive and determining factor of Segundo's theological method is his use of dialectics. It must be further noted that this methodological approach to theology is inextricably linked with an emancipatory interest[5] which conditions the values or meaning-structure of faith. Here it is useful to raise Segundo's construction of a "hermeneutic circle"[6] which provides a working structure through which his dialectical approach may be examined. The "hermeneutic circle" has four stages, which are in turn based upon two preconditions:

> They [the preconditions] are: 1. profound and enriching questions and suspicions about our real situation; 2. a new interpretation of the Bible that is equally profound and enriching. These two preconditions mean that there must in turn be four decisive factors in our circle. *Firstly* there is our way of experiencing reality, which leads us to ideological suspicion. *Secondly* there is the application of our ideological suspicion to the whole ideological superstructure in general and to theology in particular. *Thirdly* there comes a new way of experiencing theological reality that leads us to exegetical suspicion, that is, to the suspicion that the prevailing interpretation of the Bible has not taken important pieces of data into account. *Fourthly* we have our new hermeneutic, that is, our way of interpreting the fountainhead of our faith (i.e., Scripture) with the new elements at our disposal.[7]

The "ideological suspicion" Segundo refers to as the first stage of the hermeneutic circle arises from a disjunction between the representation of reality (through ideologies of either the *status quo* or traditional theology), and human beings' lived experience of that same reality. In other words, the first stage implies a growing awareness of a contradiction in reality, which leads to questions about the relationship between "the whole ideological superstructure in general," especially theology, and human experience in a specific historical context. This in turn generates a "new way" of under-standing scripture, or divine revelation, and a new interpretation of Biblical content (exegesis).

The "hermeneutic circle," then, turns traditional theological method on its head, so that human experience and historical contingency is the starting point of all scriptural analysis and its concomitant theological reflection, so that the latter is always subject to re-interpretation in the light of each particular historical period. In this way, the Bible is never read, but constantly re-read. Particular scriptural and theological reflections are constantly subjected to a process of ongoing negation which in turn generates ever-new interpretations which will inevitably dissolve as historical conditions change, and so on. Through this dialectical process of constant negation, Segundo is attempting to liberate theology from abstract ahistoricism to become a dynamic, emancipatory force in human experience. His attempt to liberate theology leads precisely to the total politicization of theology, whereby theology is of secondary importance to practical political activity so that theology follows in the service of the thoroughly historical project of human liberation. Thus, Segundo must negate theology to whatever extent that it posits an absolute, unchanging and universal truth in order to relativize theology within historical contextuality. In this way theology is subsumed by critical social theory in the sense of a transformation into a critical, self-reflexively partial and open-ended process, in the function of a particular historical goal: liberation. Human beings must begin their re-interpretation of Scripture and their theological reflection always from the point of the particular demands and needs of their given historical situation. The "human solutions" to "human problems" can only be sought by human agents, who strive together as "co-workers"[8] with God to realize the concrete goal of the liberation of humanity in history. Even though Segundo raises the issue of historical co-subjectivity, he does not develop it. He mentions it, but never explains in what sense human beings are co-workers with God. Otherwise he emphasizes the inevitable necessity of historical change occurring through the self-conscious activity of human beings committed to liberation. For Segundo, human agency is essential in the unfolding of freedom on the historical level. He remains the theologian in the view that this process will culminate in the negation of history itself, the necessary pre-condition for the completion or actualization of God's Kingdom.

Although this point will be developed further, it is important to anticipate it here, since the question of human agency is a crucial factor in an understanding of the dialectical method, especially as conceived of by Marx. It is in the area of methodology that liberation theology is most certainly indebted to and influenced by Marx,[9] and also by Hegel. Before pursuing this point, it is necessary to pause and examine in detail and clarity not only the relationship between faith and ideology, but also faith and ideology as distinct (but not divorced) concepts.

Faith

Segundo's clearest and most complete discussion of faith is to be found
in his volume *Faith and Ideologies*, where he separates faith and ideology
in order to define them as fully as possible. In *Faith and Ideologies*,
Segundo elaborates upon and extends the discussions raised in *The
Liberation of Theology* which was more concerned with expounding the
interrelationship between faith and ideology, with a fuller explanation of
ideology than faith. However, *Faith and Ideologies* presents a more
schematic analysis of faith and ideology, which results in their greater
differentiation so that the sense of their dialectical interconnection appears
weakened, although by no means absent. In this later volume, Segundo
seems to be attempting to strengthen his analysis of faith, as well as
distancing himself more from Marx, a point I will elaborate upon later.
However, the dialectical connection between faith and ideology is still
retained in *Faith and Ideologies*, which must also be read in the light of *The
Liberation of Theology*. For the moment, my discussion of Segundo's
conception of faith will be drawn mostly from *Faith and Ideologies*.

Segundo conceives of faith as an inescapable given of human psychology,
belonging to the "anthropological" dimension of human existence. In his
view, the actions and behaviour of a human being are inescapably bound up
with some form of "value-structure" which gives each person's life orientation and meaning. Given the inherent "economy of energy" that is
operative in the mental and emotional life of everyone, it is inevitable that
in deciding certain life-goals, including the values and actions that will
together realize those goals, one simultaneously excludes choosing other
values, thus closing off an unknown number of life possibilities.[10] Segundo
implies that human beings opt for basic value-structures, which they tend to
regard as absolute or ultimate in their pursuit of happiness.[11] The values
around which one builds or shapes one's life are rooted in faith, and
inevitably so, since it is impossible to empirically verify in advance whether
or not the value in question will be the most satisfying or not for that
person.[12]

The criteria by which human beings choose a particular values-structure
must then be established through the "referential witness"[13] of other human
beings which helps us assess whether our chosen value is the right or most
potentially satisfying one. Since we can never know, in advance, whether
our values are the most appropriate for a satisfying or happy life, it is only
through an act of faith that we can choose a particular meaning-structure
upon which to consecrate our lives.

Thus every option, every act of preferring one thing to another, involves the implementation of faith. Extending this to all the acts of "preference" in a human life, we can say that faith *structures* a whole life around some specific meaning. Life is valued, is considered meaningful, to the extent that concrete valuations converge towards that which has been chosen as the culminating thing in terms of value, of what ought to be. [14]

"Anthropological faith" is for Segundo a basic human characteristic, and does not necessarily involve religion. From earliest childhood onwards, human beings look to those around them, at first unconsciously, and then later consciously, for guidance and orientation as how to live and behave. For Segundo, the term "anthropological faith" applies to anything which gives meaning, direction or purpose to the life of a human being; "anthropological faith" even precedes reason and the rational choice of any valuational structure, however "scientific" or "objective."[15] Anthropological faith is so basic, so elemental to human existence, that it is "impossible" that one could "divest" oneself of it;[16] it is a dimension of human being "as universal as the human species itself"[17] and thus constitutes part of the ontological condition of all human beings.

Segundo applies Gregory Bateson's idea of "self-validating premises" to further explain what he means by "anthropological faith." The key passage in Bateson, which I quote in fuller detail than Segundo does, says:

In the natural history of the living human being, ontology and epistemology cannot be separated. His (commonly unconscious) beliefs about what sort of world it is will determine how he sees it and acts within it, and his ways of perceiving and acting will determine his beliefs about its nature. The living man is thus bound within a net of epistemological and ontological premises which—regardless of ultimate truth or falsity—become partially self-validating for him. [18]

Segundo's interpretation of Bateson's statement is a reformulation, and explanation of his own concept of "anthropological faith," which he equates with Bateson's notion of "premise." Like anthropological faith, a person's "premises" about the world precede rational process and scientific knowledge: The point here is that it is precisely the premise that is removed from reason. It precedes reason. . . . The premise is a-rational. Reason works on premises that are not created or verified by reason itself. [19]
Like anthropological faith, "ontological and epistemological premises" are part of the primary given of human existence, and constitute the values or meaning-structure at the centre of an individual's life. Referring again to

Bateson, Segundo assumes that Bateson's "premises" are easily translatable into his own understanding of values:

> Underlying the esoteric adjectives used by Bateson is a very simple human reality, precisely what I have been calling 'meaning-structure' or 'values-structure'. One of the primary tasks of that structure is to measure or gauge reality, not in terms of what is but in terms of what ought to be; i.e., in terms of its value . . . his dimension of premises is synonymous with my dimension of faith because both stand as 'self-valuating' vis-à-vis reason.[20]

The conclusion of this is that human beings hold certain premises about the world, their place and meaning in it, certain beliefs and values, because they do. It is precisely because there is no final proof or empirical verification whereby a particular values-structure is assumed by an individual, that allows Segundo to place faith, rather than reason, as the basis of knowledge and decision-making about values. Faith is thus a primary pre-rational mode of knowing that is not simply a-critical, but pre-critical and is itself impervious to critique: "Viewed from a rational standpoint, that [faith] choice is a-rational and a-scientific. . . . That is why we cannot assault the meaning-structure of anyone by waving a demonstrable 'falsehood' in front of them."[21] Faith is then incapable of either critical self-reflexivity or modification resulting from external critique. This implies that faith (religious or not) as Segundo sees it, is closed and fixed, in and of itself. [22] What can modify and mature faith, however, is ideology.

Before following this point, there are a few more remarks to be made about Segundo's concept of faith. For him, anthropological faith is both, and at the same time, absolute *and* relative, transcendent *and* immanent. Values may be relative in the sense that any given value or meaning-structure may inform one person's life, but are rejected by another. The absolute nature of values lies in the absoluteness of that value for a particular individual, which is consecrated or "crowned" as the central value of one's life. The relativity of the absolute value means that no given value can be understood as unconditional, or absolute *in itself*.

> But even in the most humble human life . . . we do encounter an absolute in the realm of value . . . there has to be something we 'prefer' for itself, not as a means or condition for some other person or thing. Here we have the 'absolute' as a value. . . . So we can say that every meaning-structure of human life is composed of things that a human being wills hypothetically (i.e. insofar as they help him or her to get something else), and of something that he or she wills absolutely (i.e. for its own sake) . . . here 'absolute' has nothing to do with something . . . metaphysical. The way in which the simplest or most superficial human being conceives happiness is that person's 'absolute'. [23]

Segundo introduces another feature that constitutes the absolute dimension or ultimacy of faith in a particular value through the idea of "transcendent datum." Segundo's discussion of the transcendent datum (or data) that is an integral part of faith allows him to show how anthropological faith may pass over into "authentic religious faith."[24] On the most simple level, the transcendent datum of anthropological faith is that criterion which makes a particular values-structure which cannot be verified in any objective, experiential way, "worthwhile."[25] The transcendent datum of any faith is that which embodies or grounds the ultimate meaning of possibilities of the universe and the human being. It must also be kept in mind that the transcendent datum of anthropological faith may, although not necessarily, refer to God, or have nothing to do with religion or metaphysics.

Segundo uses the idea of transcendent datum both formally and substantively, making it sometimes difficult to differentiate these aspects completely. On the formal level, a transcendent datum which is implicit in faith refers to the absolute nature of the particular meaning-structure which constitutes the valuational core of an individual's life, so that that specific values-structure transcends all other values, which are subordinate to it. In this sense, transcendent data mean the same thing that Bateson meant (according to Segundo) by self-validating "premises." "These premises are what I have chosen to call 'transcendent data', and they give a certain direction to one's whole values-structure." [26]

On the substantive level, a transcendent datum can also imply transcendence in a metaphysical, or religious sense. Thus the transcendent character of a person's chosen ultimate meaning-structure may easily transform into the further belief or "acquisition of transcendent data that are decisive for the realization of certain values established by anthropological faith." [27] Segundo implies that "authentic religious faith" develops as anthropological faith matures, so that the formal character of a transcendent datum of a particular value expands or unfolds into the substantive content of transcendence in the metaphysical sense. But this is one example of transcendent datum in faith; any value that informs one's life, that places it above all others, is the transcendent datum of that person's faith. Or, one could say that the *"subjective* absolutization" one gives to a values-structure constitutes a transcendent datum of that person's faith. [28]

These two aspects or features of the transcendent datum of faith merge together in Segundo's interpretations of Jesus' confrontation with the Pharisees, in Mark 2:23-28. When Jesus defends the actions of his disciples with "The sabbath was made for man, not man for the sabbath," he is not uttering a religious statement, but rather articulates his own human value-structure. In Segundo's view, "Jesus is trying to establish a scale of values"[29] in which the sabbath is relative, subordinate to the absolute value of the primacy of human welfare. Jesus speaks from a secular and religious standpoint *at the same time*, in that for him, the highest criterion, valid in itself, that places the sabbath in its proper secondary place, is the requirement of human well-being which precedes all other considerations, including religious ones. What Jesus has expressed, strictly speaking, is the preference for a "secular" value over and above a specifically religious (ritual) value. However, this preference for the secular, or human, over the religious, turns into a genuine or authentic religious value in that:

> The God of Jesus, paradoxically enough, points to human beings, their needs and their values. This explains the unexpected conclusion in the Letter of James, when it seeks to define religion that is pure and undefiled: 'To go to the help of orphans and widows in their distress . . .' [30]

For Segundo, who now introduces the distinction between authentic and false religion, "pure and undefiled" religious values are grounded in and validated by fully human criteria. Segundo develops this concept in relation to Mark 7:14-23, arguing that no amount of strict observance to ritual or commandments of religious law can render a person moral, or his actions as genuinely religious. In,

> Jesus' eyes a religious 'law' cannot give value *in itself* to any category of human acts . . . it is the intended project of a human being towards his or her fellow humans that constitutes the one and only criterion, however hazardous,for determining the 'law', the will of God. That project, in other words, is the one and only criterion for spelling out what is good in *itself*. [31]

Thus, that which is authentically moral in human beings is generated from within, and not determined by external demands; so that observance of the divine commands pertain to a "religion of the heart," whereas adherence to the laws of human religious traditions constitutes a "religion of the lips." [32] Segundo further states that according to John, the only commandment Jesus ever issued to his disciples was thoroughly human, and thus authentically religious (as opposed to instrumentally or functionally religious) since it came from God: "As I loved you, so you are to love one another." This statement of Jesus is an expression of 'pure and undefiled' religion, that is "something which is grounded in values that an alien observer would call simply 'human'." [33] Finally, what was it about Jesus that made the disciples believe in him as the son of God, what was it that made them accept him as the revelation of God? Segundo answers, "That Jesus was recognized as the revelation of God only by those people who *already* had those values." [34] Thus the disciples, and those who accepted Jesus as coming from God, already possessed faith in a values or meaning-structure which was confirmed by Jesus: "To be quite logical then, we must say that faith had to precede faith." [35]

For Segundo, the work of the Holy Spirit, the true intent of God's will, is in the service of thoroughly human values, since to love others is to do good for them, thus helping people to recover their full humanity.[36] This implies helping people to overcome alienation, the negation of those conditions and forms which prevent human beings from realizing their true human potential. The Holy Spirit works within history to realize freedom. To see God active in human history, inspiring humanity to love each other and do what is best for other people is an insight or "self-validating premise" that constitutes a transcendent datum of human faith. Thus, Segundo attempts to merge the human and the divine, anthropological faith with religious faith, in positing a transcendent datum of faith that combines those two dimensions. The value or meaning- structure of an individual's life is doubly transcendent, in the sense that the chosen value is absolute, and transcendent of all values as well as being related to God's perceived will or purpose for effecting the welfare of all humanity.

However, it is not necessary to believe either in God or in Jesus as the son of God, in order to experience transcendence in one's own faith:

> Whether we will it or not, transcendent data are operative in all structured human conduct . . . these data are not transcendent because the language is divine in its origin or because it speaks about God or some 'beyond'. One can be frankly and consistently atheistic, yet one will be forced of necessity to establish as valid certain data that cannot be verified empirically. [37]

The transcendent character of all human faith does not necessarily imply a metaphysics,[38] or a belief in God, although it can easily lead to it, and with no apparent contradiction or fundamental altering of one's faith or values-structure. Jesus Christ cannot elicit a faith-response that is *essentially* different from that elicited by Ché Guevara, since both figures stand as referential witnesses to a particular values structure that some human beings would choose as their own, simply because they would assume that "*given that this person or these persons are thus and thus so, in the end it will be seen that it was better to act in this way.*"[39] Even the resurrection does not in itself put Jesus Christ on a higher plane than a purely secular figure, like Guevara, since the ultimate object of faith is neither Jesus nor his resurrection, but the values embodied in his words and actions. Certainly, the resurrection of Jesus is a transcendent datum in one's faith in what Jesus represented, but only in the sense of any transcendent datum, or self-validating premise, or values-structure. Because the verification of the resurrection is eschatological and not empirical, it remains an object of faith *"up to the very end."*[40] It can never be known in any way other than belief. The resurrection is an additional and optional piece of the transcendent data at the centre of faith that points to or supports the ultimate meaning-structure of a Christian faith, the most important conclusion of which is, *"in the end it will be seen that it was better to act as Jesus acted and taught."*[41]

Finally, the real point of faith in Jesus is that Jesus stands as a paradigmatic referential witness or image of an "interlocutor" of those values which promote the interests and welfare of humanity.[42] And here Segundo adds a somewhat curious point: what "the transcendent data of the tradition which constitutes our faith" identifies is which God we relate to and "on whom is grounded and structured our meaning- world." [43]

Whoever this God is, it is not God which defines the values by which a human being should live, it is rather those values, the choice of which is prior to the development of religious faith, which identify or point toward that God in whom one believes. However, an analysis of the values-structures of one's life does not reveal God, but rather "various types of personal relationship with one or more interlocutors who are more or less anonymous."[44] Segundo ends his discussion on faith with a warning: "It is all the more hazardous for us to try at all cost to discover God under those anonymous interlocutors insofar as we have very good reason for erasing the name of God where it is put by many religious persons (*GS*:19)." [45]

This last cautionary sentence refers back to Segundo's distinction between authentic and illusory religious faith that he dichotomizes in terms of a "religion of the heart" over against a "religion of the lips."[46] What Segundo basically fears is that the reification of the symbols and rituals of a religious tradition will "conceal rather than reveal the authentic face of God and religion."[47] The danger is that the reification, absolutization or sacralization of religious practice through exclusive observance of the laws and rituals of a given tradition can lead to a confusion of faith and religion. An apotheosis of the sabbath, for example, leads human beings directly away from focusing on the primacy and centrality of human values, and into idolatry, wherein the thing replaces the substance. Religion is not faith, and cannot designate the values or meaning-structure of life. Religion belongs to the realm of ideology and as such, follows faith, or is an extension of anthropological faith. The demands of a religious tradition are always subordinate to the transcendent data of faith, those "self-validating premises" which constitute meaning-structure. For Segundo, religion is always instrumental, a means through which people attempt to actualize those prior values "that are independent of the God who is adopted and adored." [48] For Segundo, it is the human realm in terms of humanity and its needs and aspirations for its own welfare that is prior to the religious realm. Thus faith is always understood as attached to some particular value or meaning-structure around which one constructs one's life. Referring back to Bateson's remarks about self-validating premises, we saw that these "epistemological and ontological premises" have a certain content, which relates to the nature of the world in which we live. Segundo applies Bateson in discussing his own concept of anthropological faith, as has been shown. Even when Segundo discusses the initial basic human faith of a child through adolescence to adulthood,[49] this anthropological faith is always faith *in* someone or something. The point is, that Segundo conceives of faith as having some kind of content; it is certainly of great importance what that content is, and as far as he is concerned, it should be a values-structure that affirms the importance of human material and spiritual well-being as paramount to all other values. Faith relates to values as its grounding in the sense of a trust and commitment to a particular value, as outlined above. For Segundo, the only "truth" or ultimate truth is liberation itself.[50]

What then, can be understood from Segundo's statement in *The Liberation of Theology* that faith is "empty?" This point must be cleared up before going on to discuss ideology, and its relationship to faith. Otherwise we risk confusion about the relation between faith, values and ideology. Although more will be said about this later, it is necessary to state now that for Segundo, values, being necessarily and inevitably grounded in basic anthropological faith – "as universal as the human species itself"[51] – precedes ideology, which is the instrument or vehicle for the practical actualization of values. If values belong to the realm of faith, then how can faith be empty, even if we assume that faith and values are not identical?

The passage in question reads:

> What then, does the faith say to me in the concrete? What is its truth *content*? . . . my only response can be: *nothing*. Let me repeat that in another way. If someone were to ask me what I have derived from my faith-inspired encounter as a clear-cut, absolute truth that can validly give orientation to my concrete life, then my honest response should be: nothing. [52]

If this statement is read out of context, and taken as a final conclusion, then everything said previously becomes open to serious question, because there then appears a serious contradiction in Segundo's work, breeding an impenetrable confusion. However, the immediately following paragraph goes on the explain and qualify the immediately preceding one:

> However, we are carrying the balance of faith to an irrational extreme in talking about *one* encounter with the objective font of absolute truth. If it is in fact a matter of only *one* encounter, then there is no solution to the problem. The absolute truth would remain totally obscured behind the ideology exhibited in that one historical encounter. It is quite clear that in history we can only have historical encounters [with God] that is, encounters bound up with relative contexts.[53]

What Segundo is trying to say is that faith is empty if it focuses upon a specific religious tradition, with its historically mediated truth claims, as its proper object, rather than a value. He writes that "What is really chosen is a value, not one specific line of tradition among many others."[54] If one tries to directly apply the specific faith-based response of Biblical persons or witnesses to the particular historical demands of today, one will find oneself engaged in a hopeless and impossible task, in that one, singular "faith-inspired encounter" has *nothing* to say to a person who inhabits a different historical situation that is separated from the Biblical world by twenty centuries. The only way that one can "encounter" God in the present historical situation is through pertinent ideologies. He writes:

> Our theory, in other words, assumes that there is an empty space between the conception of God that we receive from our faith and the problems that come to us from an ever-changing history. So we must build a bridge between our conception of God and the real-life problems of history. This bridge, this provisional but necessary system of means and ends is what we are calling *ideology* here. Obviously each and every ideology presented in Scripture is a human element even though in the intensely unified psychological processes of human beings it may seem to be a direct and straightforward translation of the proper conception of the God who had been revealed.
>
> Consider the Israelites who arrived in the promised land. For them the extermination of their enemies was concretely the most clear-cut way of conceiving who God was and what he was commanding in the face of specific historical circumstances. Thus the extermination of enemies was the ideology that faith adopted, with or without critical thought, at that moment in history. And to be logical here, we must say the same thing with regard to the gospel message. When Jesus talked about freely proffered love and nonresistance to evil, he was facing the same problem of filling the void between his conception of God (or perhaps that of the first Christian community) and the problems existing in his age. In short, we are dealing here with another ideology, not the content of faith itself.[55]

Faith, then, is only empty when it confuses a particular religious tradition along with its historically contextualized faith-inspired praxis, with values, which are the proper object of faith. If one structures one's life around a value such as love of the neighbour, for example, then one has faith that it is best to live by that value, regardless of being a Christian or not. In other words, the value of love is grounded in anthropological faith, although it may be extended and confirmed in a Christian faith. Thus, if one holds this value as the ultimate value in one's life, and one happens to be a Christian, then one's religious option — Christianity — is mere "co-incidence,"[56] and actually of secondary importance. Christianity is a "pedagogical process,"[57] or what one adopts as the most appropriate way for expressing one's chosen value, although Christianity is itself not necessary to do so. If one opts for Christianity as the means (ideology) or the appropriate "educational *process* dealing with values,"[58] then one "absolutizes" this process for oneself "in a free act that cannot help but be an absolutization, since we give our all to it. And to absolutize this process is to say that God, the Absolute, is guiding it in some special way."[59]

With this point clarified, we may finally turn to the question of ideology, and its specific relationship with faith and values. This part of the discussion will bring out more clearly the dialectical[60] nature of the relationship between faith and ideology, and as I indicated earlier, it is the dialectical method that is the key radical feature of Segundo's formulation of a critical theology. The dialectical method of Segundo's theologizing, which is most clearly and fully developed in the relation between faith and ideology, has crucial implications for understanding how Segundo sees the further relation between man and God, the historical and the eschatological, between liberation and salvation — themes which will be explored later. Before broaching the issue of the dialectical relation between faith and ideology, it is necessary to examine Segundo's use of Marx, since Segundo's concept of ideology is defined in fact through a polemical dialogue that he initiates with Marx.

61

NOTES

1. Juan Luis Segundo, *Faith and Ideologies*, p. 142.

2. Juan Luis Segundo, *The Liberation of Theology*, p. 105.

3. Juan Luis Segundo, *Faith and Ideologies*, pp. 7-8

4. Ibid., p. 167.

5. Juan Luis Segundo, *The Liberation of Theology*, p. 5.

6. In using this term, "hermeneutic circle," Segundo informs his readers that it is used "in a strict sense" to describe the method of interpretation of the New Testament employed by Rudolf Bultmann. Segundo claims that the term "hermeneutic circle" applies more accurately to his methodological approach to Scripture than to Bultmann's. Since Segundo tells his readers nothing of Bultmann's "hermeneutic circle," and since he makes no further elaboration upon this particular claim, there is no reason to pursue the matter here. Segundo merely mentions Bultmann in passing, then goes on to describe his own version of the "hermeneutic circle."

7. Juan Luis Segundo, *The Liberation of Theology*, p. 7.

8. Ibid., p. 154.

9. Ibid., p. 35, n. 10.

10. Juan Luis Segundo, *Faith and Ideologies*, p. 5.

11. Ibid., p. 7.

12. Ibid., p. 5.

13. Ibid., p. 6.

14. Ibid., p. 7.

15. Ibid., p. 13.

16. Ibid., p. 13.

17. Ibid., p. 15.

18. Gregory Bateson, *Steps to an Ecology of Mind* (New York: Ballantine Books, 1972), p. 314.

19. Juan Luis Segundo, *Faith and Ideologies*, p. 92.

20. Ibid., pp. 92-93.

21. Ibid., p. 93.

22. An unnerving implication of this concept of faith is its potential for a literalism and fundamentalism that could easily serve goals and values that are directly opposed to human liberation. This is a danger Segundo never addresses, neither does he even raise its possibility. Segundo obviously relies on ideology — the correct ideology — to preclude any such danger. It might then be argued that Segundo places too much weight on ideology and its power to move human beings in the direction of liberation. If this argument is valid, then the relationship between faith and ideology loses its dialectical character. These are problems that are at least implicit in Segundo's argumentation, and should be confronted in another study of his work.

23. Juan Luis Segundo, *Faith and Ideologies*, pp. 18-19.

24. Ibid., p. 83.

25. Ibid., p. 73.

26. Ibid., p. 156.

27. Ibid., p. 78.

28. Juan Luis Segundo, *The Liberation of Theology*, p. 107. Segundo uses "transcendent datum" in very much the same way that Paul Tillich describes the "ultimate concern" implicit in faith. "Transcendent datum" and "ultimate concern" are features of that faith which places certain values in a person's life above all others. For a fuller discussion of "ultimate concern," see Paul Tillich, *Dynamics of Faith* (New York: Harper & Row, Inc., 1958).

29. Juan Luis Segundo, *Faith and Ideologies*, p. 41.

30. Ibid., p. 42.

31. Ibid., p. 44.

32. Ibid., p. 45.

33. Ibid., p. 46.

34. Ibid., p. 64.

35. Ibid., p. 65.

36. Ibid., p. 48.

37. Ibid., p. 166.

63

38. Ibid., p. 167.

39. Ibid., p. 167.

40. Ibid., p. 165.

41. Ibid., p. 165.

42. Ibid., p. 167.

43. Ibid., p. 167.

44. Ibid., p. 167.

45. Ibid., p. 167.

46. Ibid., p. 45.

47. *Gaudium et Spes, The Documents of Vatican II*, n. 19.

48. Juan Luis Segundo, *Faith and Ideologies*, p. 39.

49. Ibid., pp. 10-15.

50. Juan Luis Segundo, *The Liberation of Theology*, p. 118.

51. Juan Luis Segundo, *Faith and Ideologies*, p. 15.

52. Juan Luis Segundo, *The Liberation of Theology*, p. 108.

53. Ibid., p. 108.

54. Ibid., p. 178.

55. Ibid., p. 116.

56. Ibid., p. 178.

57. Ibid., p. 179.

58. Ibid., p. 178.

59. Ibid., p. 109.

60. There is something of a difference between the way in which Segundo actually employs the dialectic in his methodological approach to the inter-relationship between faith and ideology, and his explicit attempt to define what dialectic means to him. His own definition of the dialectic appears to be less sophisticated than his actual use of it: he defines "dialectic" as a "type of cognition," an "approach to knowledge which does not consist in the mere fact

of viewing parts as moments of a whole in process. It consists in the fact that the moments mutually interact and change" *(Faith and Ideologies*, p. 206). He is openly critical of the Hegelian and Marxian conception of dialectics as an ongoing process of the negation of the negation *(Faith and Ideologies*, pp. 206, 214) in which negation is understood as a liberating act whereby potentiality strives for self-realization through the negation of those forms which alienate itself from its self-realization. In my view, Segundo's criticism of the negation of the negation is based upon his own, perhaps not fully conscious desire to construct a permanent, fixed truth within the relativism of constant historical change. Yet his concept of faith as only meaningful when expressed in and through constantly changing, historically relevant ideologies inevitably involves the notion of negation of the negation.

Chapter III

IDEOLOGY

The Influence of Marx on Segundo's Concept of Ideology

As I said in the beginning, no serious discussion of ideology can take place without consideration of Marx's critical definition. Segundo not only engages with Marx in working out his own concept of ideology, but he also openly acknowledges the "profound" influence of Marx[1] on theology in general: "There can be no doubt about his influence on contemporary theology."[2] Marx's influence on liberation theology is particulary evident throughout the work of Segundo, most importantly on the level of methodology, which is what distinguishes liberation theology from most other forms of theological method.[3] The influence of Marx on Segundo will be analyzed in fuller detail later in the chapter, but for the moment I propose that on the level of methodology, Marx is the primary influence on Segundo, and that Segundo's work in general is a kind of polemical "dialogue" with certain central aspects of Marx's thought, especially in the area of ideology. Segundo refers to the influence of Marx on his own thought indirectly when he writes: ". . . Marx's work was such a stimulus for theology that new methods and profound questions in present-day theology are an inheritance from him. . . ."[4]

Segundo begins his dialogue with Marx about ideology by raising the well-addressed question of how Marx understood the relationship between the economic base and the ideological superstructure, realizing along with many other writers, that the exact nature of this relationship cannot be finally determined in Marx's work:

> At times Marx seems to say that the economic structure *determines* the ideologies; at times he seems to say that it *produces* the ideologies; at times he seems to say that it *conditions* them; and sometimes he even seems to say that it *is conditioned* to some extent by them.[5]

Marx's concept of ideology, as outlined in *The German Ideology*, analyzes the function of ideology as a mechanism which sustains domination in class society. While Segundo is fully aware of this aspect of Marx's thinking on ideology, there are moments when he tries to show that Marx might have thought otherwise, and that Marx's statements about ideology express a somewhat ambivalent attitude. Segundo attempts somewhat unconvincingly to prove this by selecting various passages from Marx which he hopes will demonstrate that Marx saw, to some extent, consciously or unconsciously, the emancipatory potential of ideology. Segundo offers the following quotations from Marx to illustrate his point:

> The changes in the economic foundation lead sooner or later to the transformation of the whole immense superstructure. In studying such transformations it is always necessary to distinguish between the material transformation of the economic conditions of productions, which can be determined with the precision of natural science, and the legal, political, religious, artistic, or philosophic—in short, *ideological* forms in which men become *conscious* of this conflict and fight it out. [6]

The other quotation Segundo takes from Marx refers to the necessity of the formation of a revolutionary class, "which comprises the majority of the members of society and in which there develops a *consciousness* of the need for a fundamental revolution." [7]

Segundo interprets these passages as instances where Marx equates and identifies ideology and class consciousness, so that at least at times, the two concepts as used by Marx are actually interchangeable. Segundo writes: "Marx applies the term 'ideology' to the consciousness of a culture."[8] Segundo italicizes 'consciousness' in the first quote from Marx to try to show that even Marx recognizes that ideology has the capacity to be a progressive, emancipatory force that serves the revolutionary process. In fact, Segundo misinterprets Marx by confusing in Marx, ideology with class consciousness, and he does this because he allows his own understanding of ideology—ideology as possessing the capacity to become an emancipatory, revolutionary force—to superimpose itself over Marx's concept of class consciousness. While it may be legitimate for Segundo to expand the notion of ideology to include ideology-critique and perhaps even function in the manner of a revolutionary class consciousness that comprehends the real nature of class society, it is not at all valid to claim that Marx saw ideology in the same way. Marx understood ideology and class consciousness as completely different phenomena. Ideology positively reflects the ideas which correspond to the existent structures of society, i.e., the relations of material production and their ensuing social relations. Class consciousness emerges when that segment of the exploited classes, the proletariat, sees through the ideological mystification that misrepresents the true nature of class society with the result that the proletariat becomes self-conscious of its role in that society and the necessity for its own self-negation in order to abolish class society.

The theme and importance of class consciousness in Marx's work was analyzed by Georg Lukács, from whom Segundo derives his own concept of class-consciousness.[9] Lukács preserved Marx's distinction between ideology and class consciousness when he wrote that "historical knowledge" becomes possible when the "ideology" of the ruling class is penetrated.[10] According to Lukács, the importance that Marx placed upon the necessity of a revolutionary class consciousness lay in the fact that the proletariat could only act as the bearer and subject of the revolution when it became fully conscious of the true nature of class society, and its own position in it, as I said previously. Lukács argues that for Marx, revolutionary class consciousness is the pre-condition of revolutionary praxis, so that the consciousness of the revolutionary proletariat – "the last class consciousness in the history of mankind" – must expose the real nature of class society in order to overcome it. [11]

In revolutionary class consciousness, theory and practice come together, thus bringing forth the praxis of revolution. In this sense, class consciousness is understood as a practical activity. Thus, for Marx, the consciousness of the revolutionary proletariat is a "practical, critical activity" whose goal is to change the world.[12] Revolutionary consciousness then, is a dynamic element in the revolutionary process which is "the driving force of history." Bourgeois ideology, on the other hand, is static and closed, in that it attempts to reproduce and maintain the class structure of society. In this way bourgeois ideology is an essentially affirmative and preserving mechanism of class society, while the revolutionary consciousness of the proletarian revolutionary class is the negation of itself and class society, and bourgeois ideology. When the consciousness of the proletariat "penetrates" or sees through bourgeois ideology to comprehend the real nature of class society, it also develops an ideology-critique of society or critical social theory.

Segundo distorts the meaning of ideology in Marx by blurring the boundary lines between ideology and class consciousness, causing them to overlap. Segundo is led to do this as a result of his attempt to try to rescue religion from the realm of ideology *in the pejorative sense* that Marx ascribed to it, so that he can claim religion to be ideology in the emancipatory sense. Segundo finds himself in the somewhat paradoxical position of arguing that although religion *is* ideology, it may either serve the interests of class society or it may serve as a means whereby to expose the truth within class society, becoming a form of liberatory, self-conscious, revolutionary praxis. Given what was said about the possibilities of ideology in Chapter I, it seems unnecessary for Segundo to engage in polemics with Marx to the extent that he does, even trying to prove that Marx views ideology, to whatever minuscule extent, the way he does himself.

Segundo's ultimate misreading of Marx on the question of ideology can be perhaps explained by Segundo's more general theoretical dependence on Marx, which he hopes will enable him to formulate a transformed Christian theology which can become a practical, conscious activity in service of the social and political project of liberation of Latin American society. Because Segundo is attempting to construct a particular theory of society, which has a theological - or religious - dimension to be sure, he is nonetheless engaged in a critical social analysis by definition, and in this way his use of Marx is entirely justified. Segundo is very aware of the fact that theology is incapable of positioning a theory of history and society on its own, that it cannot stand apart from its own social context if it hopes to offer a theory of society as a whole. This is why Segundo insists that "right now theologians . . . must perform the task of introducing the most fruitful elements of the social sciences into their own everyday work of theologizing."[13] This point of view is underscored by theologian Charles Davis as well: "Theology in the critical tradition cannot confine itself to religious data and evade the task of offering a general theory of society and history." [14]

Segundo's "indebtedness" to Marx rests upon the fact that Marx's theory of "historical materialism" provides him with a methodology which "enables us to discover the authentic face of reality in line with our own historical commitment."[15] Segundo has no choice but to go beyond the parameters of strictly theological or religious thinking in order to understand his own contemporary social context. The methodological premises of his theology are actually a kind of application of Marx's basic methodological approach, such as is expressed in *The German Ideology* and elsewhere. The following quotation from Marx applies equally well to Segundo's methodology:

The premises from which we begin . . . are the real individuals, their activity and the material conditions under which they live, both those which they find already existing and those produced by their activity . . . The first premise of all human history is, of course, the existence of all living human individuals. [16]

Segundo is trying to construct a critical theology through a materialist methodology, but his attempt to appropriate Marx presents him with a major problem on the question of ideology, and especially religion. If Segundo argues that ideology is a potentially emancipatory force on the practical and theoretical level, and that religion constitutes an ideology in this sense, then he must break with Marx on this particular point, since for Marx religion *is* a manifestation of ideology, and ideology is a repressive, not liberatory form of consciousness. But he does not and instead tries to see in Marx the possibility of interpreting ideology as at least an incipient form of *critical* class consciousness. If Segundo has difficulty making this case, then he at least tries to show that there is some sense of neutrality in ideology as Marx saw it: "It would seem, then, that the term 'ideology' is neutral from the standpoint of value. Depending on circumstances, in other words, laws, political structures, arts and (?) religions might be good or bad, better or worse." [17] However, Segundo cannot push this interpretation very far either, and he seems to be aware of it, when he writes: "Hence even in these passages where the term 'ideology' seems to be more neutral, it still tends to have a negative connotation for Marx." [18]

While there is no way in which Segundo can demonstrate that Marx viewed religious ideologies as progressive or even potentially serving the revolutionary process, Segundo does properly identify one possible flaw in Marx's thinking about religion, which should not be overlooked. In the *Introduction to the Critique of Hegel's Philosophy of Right*, Marx writes: "*Religious* suffering is at the same time an *expression* of real suffering and a *protest* against real suffering. Religion is the sigh of the oppressed creature, the sentiment of a heartless world, and the soul of soulless conditions." [19] This recognition of religion as the expressed "protest" of humanity against suffering could provide a fruitful avenue for exploring the liberatory potential of religion. If religion could orient itself around a central "preferential option" for the poor and oppressed, and convince human beings that God is on their side, as liberator and deliverer from "real," i.e., concrete suffering and oppression, such as the God of Exodus – all key concepts of liberation theology – then perhaps it could demonstrate a revolutionary potential. This revolutionary potential would express itself on the level of an individual and collective urge or desire for social justice, based on the belief that somehow God wants human beings to live together in peace and justice. In fact, the general orientation of liberation theology can be said to stem from just such a conviction, which is one of the reasons why the Exodus story occupies a central and paradigmatic position among Biblical narratives for most Latin American liberation theologians.

According to Gustavo Gutierrez, for example, the Exodus "is a political liberation through which Yahweh expresses his love for his people and the gift of total liberation is received." [20]

In this respect, Marx did encounter something resembling liberation theology in his own time in the form of utopian socialism, which he condemned. Marx's rejection of utopian socialism is based on his distinction between "scientific" knowledge which is able to expose the concrete nature of the forces of material production which give rise to consequent injustices in society, and religious or humanitarian impulses which might inspire the masses to revolt, but on the basis of ignorance and sentimentality. Marx's opposition to the utopian socialists, some of whom were inspired by a religious vision of the just cause of the suffering masses in their struggle to bring down the rich and mighty, is forcefully demonstrated in his angry confrontation with Wilhelm Weitling, a "tailor by profession, a wandering preacher by calling . . . a fearless German visionary . . . (who) advocated a class war of the poor against the rich," and who wrote with "fervent evangelical zeal."[21] Marx denounced this brand of socialism on the grounds of its lack of carefully thought out principles and its absence of "a strict scientific idea . . . (and) positive doctrine." [22]

A socialism that is grounded upon moral principles and a religious commitment to aid the suffering and oppressed, is open to the criticism that it merely replaces one absolute truth by another, and is based on a subjective understanding of reality that is a-historical. As Engels wrote in his critique of the utopian socialists, in all fidelity with the views of Marx: "To make a science of socialism, it had first to be placed upon a real basis." [23] Because of this sharp distinction between a scientific basis of knowledge of society as a basis for social change, and a simple protest against suffering that is inspired by religious faith, Marx could not possibly accept religion as offering any legitimate foundation upon which to construct a true class consciousness that is so crucial to the revolutionary project. He was perfectly consistent when he rejected religion as "the opium of the people," insisting that: "The abolition of religion as the *illusory* happiness of men, is a demand for their *real* happiness. The call to abandon their illusions about their condition is a *call to abandon a condition which requires illusions*." [24]

Marx rejects religion precisely as a function of the preservation of the ideological superstructure, wherein religion operates in the maintenance of class society by explaining its consequent injustice and exploitation as a "vale of tears" to be endured, rather than a set of material conditions to be abolished. It makes no difference for Marx whether religion is used as a basis of protest against suffering that is caused by concrete material conditions, because this approach to the need for social change excludes a scientific understanding of economics and its role in the forces of material production in capitalist, class society. Thus, even when religion embraces the cause of the oppressed, in Marx's view it still functions as an ideological barrier to the formation of a practical, revolutionary class consciousness, inspiring human beings to fight their oppressors in a condition of ignorance, rather than from a position based upon a scientific knowledge of society.

Segundo criticizes Marx's dichotomy between ideology and science:

> In Marx's thought ideology in the pejorative sense stands opposed precisely to social knowledge that is scientific and objective. It is knowledge distorted by (subjective) interests. However . . . this opposition is really superficial and misleading. [25]

Segundo goes on to explain why he thinks this dichotomy is illegitimate, arguing in the vein of writers like Mannheim, that science cannot be free of ideology, that it cannot be completely objective and value-free. There is no point to reproduce his argument here, as this critique of Marx has been explored in detail by the Frankfurt school, Habermas, Ricoeur and others who are critical of any positivist or "scientistic" approach to knowledge. As well-founded as Segundo's critique of Marx's separation of science and ideology may be, it does not help him in his attempt to salvage religion and ideology as being treated as progressive forces in Marx's thought. For this purpose, Segundo would do better to refer more extensively to writers like Paul Ricoeur or Clifford Geertz. Why Segundo does not do this is not at all clear. What is clear is that Segundo insists on appropriating Marx in such a way as to use Marx to support his own views on the possibility that religion may have progressive, ideological value in the process of human liberation. It cannot be too much emphasized that on this point, Segundo's task is highly problematic, at the very least. It is often difficult to determine from Segundo's writing whether he has simply misread (and thus misunderstood) Marx, or if he appropriates Marx's ideas in such a fashion as to mold Marx to his own particular viewpoint, whatever the consequences may be for an accurate understanding of Marx's thought. Segundo does not consider this, but continues to develop his own ideas and takes Marx with him.

For Segundo, religion viewed "under the lens of ideological suspicion" [26] reveals two possibilities: that religion, through a "specific interpretation" of Scripture imposed by the ruling classes can function in the material interest of these classes, or, that religion could be taken over by the proletariat and used as a "weapon in the class struggle through a new and more faithful

72

interpretation of the Scriptures."[27] In both instances, religion functions as an ideology in the service of the interests of a particular class. Segundo loses himself momentarily by claiming the superiority of one ideological standpoint over another on the basis of truth content, exactly reproducing one of his own criticisms of Marx, and precisely on this point. The question is, how is it, and by what criteria, can it be said that the proletariat is capable of a "more faithful interpretation" of Scripture than any other social group? This is exactly the question posed by Segundo himself in regard to Marx's distinction between ideology of the bourgeoisie, and the scientific knowledge that informs the insight of the class consciousness of the proletariat. Segundo makes his point against Marx through a quotation from Adam Schaff, who writes:

> The point is that knowledge is distorted only when it is conditioned by the interests of the 'descending' classes: i.e., those interested in maintaining the existing order and threatened by its disappearance. When knowledge or cognition is condition by the interests of the 'ascending' revolutionary classes, who are in favour of the social transformation in progress, there is no cognitive distortion. At this point in his reflection Marx ceased to be interested in the problem of the social factors conditioning knowledge and the whole problem of cognitive distortion. [28]

Clearly, whatever ideological expression informs the reading of Scriptures, the point is that the subsequent interpretations are themselves conditioned by a particular interest, be it in terms of sustaining the *status quo* or negating it. The fact is, and in accordance with Segundo's reasoning, that the Scriptures can be used as an ideological weapon for either (or any) interested social group, which then implies what Segundo maintains all along: that Scripture in no way stands outside of history, culture or society, but is entirely mediated by them. To continue further in Segundo's line of argumentation, what only matters is the basic interest, or values-structure which informs or inspires an ideology. At this point it is important to dwell more precisely upon what Segundo means by ideology, and its relationship to faith and values.

Faith, Values and Ideology

First, it is important to summarize Segundo's concept of faith and recall that faith is an "act of trust and surrender"[29] in a specific value or meaning-structure, which is chosen as ultimate by a human being for his or her practical life. Thus one absolutizes a particular value, and may understand oneself to have absolute faith in that particular value. Segundo's problem is how to render these values operative in praxis, or to put the same problem in a slightly different way, how to render one's faith (as attached to or grounding a specific values-structure) effective, and in his view, meaningful. It should be noted that Segundo's concept of faith and values is based on a view of humanity as socialized humanity, not as an aggregate of private individuals. Therefore, for faith and values to be meaningful and effective, in his view, they must be expressed in the social realm. And for Segundo, the only means or vehicle whereby values may be effectively actualized in history and society are to be found in ideologies, which are relative and changing because of their intimate connection with, or embeddedness in history, which is always changing and relative.

Further, in Segundo's view it is impossible to sever faith from ideologies: "faith, when properly understood, can never dissociate itself from the ideologies in which it is embodied—both in the Bible and in subsequent history."[30] And again:

> We would go further here and say the following. Even though a person living a mature life differentiates the orientation of faith from the orientation of ideology, he cannot, without diminishing his humanity, forget the fact that they are complementary, if not identical. [31]

And finally, "Faith incarnated in successive ideologies constitutes an ongoing educational process in which man learns how to learn under God's guidance."[32] Thus the importance of faith is in its functional quality, in its ability, through appropriate ideologies, "to be placed in the service of historical problems and their solution."[33] Thus faith has "sense and meaning only insofar as it serves as the foundation stone for ideologies." [34]

There is a seeming paradox, however, in Segundo's formulation of the relationship between faith and ideology which can only be resolved or at least understood if this relationship is conceived of as dialectical. As was said earlier, faith is absolute only in the sense of a subjective absolutization of a particular value that is freely placed, by the individual human subject, above all others.[35] Another absolute feature of faith is its need of or dependence upon ideologies, since ideologies mature, mediate and condition faith and its value according to specific historical circumstances.

> From the viewpoint of value, then, *ideologies* constitute the absolute feature of a functional faith; in that respect the latter is relative *to* the former. At the same time, however, ideologies ever remain *relative* to the historical circumstances that produce and condition them. No solution to an historical problem can lay claim to absolute value,

if absolute implies complete independence from the conditioning influence of historical circumstances.[36]

However, this statement cannot stand up completely since Segundo himself claims that the only truth is liberation itself.[37] So here there is a truly paradoxical situation in Segundo's thinking; he repeats that truth content of faith is always changing and relative[38] and yet at the same time absolutizes the value of human liberation, which should remain a constant value in the midst of changing ideologies. And ideologies are always changing as they attempt to realize efficiency, i.e., the effective actualization of values. Finally, it seems that what can be said is this: *both* faith and ideologies are absolute and relative in the sense that each is an absolute and necessary feature of the other, each conditioning and mediating the other. What results, then, "is a theology without a substantive norm save the process of liberation itself."[39] However, liberation as an absolute norm or value is immensely abstract, and transcendental, and can only be rendered concrete through an open-ended, indefinite historical praxis. For Segundo, ideology is the vehicle of that praxis that struggles to realize or effect the process of liberation.

Thus the question is, which ideology, or ideological version of Christianity and Biblical revelation will most effectively respond to the historical demands of Latin America? Segundo sets out to answer this question by introducing a theological method that attempts to thoroughly integrate theology into the historical, material realm of reality. He tries, on the one hand, to demonstrate that Christian theology has been deformed by ideological distortion insofar as it has functioned to help maintain an unjust social order. On the other hand, Segundo will offer an alternative ideological approach to religion which explicitly favours "the class struggle of the proletariat," thus attempting to develop Marx's nascent insight into religion to its logical conclusion: That religion can be a determining or key factor in the creation of a revolutionary consciousness with the capacity to transform the social order. Yet in order to appropriate and develop Marx's statement about religion as protest, Segundo must either negate Marx's concept of ideology or transform his own so that religious consciousness is synonymous with revolutionary consciousness.

Segundo emphasizes that in his view, religion *is* ideology — not faith, nor values — and on this point he is in agreement with Marx. Where he differs from Marx, as I have already demonstrated, is in his evaluation of ideologies, and thus religion. For Segundo, the relationship between values and ideology is functional and instrumental: religion as ideology offers a method or "procedure" that is the means whereby "pre-established values" are realized.

> The divine 'name' and the 'religion' associated with it . . . designate an 'instrument', a method, by which to attain values that have been fixed beforehand . . . the religious realm is an instrumental, essentially 'ideological' realm . . . it is definitely not the realm of faith. [40]

Segundo emphasizes his point repeatedly, that religion, as instrumental and ideological, is quite separate from the "realm of value-structure."[41] Admittedly, however, it is not always clear in Segundo's writing just what is the nature of the relationship between ideology, faith and values. Segundo insists on their separateness, yet at times it is not always so apparent that they are separate, especially when Segundo suggests that the "orientation" of faith and ideology may be even "identical."

A concrete and somewhat curious example of how Segundo views this complex interrelationship between ideology and faith is to be found in his critique of Dom Helder Camara, the former archbishop of Recife in northeastern Brazil, himself a liberation theologian and outspoken critic of the Brazilian regime. Segundo focuses on two statements by Camara made in 1976, which he quotes: "One who has Jesus Christ does not need Marx," and also, "'With the gospel message, the social encyclicals, Vatican II and Medellin, we have no need to appeal to any ideology to inspire us in our sacred commitment to foster human betterment . . .' ." [42]

Segundo interprets Camara's remarks to mean that faith in Jesus, "and specifically in the Jesus Christ who continues to live in the Catholic Church, exempts people from adhering to *ideologies*."[43] Segundo's initial objection to Camara's words are based upon his own assertion that every faith structures certain values which then must find some way to concrete realization within the complexity of the real world.[44] This view is also endorsed by the authors of both the Vatican's social encyclicals and the Medellin documents when they refer to their own texts as "applications" of the faith to specific circumstances.[45] In Segundo's view the social encyclicals, Medellin documents, Vatican II and even the gospels "fall under the category" of ideology, as Segundo understands the term. Thus, in Segundo's terms, what Camara is really saying is that Christians need no "other" ideologies, since the Christian faith "has already produced its own 'ideological' elements."[46] Segundo goes on to accuse Camara of actually lacking faith, but he does this by way of an exegesis on the relationship between faith and works in the writings of Paul and James, which I will briefly summarize, since Segundo's attack on Camara is intelligible only within this perspective.

Segundo interprets Paul's assertion that, "For we hold that a man is justified apart from works of law" (Romans, 3:28) as a caution against turning religion into an "ideology" in the reified sense, that is, in terms of a "set of sacred 'instruments',"[47] whereby the forms of religion, i.e., ritual and observance of the laws, are sacralized and absolutized as ends in themselves. If such a reification of religion occurs, whereby the outer forms replace or obscure the inner, substantive meaning-structure of religion, then religion functions as a "cover for pragmatic interests and values that have nothing to do with love for neighbour or love for God."[48] Segundo interprets Paul's notion of faith in terms of a "trust" that allows a human being to entrust "the course of one's life to another," so that one may "open one's heart — with or without religion — to a values-structure" whose source lies within one, rather than being determined by some external mechanism. If one reverses the formulation, thinking that certain actions of ritual and obedience to a set of laws bestows one's life with a valid meaning-structure, then that person is captivated by religion as ideology in the sense of enslavement, not in the sense of freedom. In other words, *In Paul's view salvation does come from faith alone, but only because faith enables a person to act, to go to work, in a certain way.*"[49] Thus justification by faith alone has nothing to do with the superiority of belief over action; rather, that faith which is part of the meaning-structure which informs a human life, liberates a person for realizing their values-structure through appropriately corresponding and thus authentic actions.

Segundo engages in a further distinction between "works of the law" (i.e., "religion of the lips") and "'works' in a good sense." [50] "The former refers to the manipulation of religion as a tool; the latter has to do with human action in history designed to flesh out values."[51] To put this distinction in another way, that exactly corresponds with Segundo's reasoning, there are regressive ideologies, embodied in religions "of the lips," and progressive ideologies, embodied in religions "of the heart"; both ideologies may be different ideological expressions of the same religion. Paul understood religion "of the heart"as the most genuine expression of faith.

Segundo offers a somewhat similar, but not identical interpretation of the relationship between faith and works in James 2:14-17. What Segundo basically argues is that when James asks, "What use is it for a man to say he has faith when he does nothing to show it?", what James means is, what is the good of faith, "i.e., adherence to a religious creed" when it is not expressed through concrete actions which will effectively ameliorate a human being's material suffering and deprivation? The issue for James is the dichotomy between religious orthodoxy, which is often mistaken for faith, and the expression of faith through "a meaning-structure and effective action in history."[52] There is no value in believing in God or in Jesus as saviour, writes Segundo, "If one's fellow humans lack daily necessities."[53] Translated into Segundo's terms, James insists that "*a faith without ideologies is, in fact, dead.*"[54] Thus, the continuity between Paul and James can be understood in the following manner: for Paul, faith frees human beings from their enslavement to the law, through which they mistakenly believe they will find salvation. Once they are free *from* the inhibitions of religious orthodoxy, they will be then free *to* "immerse themselves in a relative and changing history" wherein they will actualize their values-structure in accordance with the demands and human needs of their particular social reality.

It is neither my interest nor purpose to evaluate the above exposition of Segundo's interpretation of the relation between faith and works in Paul and James in terms of exegetical, hermeneutical or theological criteria. What this discussion does is to provide an intelligible context for understanding and assessing Segundo's rather harsh attack on Camara, to which I now return. At the heart of Segundo's dispute with Camara is an ideology-conflict wherein both theologians approach the question of faith and Christianity from different perspectives on the issue of ideology. It is this difference concerning the question of ideology which can yield varying interpretations of faith and works in the Christian Bible.

Segundo stands on his interpretation of Paul and James as a position from which to accuse Camara of lacking faith, in that the "criterion of efficacy" is absent in Camara's concept of faith, whereas, according to Segundo, faith in the Pauline sense, sets human beings free so that "their creative power can be turned into concrete, effective love."[55] Authentic faith must be effective, and only ideologies can provide the means whereby faith can possibly be effective. But Camara appears to hold to the sufficiency of the Church's interpretation of and approach to the problems of social injustice in the lines quoted by Segundo. Yet Segundo insists that this self-sufficiency does not exist, which is why theology must go beyond its own parameters and work itself out in and through other disciplines and ideologies in order to fully grasp social problems and effect concrete solutions to them. Segundo's criticism of Camara's claim for the self-sufficiency of the Vatican's social encyclicals as an important step toward "human betterment" borders on contempt in his caricature of James 2:14-7:

78

My brothers, what use is it for man to say he has faith or the social encyclicals of the church when he does nothing to show it? Can his faith or his social encyclicals save him? Suppose a brother or sister is in rags with not enough food for the day, and one of you says to them, 'Good luck to you, keep yourselves warm and have plenty to eat, thanks to the social encyclicals', but does nothing to supply their bodily needs, what is the good of that? [56]

Segundo claims that the social encyclicals have had no impact on improving the material conditions of oppressed, impoverished humanity in any country in the world, partly because most Christians are too frightened of deviating in any real or apparent way from religious orthodoxy, a fear which he insists is implied by Dom Helder Camara's repudiation of the need for ideologies. Camara,

Exemplifies the fear that anything which does not derive from the realm of religion and orthodoxy, whether the latter is effective or not, will have a pernicious result. For what? Certainly not for the solution of human problems, which are left completely unsolved, but for the only goal left: i.e., salvation. [57]

Segundo condemns Camara's "smug sense of self-sufficiency" in rejecting ideologies on the grounds that such an attitude amounts to telling the needy to go away since, "'I can't do anything for you with my faith'."[58] Segundo charges that the reason why the social encyclicals remain ineffective in concrete, social terms, is because Christians prefer and trust a faith severed from action, creating models of social duty divorced from,

an effective methodology for implementing it. Without admitting it to themselves, Christians are really trying to find some way to combine their faith with the reigning evil because the latter is so hard to uproot. So they end up with a sort of compromise. On the one hand, the real situation is unjust . . . But on the other hand, it is very difficult to effect any radical social change in the social structures responsible for this injustice. So Christian faith is reduced to merely individual acts or to the proclamation of unrealized and unrealizable values. Thus the needy go on being needy . . . The faith of the Christian is a dead faith. [59]

Segundo's emphasis and insistence that religion is ideology is a fairly clear indication that his method of theologizing is not only ideological, but *is itself* an ideology. In other words, Segundo is attempting, through his version of liberation theology, to construct a viable and alternative ideology which is both at the same time Christian and generally influenced by Marx. This partly explains the vehemence of his attack on Helder Camara's repudiation of ideology. However, Segundo is wrong to accuse Camara of lacking faith. It is not that Camara lacks faith, it is that Camara understands ideology differently from Segundo, and that he opts for the "wrong" (i.e., ineffective, in Segundo's view) ideology, such as is contained in the social encyclicals and the Medellin documents. Anyone who is familiar with the writing and activism of Dom Helder Camara could not dispute his concern and courageous efforts to change the material conditions of the oppressed people of Latin America. His opposition to the torture, murder, and imprisonment of political dissidents in Brazil, for example, is well-documented.[60] Six of his aides have been murdered, and it is only the strength of his international reputation which has protected him from a similar fate.[61] It is not that Camara lacks faith or is unconcerned to change society in order to liberate human beings, that causes Segundo to criticize him, although it is precisely on these grounds that Segundo does criticize Camara. In all likelihood, the underlying motivation for Segundo's attack has more to do with Camara's repudiation of Marxism in particular and ideology in general, as an effective means for the "betterment" of Latin Americans.[62] If one reads Segundo's charge of lack of faith in Camara literally, then one will wonder afresh what Segundo means by faith, and his whole argument will be thrown open to question.

Segundo's work reflects an attempt to persuade Christians that they have for too long understood their Christianity through the wrong ideology, which has finally resulted in some sectors of the Latin American church supporting the local social and political *status quo* historically. Segundo draws heavily upon Marx, in an effort to transform Christianity into a viable political project whose aim is to change the world. For him, "a theology worthy of the attention of the whole human being . . . stems from a pre-theological commitment to change and improve the world."[63] Theology must be re-fashioned to construct an ideology-critique (of itself included) whereby the "ideological mechanisms of established society" will be exposed, revealing the true nature of injustice and oppression that structure the social and political relations of Latin America. Unless theology is willing to develop such an ideology-critique which will also be self-reflexive, showing the ways in which Christianity has functioned ideologically in support of injustice and domination in the way Marx explained it, then theology will "become and remain the unwitting spokesman of . . . the ruling factions and classes."[64]

In order for theology to transform itself into a tool of liberative social praxis, it must adopt a methodology that is thoroughly historical and political, in which "orthopraxis" replaces orthodoxy and thus rejects an ahistorical, absolutist approach to truth. The methodological influence of

Marx is quite clear in Segundo, and cannot be over-emphasized. The result is that Segundo attempts to construct a re-constituted Christianity by developing an alternative Christian ideology that in his view will have a much greater chance of fulfilling James's concern for an effective faith in the context of Latin America.

The question, however, remains whether it is possible to engage in a theological method that is itself the negation or inversion of established theology, and still have a theology. It remains to be seen if it is at all feasible to create a theology which is dialectical in method, which begins with concrete human history, whose primary focus is humanity, and which insists that praxis, and thus politics, precedes theology, which is necessarily "the second step."[65] It is by no means clear that Christianity can be self-consciously understood as or made into a religious ideology, the basis of whose claim to superiority over other conflicting ideologies, is neither God, the Incarnation nor the Resurrection, but a system of values that places human welfare above everything else. To apply the words of Geertz to Segundo, it appears that Segundo is searching for a "new symbolic framework in terms of which to formulate, think about, and react to political problems" through a reconstructed Christianity that borders on a theological, or theologized version of Marx. The inevitable question is, does Segundo's method of theology carry within it the seeds of its own negation *as theology*?

Segundo's efforts constitute, to a large degree, a self-conscious, practical response to a specific historical situation which appears to be threatened by one of two extremely polarized political structures with their corresponding ideologies, each of which aspires to dominate Latin America. Segundo is trying to create a thoroughly integrated Christian political and religious ideology that will "salvage the sovereign liberty of the work of God"[66] in and through the thoroughly historical and political project of the liberation of the Latin American people.

NOTES

1. Juan Luis Segundo, *The Liberation of Theology*, p. 35, n. 10.

2. Ibid., p.13.

3. Ibid., pp. 5-9.

4. Ibid., p. 18.

5. Ibid., p. 15.

6. Juan Luis Segundo, *Faith and Ideologies*, p. 96.

7. Juan Luis Segundo, *The Liberation of Theology*, p. 16.

8. Juan Luis Segundo, *Faith and Ideologies*, p. 96.

9. Since Segundo's remarks about Marx's concept of class consciousness are filtered through Lukács' exposition, I, too, must draw upon Lukács' interpretation of class consciousness in order to explain Segundo's approach to class consciousness. In this way I hope to offer some critical clarification of Segundo's association of ideology with class consciousness. However, it must be clearly stated that in the writings of Karl Marx, ideology and class consciousness are entirely different phenomena. Class consciousness is the awareness of one's individual and collective position within a particular social class, which is in turn based upon the social division of labour within that society. Class consciousness further encompasses the awareness of the antagonistic nature of the contradictions of this division turning into an open struggle between these classes as the precondition of the abolition of class society.

10. Georg Lukács, *History and Class Consciousness: Studies in Marxist Dialectics*, translated by Rodney Livingstone (London: Merlin Press, 1971), p. 14.

11. Ibid., p. 70.

12. Ibid., p. 78.

13. Juan Luis Segundo, *The Liberation of Theology*, p.66.

14. Charles Davis, *Theology and Political Society* (Cambridge: Cambridge University Press, 1980), p. 130.

15. Juan Luis Segundo, *The Liberation of Theology*, p. 14.

16. Karl Marx, *The German Ideology*, p. 149.

17. Juan Luis Segundo, *Faith and Ideologies*, p. 96

18. Ibid., p. 96.

19. Karl Marx, *Introduction to the Critique of Hegel's Philosophy of Right*, in Robert C. Tucker (Ed.), *The Marx-Engels Reader*, p. 54.

82

20. Gustavo Gutierrez, *A Theology of Liberation*, p. 157.

21. Isaiah Berlin, *Karl Marx: His Life and Environment*, A Galaxy Book (New York: Oxford University Press, 1963), pp. 110-111.

22. Charles Davis, *Theology and Political Society*, p. 132.

23. Friedrich Engels, *Socialism: Utopian and Scientific*, in Robert C. Tucker (Ed.), *The Marx-Engels Reader*, p. 694.

24. Karl Marx, *Introduction to the Critique of Hegel's Philosophy of Right*, in Robert C. Tucker (Ed.), *The Marx-Engels Reader*, p. 54.

25. Juan Luis Segundo, *Faith and Ideologies*, p. 11.

26. Juan Luis Segundo, *The Liberation of Theology*, p. 16.

27. Ibid., p. 16.

28. Juan Luis Segundo, *Faith and Ideologies*, p. 112.

29. Juan Luis Segundo, *The Liberation of Theology*, p. 177.

30. Ibid., p. 181.

31. Ibid., p. 123, n. 5.

32. Ibid., p. 181.

33. Ibid., p. 154.

34. Ibid., p. 109.

35. Ibid., p. 177.

36. Ibid., p. 154.

37. Ibid., p. 118.

38. Ibid., pp. 176-177.

39. Dennis McCann, *Christian Realism and Liberation Theology: Practical Theologies in Creative Conflict*, p. 222.

40. Juan Luis Segundo, *Faith and Ideologies*, p. 39.

41. Ibid., p. 50.

42. Ibid., p. 120.

43. Ibid., p. 121.

44. Ibid., p. 121.

45. Ibid., p. 122.

46. Ibid., p. 122.

47. Ibid., p. 123.

48. Ibid., p. 123.

49. Ibid., p. 124.

50. Ibid., p. 124.

51. Ibid., p. 124.

52. Ibid., p. 126.

53. Ibid., p. 126.

54. Ibid., p. 126.

55. Ibid., p. 126.

56. Ibid., p. 127.

57. Ibid., p. 127.

58. Ibid., p. 128.

59. Ibid., p. 128.

60. Penny Lernoux, *Cry of the People: United States Involvement in the Rise of Fascism, Torture, and Murder and the Persecution of the Catholic Church in Latin America*, p. 32.

61. Noam Chomsky and Edward S. Herman, *The Political Economy of Human Rights, Vol. I, The Washington Connection and Third World Fascism* (Montreal: Black Rose Books, 1979), p. 259.

62. Segundo's attack on Camara is both scornful and ideological, in a way that reminds the reader of some of Marx's more vehement diatribes against his opponents within the same socialist camp, such as Bakunin and Proudhon. The force of Segundo's criticism of Camara is particularly sharp, perhaps, because Camara is also a liberation theologian, with a similar interest to Segundo: the liberation of the Latin American poor and suffering. Otherwise, the sharp edge of Segundo's attack is inexplicable, especially since Segundo is reacting to two statements of Camara, and to nothing else Camara has said publicly, or written, as far as is apparent here.

63. Juan Luis Segundo, *The Liberation of Theology*, p. 39.

64. Ibid., p. 39.

65. Ibid., p. 71.

66. Ibid., p. 39.

Chapter IV

THE DEBATE WITH MARX

Most liberation theologians in Latin America do not acknowledge as heavy a theoretical debt to the thought of Karl Marx as does Juan Luis Segundo. There are some liberation theologians, such as Gustavo Gutierrez, who use certain Marxian categories (for example, class conflict), as analytical tools in their social critique of Latin America. While many other liberation theologians refer to Marx, especially to his criticism of religion, none enter into as sustained and profound a confrontation with his thought as does Segundo. He is one of the few Latin American liberation theologians who attempts to openly appropriate Marx's thought and present it sympathetically, for the most part, and who makes an effort to incorporate what he deems to be those "proper" and "positive" elements in Marx's thought into his own theology.[1] Segundo's main concern is to put forward a critical, practical theology that is capable of becoming a form of liberatory activity with the goal of changing Latin American society, through an analysis that will adequately address its severe problems as well as offering a means whereby they may be abolished. Since the problems that inflict Latin America are basically a result of extreme material deprivation characteristic of a blatant class society, structured along the lines of a well-off minority over a huge, impoverished majority population, Segundo needs a theory of society which can explain how that situation came about and is sustained. Segundo finds in Marx the social analysis required to expose the nature of economic and social reality in Latin America. Theology by itself cannot account for this situation, since traditionally it is too far removed from the complex, material reality of concrete existence, which is one of the points Segundo makes in his book *The Liberation of Theology*. Thus Segundo goes beyond the boundaries of traditional theological discourse to apply Marx's conception of society and history to Latin America while at the same time attempting to preserve some elements of theological discourse, but in a transformed way. However, it should be clear by now that Segundo faces some major difficulties in attempting to render Marx compatible with

Christian theology, even in the form of liberation theology, as we saw earlier in relation to ideology.

My aim here is to extend the analysis of the ways in which Segundo tries to harness Marx into his own theological thought, and pinpoint the difficulties, contradictions and inconsistencies that arise as a result of this effort. A Christian-Marxist dialogue is one thing; a theologized Marxism, or a Marxist theology is quite something else, and it is when the dialogue passes over into an attempted synthesis that Segundo becomes caught in major problems that are very difficult to untangle, let alone solve. Before pursuing this line of critique, it is necessary to summarize and highlight briefly some general points of similarity between the theoretical methodology of Marx and Segundo. The relationship between Marx and Segundo cannot be framed in terms of a direct, one-to-one correspondence. My purpose here is to draw out the general, yet pervasive impact of Marx's thought on Segundo's theology, pointing out as clearly as possible their explicit theoretical links, but also their deep differences. Segundo, unfortunately, is not always clear about what he wants to say about Marx, so that one is required to make as explicit as possible what is often in Segundo implicit or even vague. Thus at times I will introduce certain ideas and concepts from elsewhere, but which permeate Segundo's thought, in order to clarify and order his argument. It remains to be seen whether Segundo is successful in his efforts to appropriate Marx, or if he instead ends up entangled in some impossible and irreconcilable contradictions.

The most explicit points of contact between Marx and Segundo are almost strictly and straightforwardly methodological and readily apparent if one compares, for example, Marx's *Theses on Feuerbach*[2] and almost any of Segundo's statements about his own theological method which has to do with social and political analysis. In Thesis II, Marx defines the "question of objective truth" as a "practical question," not a theoretical one, in which theory is "isolated" from practice. He emphasizes the concrete, "this-sidedness" of thought wherein theory and praxis are linked in the practical, critical activity of human consciousness which itself is engaged in the process of social change and liberation. Marx understands that the real task of theory is to bring about a dynamic unity between subject and object, so that theory's grasp of societal contradictions does not merely name the concrete historical situation, but rather acts as a force within it to initiate concrete, social change. This applies to the way in which Segundo conceives of theology in the following statement, quoted earlier:

The most progressive theology in Latin America is more interested in *being liberative* than in *talking about liberation*. In other words, liberation deals not so much with content as with the method used to theologize in the face of our real-life situation. [3]

In Thesis VI, Marx defines "the human essence" as "no abstraction," but "in reality it is the ensemble of the social relations." Marx negates the concept of the ideal, abstract human individual who embodies "human essence" in order to affirm human beings as conditioned by their material context and concrete life conditions, which are deeply bound up with the material forces of production and the social relationships to which they give rise. This point will become important further on because it points not only to a possible misunderstanding of Marx by Segundo, but also to a contradiction in Segundo's own thought, which again appears later. Segundo does not dwell upon the abstraction of individual man, or address the question of "human essence" in any sustained, systematic or philosophical fashion. He too is concerned with human beings in the context of their material conditions and social relations, which comes through when he writes of the "proletariat" and his "own historical commitment"[4] for the liberation of the proletariat (which is the equivalent for Segundo of all the oppressed people of Latin America) from real, concrete suffering and deprivation. Segundo's main interest is practical, involving the transformation of society on the concrete material level, which is evident, for example, in his theological interpretation of the meaning and importance of Jesus' assertion that the Sabbath was made for man, mentioned earlier.

Segundo is fully aware of the fact that his theology is thoroughly contingent upon and conditioned by the "realm of human options and biases" and that it is "intimately bound up with the psychological, social or political status quo."[5] For him, theology exists within a given cultural milieu, and as such is inevitably mediated by it and if it is to be relevant to that context, it cannot remain within its own immanent realm. Thus any major changes in theological thought and method in any given period must be seen, at least in part, as a response to that specific cultural and historical situation, a point Segundo makes repeatedly in his discussion about the need for ideologies in Biblical interpretation cited earlier. The remarks of the Spanish theologian, Alfredo Fierro, regarding the influence of Marx on Western thought in general and theology in particular are especially relevant to Segundo: "It seems hard to deny the correspondence existing between the incorporation of Marxist thinking into the awareness of Western culture and the sudden flowering of a political hermeneutics of the gospel message."[6] Fierro locates the specific elements of Marxist thought that constitute the main influence on political (and liberation) theology in "dialectical reasoning" and "historical materialism." As a result of these influences, Segundo is able to construct a theology which proposes a negative critique of the existing social order in Latin America with a progressive goal of liberation in history. Thus his theology aspires to be a practically engaged, transformative, emancipatory activity.

Some of the problems of Segundo's specific cultural context, to which he proposes a response, involve the revolutionary activity of various guerrilla groups and severe government and military repression characteristic of authoritarian and/or military regimes. It becomes apparent in Segundo's work that the traditional discourse of Christianity, its logos about God expressed through the language of symbol and representation, is no longer adequate to address the "systematic" injustice[7] of Latin America, which has to do with concrete happenings and the material conditions of life. Segundo's aim is to place theology in the service of the liberation process, through which he hopes his society will experience structural transformation and widespread changes. Thus the specific symbolic language of theology dissolves as a separate form of discourse, giving way to the discourse of politics, since it is in the political realm, not the theological, that Segundo sees changes in society as occurring. Recall his disillusionment with the social encyclicals of the church, which he claims have not been put into practice in a single country in the world. His point is that appeals to charity and God's command to love the neighbour are insufficient as effective forces, by themselves, for practical social reformation or transformation.[8] This is why Segundo cites Gutierrez's declaration that theology is the "second step," and is necessarily *a posteriori* to politics. To reinforce his view he invokes Gustavo Gutierrez's definition of politics:

> Human reason has become political reason. For the contemporary historical consciousness, things political are not only those which one attends to during the free time afforded by his private life; nor are they even a well-defined area of human existence. . . . It is the sphere for the exercise of a critical freedom which is won through history. It is the universal determinant and the collective arena for human fulfilment. . . . Nothing lies outside the political sphere understood in this way. Everything has a political color. . . . Personal relationships themselves acquire an ever-increasing political dimension. Men enter into relationships among themselves through political means.[9]

For Segundo, this means that whatever the gospel message seems to convey, for example, or whatever Jesus said, "must be translated to an era in which real-life love has taken on political forms," since in modern times, "politics is the fundamental human dimension." [10]

This view of politics as a "fundamental human dimension", implies that all human activity, including thought, belongs to the practical sphere of human existence, so that human beings must look for truth and its verification in concrete practice. If one accepts Marx's assertion that existence is prior to consciousness, then knowledge is not a matter of discovering the ultimate, fixed truth that is meant to explain reality. Rather, knowledge is understood as an open-ended, partial historically-embedded process which *per definitionem* will never yield or reveal any final truth, since such truth does not exist. This kind of approach to reality focuses upon the possible as opposed to the absolute given, resulting in critical social theories which search for viable, historical alternatives to the existent state of affairs. Such a critical social theory is the negation of the existent, in all its unfreedom and consequent human alienation. A critical theoretical perspective on social reality rejects the mere factuality of the existent in order to discover the possibilities for a more authentic, unalienated and socialized humanity, in which the needs of the individual and the community are interdependent, and self-consciously understood as such. Again, to borrow Herbert Marcuse's language, negation of the existent is positive, because it has a liberating function in its "Great Refusal to accept the rules of a game in which the dice are loaded," and in its ability to make the absent present "because the greater part of the truth is that which is absent."[11] The negation of the existent also means the negation of the social order, so that negation is "political negation" which may find expression in non-political language, since "the entire dimension of politics becomes an integral part of the status quo." [12]

Segundo shares Marcuse's view of the relation between theory and practice, and the primary place of politics. If Segundo is approached from the perspective of the general features of critical theory, then his own theological method and intent assume greater clarity and coherence. Certainly it cannot be said that Segundo is completely unfamiliar with the central tenets of critical theory, and he is familiar with the work of Marcuse. This is hardly surprising, especially if one considers, along with Alfredo Fierro, that critical social theory has had an irrevocable impact on contemporary theology in general:

> Lack of conformity with, or negation of, existing reality, then, has come to form an intrinsic feature of theology just as it has come to form an intrinsic feature of knowledge in the school of dialectical thinking — and the Frankfurt School especially. [13]

However, Fierro applies this statement to the political theologians of Europe, but not to the liberation theologians of Latin America, whose "reading and interpretation of Marx proceeds from different suppositions, [and] is not filtered through the Frankfurt School of thinking, and is usually closer to Orthodox Marxism."[14] We have seen, for example, that Gutierrez linked liberation theology to critical theory. Fierro does not take this into account, nor does he make any reference whatsoever to Segundo, but more importantly, his distinction between political and liberation theology is too sharp. Certainly both "schools" of theology are familiar with the other, and with the major thinkers of modern times. The most Fierro can do is to point out basic orientations of various theological approaches. However, the issue is not to prove that Segundo is directly influenced by the Frankfurt School, or that he is explicitly and consistently applying their thought to his theology. The point is to try to draw out of Segundo's own thought its overall features and implications, and to do this, it is helpful to read his work from the perspective of critical theory, which is closer to Segundo's own thought than any self-professed "orthodox Marxism," a highly debatable term in itself. I have no intention to now introduce a lengthy discussion about the Frankfurt School. The point is, rather, to try to identify, if at all possible, what the basic orientation is in Segundo's approach to social analysis, and in what ways or by what other theoretical influence, if any, he has appropriated Marx.

This, however, is no easy task, since it is very difficult to determine any predominant or easily identifiable Marxist interpretation reflected in Segundo. What Segundo does is to select certain ideas from Marx's writings and apply them to his own theoretical method as ever he can, in very much the same way as he tried to bring Marx into line with his own concept of ideology. Although Segundo will use a writer like Adam Schaff or Georg Lukács occasionally to underline or interpret a particular point in Marx that is compatible with his own critique of Marx, he never does so in any systematic and consistent manner, making it very difficult to understand just how he interprets Marx. Part of the reason for this is that Segundo cites very few passages from Marx, which are in turn based upon a relatively small selection of texts. Segundo focuses very narrowly on limited, specific points in Marx, which he labels as those "proper and positive dimensions"[15] in Marx's work that are most useful for him. Segundo does not engage in a sustained critical analysis of Marx, and perhaps there is no reason why he should, since his interest in Marx is more or less limited to strictly method-ological issues. Yet this can create problems for Segundo's readers, since it is the reader who must develop themes and concepts that are latently (but sometimes more manifestly) present, such as the use of the dialectic and negation in order to comprehend Segundo. Segundo tends to move in and out of a polemical dialogue with Marx throughout both *The Liberation of Theology* and *Faith and Ideologies*, but abandons this enterprise in *The Historical Jesus of the Synoptics* and *The Humanist Christology of Paul*, which follow *Faith and Ideologies* as subsequent volumes. This fact is significant, since the earlier books are almost exclusively concerned with methodology, while the latter are direct applications of Segundo's methodology.

Nonetheless, Segundo's relationship with Marx is an uneasy one, a situation which Segundo generates himself by attempting to impose on Marx certain interpretations and implications that are highly questionable. Segundo's understanding of "historical materialism" is one illustration of this. Segundo tries to question the strict "materialism" of Marx's approach to social relations (without defining what "materialism" is as he comprehends the term) concluding that by "material," Marx recognizes *both* material *and* spiritual dimensions as implied in the relations of material production and their consequent social relations.

> The term 'mode of production' is much less *materialist* than is often assumed by both its advocates and its opponents. As Marx repeatedly stresses, the mode of production — or, the concrete economic structure — does not just take in the organization of the means of production: i.e., its more quantitative and hence 'materialist' type of production in question and by the appropriation of the means of production. And in these relations between human beings, effected in and through work, are included many elements which we could rightly call 'spiritual' and which are not nebulous idealizations. The concrete is complex. It is material and spiritual, even for historical materialism — or at least for the materialism of Marxism's founders. [16]

Beside the fact that Segundo begins the passage with Marx himself, and ends with "Marxism's founders," whom he does not name, the more serious problem lies in the vulgar understanding of materialism that Segundo attributes to Marx. It seems that Segundo interprets "materialism" in the most literal sense of the word, so that he can designate all other aspects of social relations — which he, *not* Marx, calls 'human relations' — as "spiritual." Although Marx's concept of the relations of material production and social relations is indeed complex and multidimensional, he does not use the term "spiritual" to describe them. Consider this passage from his *Preface to A Contribution to the Critique of Political Economy*:

In the social production of their life, men enter into definite relations that are indispensable and independent of their will, relations of production which correspond to a definite stage of development of their material productive forces. The sum total of these relations of production constitutes the economic structure of society, the real foundation, on which rises a legal and political superstructure and to which correspond definite forms of social consciousness. The mode of production of material life conditions the social, political and intellectual life process in general. It is not the consciousness of men that determines their being, but, on the contrary, their social being that determines their consciousness. [17]

Human beings, then, for Marx, cannot be divorced from the material conditions of concrete existence, and concrete existence includes all social relations and intellectual life "up to (their) furthest forms."[18] Consciousness is "conscious existence, and the existence of men is their actual life-process."[19] Consciousness relates to the material, and not the spiritual, to which Marx gives no legitimate credence as a category in any case. Segundo may well attribute a spiritual dimension to human experience, but Marx does not, and cannot be read to do so.

For Marx, "spirit" has more to do with Hegel's idealist philosophy, which he questioned as sheer abstraction. In applying the term "spiritual" to Marx's material conception of history, Segundo simply engages in a reductionism of Marx's understanding of the complex interconnection between the productive forces of society, the relations of production and social relations. The problem is compounded further by Segundo's lack of clarity about what exactly he means by spirit.

The spirit . . . is concrete. And consciousness, its organ or product par excellence, must return to the concrete in order to construct its practical projects. . . . Theoretical praxis which seeks to transform the world is precisely the activity of the spirit geared toward the creation of a new world. Hence 'materialism' cannot be an alternative to the spirit and its functions. [20]

This is not Marx, and if anything is closer to Hegel, and it is surprising that Segundo even tries to elaborate upon Marx's material conception of history by a superimposition of a Hegelian philosophy of history, and not realize it. This particular passage shows that Segundo has actually turned Marx upside down, which is perfectly understandable if his intention is to insert the notion of spirit into Marx. But in that case, Segundo would do better to pursue this line of thought vis-á-vis Hegel, and not Marx.

In fact, Segundo might have fewer theoretical problems altogether if he had chosen to dialogue with Hegel, since Segundo's theory finally cannot dissociate itself from relying on an absolute 'something' as a conditioning or guiding element in his own approach to history and human praxis. Even though Segundo's theological method begins with and emphasizes the primacy of practical action of human beings in their concrete environment, he remains disturbed by the problem of relativity. He asks:

> How and from where can there arise an absolute that will put order into all that relativity in a praxis? . . . action cannot be structured without something unconditioned that subjects everything else to unity. That unconditioned need not be God or a metaphysical entity, but is has to be a value. [21]

Here Segundo introduces an abstract category that implies a dialectical relation between an absolute, unconditioned value — which could be God, a metaphysical entity, or Absolute Spirit — and historical contingency and change. This approach to the question of relativity and history actually drives Segundo closer to Hegel than to Marx, and it raises the question of who, or what is the subject of history, in Segundo's view. But Segundo dismisses Hegel, charging that Hegel's "idealism" is "characterized by a valuational indifference on the part of the philosopher (and the dialectic itself)."[22] Here one must proceed carefully, since Segundo does not enter into a serious analysis of Hegel's philosophy. Segundo's charge of idealism, then, is not the issue, as it turns out, but simply that Hegel's philosophy is not partisan, which is really what Segundo means by valuational; that is, it lacks a specific commitment to a particular social, historical group:

> Neither the lord nor the bondsman, the sceptic or the stoic, incarnate a value or get any preference. If there is any value in Hegel's dialectic, it is to be located in the opposition itself, not in either one of the antagonists. Values are conveyed by the process of opposition only. [23]

Segundo, then, in actual fact rejects Hegelian dialectics on the grounds that it posits the wrong category as the "unconditional" of human history and praxis. Where Hegel sees the dialectical movement in history as initiated by Absolute Spirit, Segundo prefers an engaged value as the motivating historical force. Methodologically speaking, there seems to be very little difference here between Segundo and what he claims was meant by Hegel, as long as Segundo fails to break with metaphysics. Then Segundo abruptly declares his preference for Marx, who "brought dialectic back down to realism, to 'real human beings'."[24] But then Segundo explains Marx's methodology, i.e., his material conception of history in which the human being is the only subject, as actually depending upon a moral judgement of the just cause of the proletariat, which makes Marx's theory value-laden.   Here Segundo treads on dangerous ground, because he obscures the fact that the decisive difference between Marx and Hegel is located in their opposing conceptions of the subject of history, which for Marx is man, but for Hegel, Absolute Spirit.   When Segundo rejects Hegel's dialectical method on the grounds of it being valueless, he confuses the crucial point, thus reducing Hegel to some kind of dilettante or immoralist. He further fails to recognize that his location of value as the unconditioned absolute of human praxis and history raises serious questions about the historical subject in his own theory, questions which take him far away from Marx.   One wonders how Segundo can claim to dissociate himself from Hegel on the point of the subject of history, and why he does so, and then identify with Marx who clearly rejected any such notion of an "absolute" or unconditioned element as a legitimate feature of a materialist and dialectical methodology.

To reject Hegel on the grounds of his dialectics, dismissing the importance of the dialectical method in general, is also far from Marx. In Volume I of *Capital*, Marx writes:

> My dialectic method is not only different from the Hegelian, but is its direct opposite. To Hegel, the life-process of the human brain, i.e., the process of thinking, which, under the name of 'the Idea', he even transforms into an independent subject, is the demiurgos of the real world, and the real world is only the external, phenomenal form of 'the Idea'. With me, on the contrary, the ideal is nothing else than the material world reflected by the human mind, and translated into forms of thought. [5]

The key difference between Marx and Hegel lies within the location of the historical subject, not in the dialectical method *per se*. Segundo slides over this point because his central interest is to show that Marx's theory rests upon an anthropological faith in a value, and he refers to Marx's realist "relocation of the dialectic" which,

> inevitably entails the accentuation of some *predialectical 'faith'*. . . .   It is not the dialectic that leads Marx to place himself on the side of the proletariat. . . . Marx's position is not one of opportunism abetted by predictions which the dialectic makes possible. . . . His option is an effort to change the world by establishing values. [26]

Marx's "relocation of the dialectic" has nothing to do with values or taking sides.   Segundo cannot legitimately reduce Marx's insistence on human beings as historical subject to a partisan preference for one historical group over another, based upon an abstract value. This is to read Marx as a moralist, which he was not.   Moreover, Segundo's rejection of the dialectical method on the grounds of the absence of values makes no sense. Marx's method is also dialectical, and he inherited it from Hegel, and it has nothing to do with values in the sense Segundo means. Marx acknowledges how he had "openly avowed" himself as "the pupil of that mighty thinker" (Hegel) from whom he inherited the general theory of the dialectic, while disagreeing with Hegel about its location:

> The mystification which dialectic suffers in Hegel's hands, by no means prevents him from being the first to present its general form of working in a comprehensive and conscious manner. With him it is standing on its head. It must be turned right side up again, if you would discover the rational kernel within the mystical shell. [27]

Marx also stresses the importance of negation in dialectics, another element taken from Hegel, with its power for "breaking up" the "existing state of things,""because it regards every historically developed social form as in fluid movement, and therefore takes into account its transient nature not less that its momentary existence; because it lets nothing impose upon it, and is in its essence critical and revolutionary."[28] Like Hegel, Marx also understands dialectics as negative dialectics, which Segundo for some reason repudiates only in Hegel, whom he dismisses as using "the negation of the negation" as an irritating "manner of speech," "*ad nauseum.*"[29]

Segundo unfortunately interprets Hegel's concept of negation in a literal, vulgar way:

> Unlike a small child, an adult human being knows that a chair is not really the negation of a table, ever. Nor is the canine carcass the negation of the dog . . . mere differences are not negations. . . . *Only if I want to sit down*, and deliberate where to sit down, can the chair become metaphorically the 'negation' of the table, and vice versa. [30]

There is no point to debate with Segundo about Hegel's concept of negation, and its importance for the overcoming of alienation, for example, since Segundo offers a simple caricature of Hegel in the above quoted paragraph, and seems to show no interest in a serious discussion of this point. My aim is, however, to show that his disagreement with Hegel and his siding with Marx on the issue of dialectics as a question primarily of values is misplaced and unnecessary. There is no reason for Segundo to dismiss Hegel, before even entering into a serious evaluation of his philosophy. This whole confusing discussion in Segundo about Marx, Hegel and dialectics is finally irrelevant to Segundo's real purpose, which is to try and show that Marx's theory is grounded in a "pre-dialectical" values-structure. To state the matter very directly, there is no way Segundo can convincingly prove it, and at the end of his discussion about the above-mentioned themes, the reader is left somewhat bewildered. It should be finally noted that Segundo at some point drops the term "materialism" in favour of "realism," so that Marx's critique of Hegel is understood as a *"realist* reworking of Hegel's dialectic." [31]

However, the important issue for Segundo at this point is not the methodology of a materialist conception of history or dialectics, which was very important to his theory before; it now appears as secondary to the question of faith and values:

> Neither historical materialism nor dialectical materialism can claim to determine the value (the 'ought-to-be') possessed in and of themselves by premises which are, by definition, *self-validating* — i.e., which belong to the realm of meaning. [32]

For Segundo, faith, and the values which proceed from it, are beyond the boundaries of theoretical methodology.[33] Values constitute therefore an absolute, unconditioned and fixed transcendental truth which grounds and mediates both theoretical and practical methodology. Segundo thus undermines the internal consistency of his own theory by reverting back to ahistorical categories as the foundations of historical analysis. He suddenly abandons humanity as the proper subject of history. It is precisely here that Segundo reveals the idealist strain within his thought. But this becomes extremely problematic as he consistently tries to impose this view on Marx, asserting that Marx's "realist dialectic" is itself grounded in a "particular conception of meaning and value," and even further that "only those who share this meaning and values structure can use Marx's method of cognition and action in a logical, effective way."[34] One wonders if this is a purely descriptive, or moralistic statement. It seems to imply that the underlying motivation of Marx and anyone else concerned with the abolition of class society and the liberation of the oppressed (and all humanity) necessarily arises from an abstract principle or value concerning the just cause of an alienated humanity. Segundo thus turns Marx into a kind of utopian socialist, never confronting Marx's repeated attacks on utopian socialism in favour of a scientific, materialist analysis of the concrete laws and processes of history.

Segundo actually wants to interpret Marx in terms of Marxist humanism, which places him closer to those groups of thinkers who have attempted to read Marx by way of a socialist humanism, such as is found in the work of the Frankfurt School and the *Praxis*[35] philosophers, which include writers like Herbert Marcuse and Erich Fromm. These philosophers and critical theorists are two important examples of those intellectual efforts to reclaim Marx from distortions derived from mechanistic and deterministic interpretations that have so unfortunately reified Marx's thought through Leninist and Stalinist ideologies. Segundo acknowledges that he reads Marx in a humanist key, although he does not explain very fully what this means. He speaks of the humanism of Marx, but makes no effort to develop this idea beyond a very specific point. He quotes Fromm to support his position that Marx was a humanist: "It must be noted that labour and capital were not at all for Marx only economic categories; they were *anthropological* categories, imbued with a *value judgement* which is rooted in his humanistic position."[36] (Segundo's italics). Then Segundo goes into a very brief and descriptive discussion about Marx's humanism in which he acknowledges the existence of the large body of literature on the subject, with its controversial debate. Segundo does not delve into this debate, however, but asserts that Marx does indeed have an ideal concept of human being which is "partially derived from Hegel,"[37] and that Marx does profess, "The essence of the human being," which Segundo immediately labels as a *"transcendent datum par excellence."*[38] Segundo proceeds to assert that such a humanism has nothing to do with science, and that its "premises" are based upon an idea of "essence" which "looks an awful lot like one of Bateson's 'self-validating premises'."[39] Segundo comes dangerously close to postulating an idealist tendency in Marx's thought, but cannot convincingly prove it.

But then he concedes that the concept of "human essence," while present in Marx, is also "renounced" by Marx in his sixth thesis on Feuerbach, but does not explain this apparent contradiction. However, the sixth thesis on Feuerbach is by no means the only text where Marx explicitly repudiates the notion of a human essence, in an abstract, idealist sense:

> Circumstances make men just as much as men make circumstances. This sum of productive forces, capital funds and social forms of intercourse, which every individual and generation finds in existence as something given, is the real basis of what the philosophers have conceived as 'substance' and 'essence of man'.[40]

Finally, it is impossible to conclude just how Segundo in fact understands Marx's sixth thesis on Feuerbach, or why he even mentions it. In any case, Segundo does not reconsider any of his immediately preceding assertions about Marx's humanism as based upon the premise of an ideal concept of human being that the "young Marx brought to all his writings."[41] Again, another general statement about "all" the writings of the young Marx, with no references or quotations, since Segundo "won't go into the very specific content which Marx saw in that concept of the human being."[42] It must be remembered that the *Theses on Feuerbach* were written in 1845, in the period known as the young or early Marx, and *The German Ideology* was written in 1845-1846, also when Marx was young. Segundo's claim about the idealist notions of human essence in the young Marx is then open to serious doubt.

There is another point that must be raised with regard to Segundo's interpretation of Marx, and that is his assertion that Marx's "materialism" is not incompatible with belief in God. Segundo states that all Marx's theory does is to criticize or "combat religion in one of its historical forms,"[43] although he does not explain what he means by this, or which historical form he has in mind. Segundo tries to demonstrate that there is no intrinsic connection between Marx's thought and atheism:

> There is no more a relationship between atheism and a materialism consistent with the thought of Marx (be there one Marx or two) than there is between atheism and historical materialism, or atheism and dialectical materialism. [44]

Although Segundo is partly correct, this assertion is misleading if one looks to the writings of Marx himself, who clearly rejects not only religion and theology as forms of ideology, but also the notion of God itself, although not strictly from the point of view of an atheist. In the *Economic and Philosophical Manuscripts* (1844), Marx writes:

> A *being* only considers himself independent when he stands on his own feet; and he only stands on his own feet when he owes his *existence* to himself. A man who lives by the grace of another regards himself as a dependent being. But I live completely by the grace of another if I owe him not only the sustenance of my life, but if he has moreover, *created* my *life* – if he is the *source* of my life. [45]

Marx continues this passage to nullify the doctrine of Creation, citing the "*Generatio aequivoca* [as] the only practical refutation of the theory of creation" of the world; he then rejects the doctrine of the creation of Man, even physically by any force other than human: "even physically man owes his existence to man . . . by which *man* repeats himself in procreation, thus always remaining the subject."[46] Marx goes on to undermine the very question of atheism as a legitimate question, claiming that it is not an issue for socialist man: "Since for the socialist man the *entire so-called history* of the world is nothing but the begetting of man through human labour," so that man has:

The visible, irrefutable proof of his *birth* through himself, of his *process* of *coming-to-be*. Since the *real existence* of man and nature has become practical sensuous and perceptible . . . the question about an *alien* being, about a being above nature and man . . . has become impossible in practice. Atheism has no longer any meaning, for atheism is a *negation of God*, and postulates the *existence of man* through this negation; but socialism as socialism no longer stands in any need of such a mediation. It proceeds from the *practically* and theoretically sensuous *consciousness* of man and of nature as the essence. Socialism is man's *positive self-consciousness* no longer mediated through the annulment of religion. [47]

Segundo refers to the first part of this quotation as Marx's "reason" for atheism.[48] It is not clear what Segundo means by this, or why he even raises it. Marx is not promoting atheism, because atheism is the negation of theism, and as such accepts the question of the existence or non-existence of God to be legitimate. Marx does not accept the theist/atheist dichotomy to be relevant because it still formulates, or mediates the question of concrete human existence in relation to a Creator, thus obscuring the fact of historical human subjectivity. If the root of man is man himself, there is no need to even think about God; socialist man, free of the alienation produced by class society and reflected in religion, one of its ideological forms, understands himself as his own "root" or essence. "Socialism is man's *positive self-consciousness* no longer mediated through the annulment of religion," wrote Marx, and Segundo does not take this statement into serious account. He simply wants to state that Marxism and atheism are not mutually exclusive. Here again, it is necessary to show that Segundo displays a tendency to reduce or simplify Marx at certain points in order to not only build his own position, but to try to enlist Marx's support for it by his analysis and interpretation of the texts of Marx. Thus "Marx's work" is not "an ontology loaded with the transcendent datum that transcendent data do not exist at all."[49] If by "transcendent data" Segundo means God, then he would be hard pressed to show that there is any text in Marx that even allows the possibility of the existence of God. If there were, then theology (i.e., *logos* about God) would have to be seen as a legitimate activity for Marx. But for him, theology is nothing more than "philosophy's spot of infection."[50] But Segundo drops the matter, content with his unfounded assertion that Marx's thought does not necessarily imply denial of the existence of God.

In *The Liberation of Theology*, Segundo tries to construct a critical, materialist methodology for liberation theology, mostly by way of Marx. He began his approach to theology by placing man as the centre of human history so that the focus of his theology would be man in his concrete, material context, and whose purpose would be to change the structures of society for the liberation of Latin Americans. However, man as centre, in the methodological sense, does not necessarily imply man as the sole subject of history. This is a highly important distinction. For Marx, man is clearly and unequivocally the subject of history, while for Segundo, he is the centre or central *focus* of history; however, subject and centre are not the same. Man as centre implies that God is the subject of history working out his divine plan through humanity. To try to resolve the confusion of historical agency through a concept of God and human beings as "co-workers"[51] in history implies a false equality between the transcendent and the immanent, and does little to clarify the motive force of history.

In *Faith and Ideologies*, Segundo goes much farther in his appropriation of Marx's methodology so that he tries to force Marx into a position that is actually compatible with his own re-thinking of Christian theology, so that there is no unbridgeable disagreement between himself and Marx on the questions of ideology, faith and values and even theism. In order to do this, Segundo engages in a polemics with Marx which is based not only on a highly selective and eclectic reading of Marx's texts, but also on an extremely questionable interpretation of those texts, many of which I have tried to expose. Segundo tries to soften Marx's harsh critique of religion by introducing a distinction between faith and ideology, by redefining ideology and arguing that faith and values are not only untouched by Marx, but become an intrinsic part of Marx's own theory. Segundo also attempts to separate faith and values from ideology in such a way as to preserve their "inextricable" interconnection, and somehow show that his working out of these themes can be validated by a reading of Marx. In my view, this effort and the conclusions Segundo draws from it do not stand up under critical scrutiny. Segundo seems to be constructing a revised Christian theology which is openly influenced by a Marxist theory, and unsuccessfully so. While it may be perfectly legitimate to use Marx's materialist conception of history and dialectics as a methodological framework in which to formulate a critique of Christianity for the purpose of transforming Christianity into a more relevant or sensitive response to the concrete historical problems of a given social context as in Latin America, it is rather something else to try and digest Marx into a critical theology as part of its thematic substance in the way Segundo does.

It is perfectly understandable that Segundo attempts to bring Christian theology into synchrony with his own particular cultural and historical situation, working out a new basis for its validity, which obviously rests upon its relevance to the Latin American setting. Segundo's aim is in direct agreement with Fierro's statement that, "A theology is well-grounded when it makes the gospel of Jesus Christ meaningful to its contemporaries." [52]

The question remains to be fully answered as to why he insists that Christianity is an ideology with progressive, programmatic potential, with the power to make a constructive and meaningful intervention in the problems of contemporary Latin America. What other ideologies are present in Latin America, and how do they threaten or undermine Christianity, or compete with it on the popular level, if at all? In the next Chapter I will discuss some of the representative ideologies in Latin America that are in direct competition with each other for popular allegiance.

NOTES

1. Juan Luis Segundo, *Faith and Ideologies*, p. 300.

2. Karl Marx, *Theses on Feuerbach*, in Robert C. Tucker (ed.), *The Marx-Engels Reader*.

3. Juan Luis Segundo, *The Liberation of Theology*, p. 9.

4. bid., p. 14.

5. Ibid., p. 13.

6. Alfredo Fierro, *The Militant Gospel: A Critical Introduction to Political Theologies*, translated by John Drury (Maryknoll, N.Y.: Orbis Books, 1977), p. 80.

7. Juan Luis Segundo, *Faith and Ideologies*, p. 278.

8. Again, I would cite Max Horkheimer, who made a similar point about the necessity of an effective Christian love when he stated that the "meaning of the concept [of Christian love] would become apparent if it were explicated in the form of a theory of reality — of those real situations in which it should be tested." *Critique of Instrumental Reason*, translated by Matthew J. O'Connell and others (New York: The Seabury Press, 1974), p. 48.

9. Quoted in Juan Luis Segundo, *The Liberation of Theology*, p. 71.

10. Ibid., p. 71. The inescapable conclusion of Gutierrez's definition of politics, which is endorsed by Segundo, is that liberation theology assumes the politicization of the totality of human existence. Thus politics in this way assumes the status of an ontological category. And thus, the recurring question: what place and meaning does theology have in this approach to politics? Certainly theology ceases to exist in the sense of referring to a separate realm of reality and human existence, since as a separate realm of meaning, theology becomes irrelevant. These questions are taken up again later.

11. Herbert Marcuse, "A Note on the Dialectic," in *The Essential Frankfurt School Reader*, edited by Andrew Arato and Eike Gebhardt (New York: Continuum Publishing Company, 1982), p. 448.

12. Ibid., p. 449.

13. Alfredo Fierro, *The Militant Gospel*, p. 108.

14. Ibid., p. 109.

15. Juan Luis Segundo, *Faith and Ideologies*, p. 300.

16. Ibid., p. 180.

17. Karl Marx, *Preface to a Contribution to the Critique of Political Economy*, in Robert C. Tucker (ed.), The Marx-Engels Reader, p. 4.

18. Karl Marx, *The German Ideology*, p. 154.

19. Ibid., p. 154.

20. Juan Luis Segundo, *Faith and Ideologies*, p. 180.

21. Ibid., p. 184.

22. Ibid., p. 234.

23. Ibid., p. 234.

24. Ibid., p. 234.

25. Karl Marx, *Capital: A Critique of Political Economy*, Volume I, translated from the third German edition by Samuel Moore and Edward Aveling, edited by Frederick Engels (New York: International Publishers, 1967), p. 19.

26. Juan Luis Segundo, *Faith and Ideologies*, pp. 234-235.

27. Karl Marx, *Capital*, Vol. I, p. 20.

28. Ibid., p. 20.

29. Juan Luis Segundo, *Faith and Ideologies*, p. 210.

30. Ibid., p. 210.

31. Ibid., p. 235.

32. Ibid., p. 225. What Segundo does not seem to realize is that when he rejects the notion of Absolute Spirit as the motive force of history, he removes God. For Hegel, Absolute Spirit was the concept of God, brought to its philosophical notion.

33. Ibid., p. 225.

34. Ibid., p. 236.

35. The *Praxis* group refers to the most significant group of Yugoslav philosophers and sociologists, mostly from Zagreb and Belgrade universities, who in the sixties and seventies published the influential and internationally-known philosophical journal, *Praxis*. This journal explored themes concerning freedom, emancipation and revolution from a socialist-humanist perspective. A fuller discussion of Praxis, including its association with well-known thinkers outside Yugoslavia, is to be found in Erich Fromm's *Socialist Humanism: An International Symposium* (Garden City, N.Y.: Anchor Books, 1966) and in Gerson S. Sher's *Praxis: Marxist Criticism and Dissent in Socialist Yugoslavia* (Bloomington: Indiana University Press, 1977).

36. Juan Luis Segundo, *Faith and Ideologies*, p. 239.

37. Ibid., p. 240.

38. Ibid., p. 240.

39. Ibid., p. 240.

40. Karl Marx, *The German Ideology*, p. 165.

41. Juan Luis Segundo, *Faith and Ideologies*, p. 240.

42. Ibid., p. 240.

43. Ibid., p. 241.

44. Ibid., p. 241.

45. Karl Marx, *Economic and Philosophical Manuscripts of 1844*, in Robert C. Tucker (ed.), *The Marx-Engels Reader*, p. 91.

46. Ibid., p. 92.

47. Ibid., pp. 92-93.

48. Juan Luis Segundo, *Faith and Ideologies*, p. 247, n. 41.

49. Ibid., p. 241.

50. Karl Marx, *Economic and Philosophical Manuscripts of 1844*, p. 70.

51. Juan Luis Segundo, *The Liberation of Theology*, p. 148.

52. Alfredo Fierro, *The Militant Gospel*, p. 125.

Chapter V

BETWEEN NATIONAL SECURITY AND REVOLUTIONARY MOVEMENTS: THE NEED FOR A NEW IDEOLOGY

According to André Gunder Frank, the "battleground" upon which the revolutionary struggle for social change in Latin America will take place "includes the field of ideology."[1] It is the "field of ideology" that Segundo is addressing in his efforts to create a theology that is capable of being more relevant to the needs and problems of Latin America. He is trying to promote an approach to social change that is practical and effective but that is also solidly grounded in certain human values which he finds confirmed and proclaimed by "the historical Jesus." By "historical Jesus", Segundo means the living human person Jesus, who acted and spoke in the presence of other real life human beings, and whose life and deeds actually bore witness to a "process of humanization" which is relevant for human beings today.[2] Segundo views Jesus first and foremost as one who *"bore witness* to certain human values,"[3] that were meant to be lived in the concrete world of human experience and action. This is one of the reasons why he insists on the necessary interdependence of faith (in values) and ideology, which he describes in terms of "the complementarity existing between faith and ideology."[4] Segundo is concerned that ideologies without values will degenerate into mere rigid instrumentality, while values (or faith) divorced from an appropriate vehicle or structure for realizing them in practice, will be meaningless and dead, as far as human action is concerned.

Latin American society is not devoid of ideologies, including political ideologies which exist in a lethal competition with one another. In this sense, Latin America does indeed present a battleground of opposing and warring ideologies, which interlock in a perpetual spiral of violent instability and material impoverishment. The two most important ideological extremes which exist in Latin America, and which stand in direct opposition to one another, have to do with the ideology of "National Security" on the one hand, and various forms of revolutionary and guerrilla ideologies on the other. Although Segundo refers to the ideologies of both National Security and revolutionary movements (which in his terminology includes guerrillas, subversives, and "the Left"), he does so only briefly and very generally, without any coherent explanation of what these ideologies express, or whom they specifically represent. Furthermore, it is apparent that Segundo is attempting to open the possibility of an alternative ideology to the existing ideological extremes, thus formulating something of a mélange of those "proper and positive" dimensions of both Marx and Christianity.

In Segundo's work, liberation theology becomes a progressive Christian ideology that rests upon both faith in the basic values that stress human welfare and a generally social and historical analysis of Latin America derived from the political economy of Marx. In Segundo's view, the possibility for such a theology first appeared with Vatican II, and was later elaborated upon and applied to the Latin American context in the documents of the Second Latin American Bishops' Conference (CELAM II) at Medellin, Colombia, in 1968:

> It can be said that the Catholic Church in Latin America was the first Catholic community to set out resolutely on the new pathway opened up by Vatican II. The new pathway was based on the assumption that faith has as its function the task of guiding the human mind towards more fully human solutions in history; that the Church does not possess those solutions in advance but does possess elements that have been revealed by God; that these revealed elements do not preserve the Church from ideologies; that instead the Church must take advantage of those elements to go out in search of (ideological) solutions to the problems posed by the historical process; and that such solutions will always remain provisional.... At Medellin the bishops adopted ideologies that went counter to the status quo. This enabled a large number of Christians to perceive the intermingling of faith and ideology for the first time. [5]

Segundo assumes that his attempt to construct a progressive Christian ideology has a far better chance of finding support among the Latin American people than either the ideology of the National Security State or the ideology of what he calls "the Left,"[6] which he never defines, but which seems to randomly include "subversives," and guerrillas and even left-wing political parties. In his view, the reason why liberation theology (as a progressive Christian ideology), has a good chance of gaining ideological hegemony in Latin America is because:

> The Latin American Church is supremely sure of its membership. Despite dire problems and predictions, and in a society that is urban for the most part, more than ninety percent of all Latin Americans still call themselves 'Catholic'. [7]

Before proceeding with Segundo's somewhat esoteric analysis of the ideological conflicts within Latin America or exploring his own attempts at constructing an ideological alternative, it is important to present a more explicit picture of the ideological context in which Segundo is writing, and about which he is critical. Segundo himself is vague with regard to the content of these ideologies, which renders the basic features of his critique somewhat abstract. At this point I will try to present a general overview of both the National Security ideology and the main ideological tendencies which generally characterize some of the Latin American revolutionary movements since the 1960's to the present.

The Ideology of the National Security State

Shortly after World War II, the United States government established the National Security Council (NSC) and the Central Intelligence Agency (CIA), two political agencies whose existence produced serious repercussions throughout Latin America in the following decades. In Latin America, prior to World War II, there were some fascist movements of minor importance, modelled after those that existed in Germany and Spain.[8] Although these movements were neither widespread nor popular, they resurfaced in a much stronger form after World War II when many Latin American countries developed their own imitations of the American National Security Council and the Central Intelligence Agency. According to Brazilian theologian José Comblin, "the national security system has come to dominate most Latin American nations and is likely to conquer the rest very soon."[9] The basic features of what Comblin calls "national security ideology" are:

> The integration of the whole nation into the national security system and the policy of the United States; total war against communism; collaboration with American or American-controlled business corporations; establishment of dictatorship; and placing of absolute power in the hands of the military.[10]

The effects of this national security system have become particulary devastating in Latin America since the mid-1960's during and after which a series of military dictatorships took over several Latin American countries, and which very largely abolished whatever democratic governments there were along with most structures of civil society. The recent history of the political situation in Uruguay provides a representative picture of the situation existing in many Latin American countries. A brief discussion of Uruguay is also relevant here, since Segundo lives in Uruguay. Prior to the military takeover in 1973, Uruguay was one of the most stable, economically prosperous and democratic countries in Latin America.[11] Since the military took power, the economy has deteriorated severely, and all the fundamental human rights have been abolished. State terror is regularly used to repress any and all forms of protest; recently Uruguay was thought to have the highest per capita number of political prisoners in the world.[12] The approximately one thousand or more political prisoners (in a total population of just over two million) incarcerated in the infamous *Libertad* and *Punta de Rieles* prisons live in conditions,

> deliberately designed to bring about the physical and mental breakdown of the prisoners who are forced to live in an atmosphere of permanent fear and insecurity. These conditions are an extension of the torture inflicted on the majority, if not all political prisoners immediately after arrest in Uruguay. [13]

Uruguay is known as a "classic example" of a state based upon the principles of the national security system.[14] The Uruguayan regime implements the national security ideology through a "sophisticated system of control in which repression is embedded in the very structures of society."[15] The practices of the Uruguayan state are typical of those regimes "committed to the ideology of the national security state"[16] which include the dismantling of the constitution, the dissolution of Parliament, the abolition of an independent judiciary and the establishment of laws through decree. The military has authority to arrest, try and sentence civilians suspected of "political" crimes, interrogate them routinely under torture and incarcerate them in military prisons under military discipline.[17] These prisoners have no access to fair trials or appeals. The last human rights organization to exist in Uruguay, "Service for Peace and Justice" (SERPAJ), established in 1980, was officially banned in August, 1983. This group used to publish monthly reports which monitored the situation of the political prisoners and prison conditions, as well as providing information and documentation to the relatives of the "Disappeared," as well as keeping international organizations abreast of the general political situation in Uruguay.[18] Meanwhile, economic conditions continue to worsen in Uruguay, which experiences inflation rates of 45%, with a 17% unemployment rate, and a four billion dollar foreign debt.[19] The *Tupamaros*, or *Movimiento de Liberacion Nacional* (MLN), an Uruguayan guerrilla organization operating against the status quo, has been severely repressed, with its leaders serving prison terms of thirty-five to forty years.

This is what the situation looks like in a country dominated by the national security system and its corresponding ideology. The Latin American version of the national security state is particularly dangerous because it operates unchecked by those limitations which would normally be imposed by constitutions or other independent government bodies.

> There is no longer either a constitution or a functioning congress in most Latin American countries. Sometimes appearances are maintained, but they are only appearances. In Brazil, for example, there is a puppet congress that meets but has no power. The National Security Council and the NIS (National Information Service) are able to determine events without restrictions. This is true in most of the countries where the new institutions have replaced the former organs of the state. They are building a new pattern for the state wherein the traditional legislative, executive and judicial powers are nothing but administrative services functioning under the real power — the new institutions . . . (its) ideology . . . covers virtually all individual and social activities of the nation and gives new meaning to all human existence, (and) is universal enough and totalitarian enough to exclude any interferences by another philosophy. [20]

One of the basic ideological assumptions of the national security system is that its country is in a state of permanent, total war in which the battle is waged against an internal enemy which is usually branded as "communism." This idea assumes "all politics (to be) a politics of war,"[21] a clear example of which can be found in Peru. Since 1980, there exists in that country an all-out war waged by the Peruvian state, through the military and counter-insurgency police, known as *Sinchis*, against the "Maoist" guerrilla organization, *Sendero Luminoso*, about which more will be said later. Peru is a clear example of a country engaged in total war against an internal, "communist" enemy, which is the case in most Latin American countries. The ideology of National Security holds that the very survival of the nation is endangered, so that anyone remotely suspected of "subversion" or sympathy with "subversive", "communist" elements in the society, must be severely punished and even eliminated. In such an extreme situation of suspicion, every citizen is a potential enemy of the state. In order for the nation to survive and remain strong so that is can pursue its "national goals" — whatever they may be — the state must have full power and control to take whatever measures are necessary to eradicate its "enemies." "National security is the final and unconditional point of reference for everything, the absolute necessity, the unqualified Good; national power is the radical characteristic or nature of all things." [22]

In the ideology of the National Security State, the military is seen as the guarantor of the national power and survival. The power of the military in most Latin American countries, whether it is in direct control or closely aligned with civilian governments, is justified on the assumption that the large majority of the population, which includes mostly peasants, urban poor and workers, cannot be trusted to be totally loyal to the ruling power.[23] As was said earlier, communism and/or Marxism is perceived as the single most insidious threat to national security, so that only the military can "regenerate" and protect the nation. "What gives them this ability to regenerate the nation?" asks Comblin.

> Nothing other than force and power. Their entire doctrine is based on their ability to create force and violence. The essence of the state is force and power. The military are in possession of power. Consequently, the military alone are able to give power to the state again. Within such a system, military force reaches the level of a metaphysical attribute: life is power, military power; the essence of being is violence. [24]

Paradoxically enough, National Security ideology, which is of course supported by the military, embraces the principles of both democracy and Christianity:

> According to their [the military regimes'] own declarations, the only purpose of their entire politics is the salvation of democracy and Christianity. They all want to create a new society based on Christian principles. Reading the Declaration of Principles of the Chilean junta, one has to weep tears of joy and wonder—surely no government in the modern world has ever had such a Christian purpose. [25]

As part of their efforts of self-legitimation, the military regimes attempt to actively co-opt the Latin American Church, and in fact do enjoy a measure of support within various Catholic movements, as well as within the Catholic Church itself.[26] One of the main reasons for this support is the opposition of the official church to communism and Marxism. This point is important for understanding Segundo, and his attempted appropriation of Marxism, and his disagreement with the Vatican on this particular point, which will be the subject of the next chapter. When the Catholic bourgeoisie and the Church enter into "coalitions" or agreements with the national governments of a Latin American country, they do so partly because they share some common concerns and goals expressed by National Security ideology, namely the fear of communism and the desire for a rejuvenated Christian society in which the Church has an important decision-making role.[27] Underlying these concerns of the Church is a much deeper issue, and that is the question of the survival or at least strong influence of the Church in Latin America.

From the point of view of the Church, this is a real and legitimate concern, but unfortunately has lead some sectors of the Church, at least, into the "temptation" to forge what Comblin describes as "the new Constantinian agreement"[28] with the ruling powers in some countries. The Church in Latin America very much opposes the spread of communist and/or Marxist ideology, which has become an increasingly powerful force in some Latin American countries as a result of growing revolutionary movements, and the increased dissatisfaction of the population with the governments. However, it is by no means true that there is any consensus or even majority agreement either among Catholics or within the Church to adopt a "Constantinian" alliance with the governments or military regimes.

> The majority in the Catholic Church have not fallen into the trap, have not succumbed to the very temptation. There is a virtual break between church and state that is apparent in a good many circumstances. At the same time, there is a split within the church itself between those who accept and those who do not accept the new Constantinian agreement (although each party has given up any hope of converting the other party).[29]

Nonetheless, the Latin American Church has not produced "a Christian doctrine" (ideology-critique?) which can effectively challenge or counteract the "dominant" national security ideology.[30] This is a necessary task that must be assumed by Latin American theologians.

However, Segundo has begun to take up this effort in the form of creating an alternative ideological response to the dominant National Security ideology. Segundo is proposing an ideology that expresses a political and theoretical association between Marx and Christianity. There is one further aspect to this that should be clarified: the connections between Marx and Christianity as Segundo interprets them, exist mostly on the level of a shared anthropology, which Segundo tries to demonstrate by postulating a humanist values-structure at the core of Marx's thought. Marx does discuss the theme of human alienation, for example, which is produced by capitalist, class society, and the possibility of human beings overcoming that alienation through the establishment of a socialist, or communist society. The point, however, is not to open up a new debate around Marx's anthropology; Segundo has already done this, and it has been discussed here. The point is, rather, to understand Segundo's appropriation of Marx's anthropology. Segundo thinks that Marx assumes, like he does, that human beings justly deserve lives free from material deprivation and oppression as a given moral principle. This very general view of human beings centres around an absolute value that places human welfare above all other considerations, which for Segundo is rooted in love, which also happens to be the absolute value of Christian ethics. The ideology of the National Security system in Latin America, however, holds an opposite anthropology that is primarily Hobbesian, and thus the negation not only of Segundo's anthropology, but of Christian anthropology in general. The anthropology inherent in a National Security ideology assumes that:

> The human is, above all, a weak and limited being, existing in permanent danger, always afraid and living in a feeling of permanent insecurity. Between human beings there is not spontaneous agreement. By themselves, human beings are not able to put peace or order or reason into the world. Human beings are wolves to other human beings. Any human is a danger to any other. Human life is fight, competition, struggle, survival of the stronger individuals – of the fittest. [31]

Thus, in the National Security ideology, there is no possibility of a shared anthropology with Christianity, since the former holds no concept of love, forgiveness, nor reconciliation, the central values of Christianity.

However, in line with Segundo's logic, these values (or any values) are not sufficient in themselves to be effective in the concrete lives of individuals. Values are in need of a mechanism, or strategy whereby they may become actualized in human praxis, and this mechanism Segundo of course identifies with ideology, as has been discussed. Yet the ideology of the National Security state is not the only ideology to which Segundo must respond. In Latin America, there are also the various ideologies of the different revolutionary movements and guerrilla groups which are struggling against the government and military forces in many Latin American countries. The ideology of the National Security system is more or less the common ideology of the military and civilian governments in most Latin American countries, and as such, can be generally identified and described in terms of common features. There is no such homogeneous revolutionary or guerrilla ideology common to the many groups operating in Latin America. However, it must also be pointed out that the various rural and urban guerrilla organizations existing throughout Latin America since the Cuban revolution, can be loosely classified within either a Leninist or Maoist theoretical orientation.

Those revolutionary movements and groups which would be termed "Leninist," base their struggle in the urban areas and rely upon the industrial working class and university students to wage the revolution. Those whose revolutionary project can be traced back to the historical experience of the Chinese revolution, more commonly labelled "Maoist" (which itself could be traced further back to the Russian revolution) seek their revolutionary social base in rural areas among the peasants. More recently, there emerged a third model of revolutionary struggle, based upon a combination of the urban and rural guerrilla movement as was the case in the revolutionary war in Nicaragua. However, it serves no useful purpose to now embark upon a detailed anatomy of the various revolutionary movements with Latin America. The point is to offer some indication of the existence of both the range of revolutionary movements and their corresponding ideologies. In order to more fully understand the ideological context within which Segundo is attempting to formulate his ideological alternative, this time vis-à-vis the various left-wing revolutionary movements, I will present a brief picture of four fairly representative revolutionary ideologies. Hopefully, this effort will allow a more concrete comprehension of what Segundo is writing about when he freely interchanges terms like "the Left," "guerrillas," "terrorists," "revolutionaries" and "subversives" without explaining who they are or what they think or do. Unless we have some clearer idea of the various ideologies that proliferate throughout Latin America and their basic theoretical orientation, it will remain difficult to determine what ideological alternative Segundo wishes to support.

Illustrations of Revolutionary Theory and Practice in Latin America

Carlos Marighella

Carlos Marighella was a Brazilian, born into the middle class, who joined the Communist Party in the 1930's, which he left in the 1960's to form his own revolutionary organizations called *Ala Marighella* (Marighella Wing). He also organized a coalition of urban terrorist groups, and wrote the *Minimanual of the Urban Guerrilla*, which became their operational handbook. This small book is now considered a classic of its type.

Marighella's 'Minimanual', although written for the Brazilian struggle, became influential and widely read by urban guerrilla groups around the world. It basically outlines the mechanics of revolutionary struggle, which include what types of guns and ammunition are best suited for a guerrilla war, as well as identifying the legitimate targets of guerrilla attack. For example, Marighella urges the use of the light machine gun, whose greatest advantage is that it is "greatly respected by the enemy."[32] The proper targets of guerrilla actions are: all government property and institutions, banks, police stations, mass media, North American firms and possessions, and government transportation vehicles. He outlines a detailed series of "action models" for the urban guerrilla, which include: executions, kidnappings (in order to bargain for imprisoned guerrillas and force the suspension of torture in jails), sabotage and terrorism. Marighella recognizes that terrorism can be very important in undermining the security and confidence in the government and military, as well as corroding their strength and legitimacy in the eyes of the people. "Terrorism is an arm the revolutionary can never relinquish." [33]

Marighella also devoted part of his 'Minimanual' to a discussion of the personality of the urban guerrilla and the importance of ideological purity. The urban guerrilla is "morally superior"[34] to all other men, and his principle duty is to "attack and survive." His goal is strictly political, to attack only government forces, "big capitalists," foreign imperialists, and "particularly North Americans." The guerrilla selflessly and relentlessly pursues his goal, subordinating all other considerations, especially personal ones, to the fulfilment of his aim, the overthrow of the existing social order. In fact, the "urban guerrilla's reason for existence, the basic condition in which he acts and survives, is to shoot."[35] Thus the urban guerrilla loses all sense of personal subjectivity, transforming himself into a single concentrated, pure function of the revolution. The implied anthropology of this concept of the urban guerrilla is that he or she is actually not a human being but a technician of armed combat, a virtual extension of the machine gun. The guerrilla is thus reduced to the simple, mindless function of shooting the enemy, and therein lies his or her supreme value.

The urban guerrilla must adhere unwaveringly to ideological principles and "correct methods" of thinking and practice, and here Marighella shows the influence of Lenin. The guerrilla unit must be a tightly knit, ideologically inflexible group, which must protect itself from ideological "contamination." For this reason, extreme caution must be exercised when choosing new recruits. The urban guerrilla is the ideological and strategic "backbone" of the revolutionary war, and is instrumental in building up a revolutionary army of national liberation. Although Marighella acknowledges the importance of cultivating popular support, he sees the revolt of the masses as subordinate to the leadership of the vanguard, who are intellectuals. He also acknowledges the important role of Christians in waging the revolution:

Churchmen . . . those ministers or priests and religious men of various hierarchies and persuasions — represent a sector that has a special ability to communicate with the people, particularly with workers, with peasants and the Brazilian woman. The priest who is an urban guerrilla is an active ingredient in the ongoing Brazilian revolutionary war, and constitutes a powerful arm in the struggle against military power and North American imperialism. [36]

Marighella knows very well that the presence of clergy and lay Christians in the guerrilla movement constitutes a powerful ideological tool or inroad into the popular culture of Latin America, which is predominantly Christian. What Marighella implies, is that Christianity is the chief cultural, public "ideology" in Brazil, and that to involve clergy in the revolutionary struggle is also a struggle for cultural hegemony. Segundo too, is well aware of the fact that Catholic Christianity is an intact cultural force in Latin America, with a fairly long historical tradition: "In Latin America . . . religion is intricately bound up with the whole system of relationships that governs the mentality of the people."[37] Assuming this to be the case, Marighella will obviously hope to co-opt Christians into the revolutionary movement as an important means of gaining popular support. Both Fidel Castro and Ché Guevara have also referred to the importance of Christian participation in Latin American revolutions. Although Segundo has a measured understanding and perhaps even sympathy with the revolutionary movements in Latin America, he by no means desires that Christianity becomes subsumed or co-opted by guerrilla movements. His critique of these movements is discussed later in this chapter. Although Segundo never dismisses the efforts or good intentions of revolutionary movements, he is careful to distance himself from them:

My purpose . . . is certainly not to discredit the revolutionary good faith of any group or movement. Nor is it to claim that real revolution is impossible, although it certainly is a far more difficult process than (sic) any revolutionary handbook might suggest. [38]

Régis Debray

Régis Debray also emerged as an important and influential theoretician of revolutionary and guerrilla movements in Latin America, and although he is not Latin American himself, he must nonetheless be taken into account, at least briefly. Whereas Marighella is a political-military thinker, whose basic focus is on the mechanics of the revolution, Debray is a more political thinker of the revolution. Like Marighella, he too believes that the guerrilla unit must be the vanguard of the people, acting as a self-conscious minority within the population, to lead the people through revolutionary struggle to victory. As a personality, the guerrilla must be single-mindedly concentrated on the revolutionary cause, prepared to "stake all" and "lose all" in order to "win all."

> To risk all means . . . the fighters must wage *a war to the death*, a war that does not admit of truces, retreats, or compromises. To conquer is to accept as a matter of principle that life, for the revolutionary, is not the supreme good. [39]

The first prerequisite for a guerrilla is not ideological education, which will come inevitably in Debray's view, through direct, armed confrontation with the enemy. This experience is, according to Debray, the best teacher of Marxism-Leninism.   The chief prerequisite for the guerrilla fighter is "physical aptitude," the "most basic" of all skills needed in waging a war.[40]
    The most significant aspect of Debray's thought is his insistence on the unity of the military and the political wings of the revolution, which cannot be separate but must be concentrated in an "organic whole": "The guerrilla force is the party in embryo."[41]   What the guerrilla movement does, according to him, is to overcome the split between revolutionary theory and practice by combining political and military leadership, so that the military forces are not controlled by a separate party structure.[42] In a very revealing passage, Debray develops his concept of political and military unity of the guerrilla movement through a visual metaphor, in which the uniforms of the leaders of the Cuban revolution signify the integration of the political and military:

> A foreign journalist in Cuba was astonished one day to see many Communist leaders in battle dress; he had thought that battle dress and pistols belonged to the folk-lore of the Revolution, that they were really a kind of martial affectation. Poor man! It was not an affectation, it was the history of the Revolution itself appearing before his eyes, and most certainly the future history of America. [43]

Here Debray is indulging in primitive hypostasis, where the revolution becomes reified in the cult of the personality in uniform. The battle dress of the Cuban revolutionary leaders, as interpreted by Debray, stand as sheer representation, reducing the Cuban revolution to historical spectacle. It is reification of the Stalinist kind, and implies only one possible outcome: the absolutization and thus dictatorship of the party, embodied in the leadership of one man, as is the case of Cuba. Debray actually envisions a future socialist society in the symbol of a military uniform: "This," writes Debray, "is the staggering novelty introduced by the Cuban Revolution."[44] Debray's concept of revolution is the struggle toward a new dictatorship, the potential horrors of which are so obvious that a critique at this point is actually unnecessary.

What Marighella and Debray represent is a "Marxist" concept of revolution of the Leninist-Stalinist version, which is very different from the socialist humanist thrust of Segundo's writing, and his corresponding interpretations of Marx. With Marighella and Debray, revolution is a strictly military and political affair, constructed upon an inflexible, instrumentalist rationality, that sees the revolution as an end in itself, embodied in the domination of a particular leadership, vested in a group or single person. What Debray advocates is precisely that which the Christian theologians of liberation such as Segundo specifically reject, and that is the sacralization, or absolutization of any particular revolutionary struggle or social order. For that matter, so did Marx. If the theories of revolution put forward by Marighella and Debray do exert ideological appeal and influence on the revolutionary struggles throughout Latin America, then Segundo's insistence on the need for human-centred values as the grounding of ideology makes sense. As was pointed out earlier, Segundo fears that ideology without values or meaning-structure threatens to produce a rigidity and inflexibility which can easily lose sight of the authentic goals of revolution: the liberation of real human beings in Latin America from the misery and poverty in which they now live. An ideology detached from human values postulates the revolution as an end in itself, not a process toward human liberation, which is what is expressed in Marighella and Debray. If this kind of revolutionary ideology is the only alternative to National Security ideology, then the people may accept this concept of revolution as their only hope against the increasing repression and violence produced by their governments. Segundo seems to fear that such revolutionary ideologies will result in the further breakdown of Latin American society, which he calls the destruction of the "social ecology," which will be discussed later in this chapter.

Ernesto 'Ché' Guevara

Any discussion of revolutionary theories must include Ché Guevara, who perhaps still exercises the most popular appeal in Latin America than any other revolutionary fighter in recent history. Guevara differs from Marighella and Debray in that he has a strong sense of what can be termed a socialist humanism, or a sense of what Segundo means by human values. He is not a strict ideological purist or mechanistic tactician in the mold of a Marighella or Debray. His writings reflect a strong sympathy with the plight of poor Latin Americans, and indicates that his participation in the revolutionary struggles of Latin America was motivated by his own protest against the "horrible conditions of exploitation"[45] in Latin America. This humane motivation is particulary clear in a speech, "On Revolutionary Medicine." Here Guevara shows the underlying human values of his revolutionary activity, values which he learned as a doctor in Latin America:

> Because of the circumstances in which I travelled, first as a student and later as a doctor, I came into close contact with poverty, hunger, and disease; with the inability to treat a child because of lack of money; with the stupefaction provoked by continual hunger and punishment, to the point that a father can accept the loss of a son as an unimportant accident, as occurs often in the downtrodden classes of our American homeland. And I began to realize at that time that there were things that were almost as important to me as becoming a famous scientist or making a significant contribution to medical science: I wanted to help those people. [46]

There is a humane quality to Guevera's writings that is largely absent in Marighella and the young Debray, and which constitutes an important distinction between Guevara and them, which must not be ignored.

However, Guevara is in accord with Debray on the role of the guerrillas as the revolutionary vanguard, "the people's fighting vanguard" which relies upon the support of the masses, not only to win, but as a moral legitimation of its vanguard role. Unless the guerrillas achieve the popular support of the "masses of peasants and workers," Guevara maintains that "guerrilla warfare is unacceptable."[47] Nevertheless, Guevara stresses the necessity of the guerrilla vanguard, as the "subjective condition" necessary for victory. But Guevara does not seem to reduce the masses to mere foot soldiers of the revolution, whose sole purpose is to support the fighting guerrillas, in the way Marighella and Debray imply, and neither does he indulge in excessive glorifications of the personal qualities of guerrilla fighters, although their military function and importance are highly stressed. Guevara even reveals a sense of human community when he writes that there is a "close dialectical unity which exists between the individual and the mass, in which both are interrelated, and the mass, as a whole composed of individuals, is in turn interrelated with the leader." [48]

Thus Guevara shows an approach to revolution that is somewhat reflective rather than strictly technical and tactical, so that revolution becomes a vehicle for the realization of the "new man": "To build communism, a new man must be created simultaneously with the material base."[49] The emergence of the "new man" or socialist man, will develop parallel to the creation of new economic forms, and the revolutionary society will be a society of man "freed from alienation."[50] Guevara stressed the "two pillars of socialism" as the formation of the new human being as well as the development of technology and material conditions which would serve the concrete needs of a socialized humanity. It was this humanist concern with both human alienation and material deprivation that allowed Guevara to proclaim that the "true revolutionary" is motivated by "strong feelings of love."[51] Thus the guerrilla fighter must combine in himself an "impassioned spirit" with a "cold mind," inspired by an indivisible, idealized love for both the people and the revolutionary goal (the "hallowed cause").[52] The revolutionary's love for the people must be expressed daily in "concrete deeds" that will set an example for all, inspiring and mobilizing the masses to embrace and support the revolutionary struggle with the dual aim of transforming human beings *and* the social order.

Guevara's emphasis on the necessity of "profound internal changes" in individuals along with "profound external changes" in social structures, is not incompatible with the views of Segundo, because Guevara also recognizes the importance of human values, and appears to view revolutionary struggle, in part, as the means whereby those values may be realized. [53]

Sendero Luminoso ("Shining Path")

Very little is known about this rural based guerrilla organization, which emerged in 1964 as the result of a Sino-Soviet split within the Communist Party of Peru.[54] It is not a group which publishes statements nor does it often publicly claim responsibility for actions, or grant interviews with journalists.[55] Ideologically, it seems to mix Maoism and Inca nationalism, adopting the classical Maoist strategy of a "prolonged popular war encircling the cities from the countryside."[56] Its leader is a former university professor of philosophy, Abimael Guzman, from the southern Andean *departamento* of Ayacucho, one of the poorest, most marginalized areas in Peru. Although the group has its roots in the San Cristobal National University in Ayacucho, it sends its cadres into the surrounding peasant communities, where they have learned the local Indian language, Quechua, and "nurtured the messianic tradition of Inca rebellion against the conquistadors and landowners." [57]

It seems that *Sendero Luminoso*, or "Shining Path", derives its name from a statement once made by the Peruvian Marxist-Leninist, José Carlo Mariatequi: "Marxism-Leninism will open up the shining path to revolution."[58] Some observers compare *Sendero Luminoso* to the Khmer Rouge, because of its efforts "to create a peasant-worker republic, reject modern technology, prevent food storage, keep money out of the economy, and restore a traditional economic system" based on commodity exchange.[59] One of *Sendero's's* basic strategies is the total integration of its members into the local, indigenous culture.

In 1980, the *Senderistas* declared a "prolonged popular war" against the newly elected civilian government of Peru after which they began to bomb public buildings and power stations, and were so successful that they cut off the power supply to Lima in 1982. They hold "popular trials" and commit "executions" of local policemen, landowners, politicians and even peasants whom they suspect of being informants or opposed to their cause.[60] Since 1984, *Sendero* has been increasingly active in Lima, bombing buildings and assassinating policemen and other officers. Some observers refer to *Sendero Luminoso* as "one of the most brutal guerrilla organizations to appear" in Latin America.[61]

The appearance and violent actions of *Sendero Luminoso* have resulted in an equally violent counter-insurgency strategy on the part of the government, which by 1985, placed twenty-six provinces in Peru under direct military control – unleashing a classic "spiral of violence" situation. In the declared "emergency zones" of Peru, the *Sinchis*, or special counter-insurgency police, are given full power to arrest anyone suspected of having contacts with the Senderistas. The tactics of the *Sinchis* and the military have resulted in mass arrests, increased torture, disappearances and extra-judicial executions, for which the military and government authorities often blame *Sendero*. The peasants are of course caught in the middle of this spiralling violence and counterviolence, terrorized by both sides. It is a situation which corresponds to the ideology of the National Security State, in which the national forces understand themselves to be in a state of all-out war with an internal enemy. This ideology of total war to the end is also to be found within revolutionary movements, and which is articulated by Debray, as quoted earlier. In this way these two opposing ideologies share a common goal of each annihilating the other, and thus establishing a new social order in which the leaders of the struggle become the political leaders of the new society.

Although brief, the above presentation is fairly accurate account of the polarized situation that exists in most Latin American countries, in terms of the opposing forces of the National Security system and the revolutionary and guerrilla movements. My central interest is to indicate the basic ideological features of those forces in order to more clearly understand the general ideological context in which Segundo is writing. Since Segundo rarely goes into concrete detail about anything, it is all the more urgent to have a sense of what opposing ideological forces are operating in Latin America and then gain some comprehension of what Segundo faces in his efforts to create a credible ideological alternative.

Toward an Ideological Alternative

Segundo states that the period of "awareness" among some sectors of Latin America, most notably in university settings, of the "structural, systematic character" of injustice[62] developed from 1950 onwards. He attributes this growing awareness to the suspicions raised by certain ideologies critical of the *status quo*, although he does not identify these ideologies or the social groups to which they correspond. He then refers to a "politics of the Left" that exists "in some countries," which are "associated more or less closely with Marxism and its theoretical systematiz-ation"[63] although he gives no details nor makes any distinctions among those groups embracing a "politics of the Left." As has been pointed out here, such distinctions do exist and are important, yet at no time does Segundo delve into this question. He simply refers to the "revolutionaries" or the left as if they were all the same, which they are not. Nonetheless, Segundo maintains that only "the Marxist ideology," when applied to Latin America, is able to give an accurate interpretation of the "situation" in Latin America, i.e., the systematic, structural nature of the injustice, exploitation and violence that permeates Latin American society:

> Nor should it surprise anyone that the Marxist view would be influential in spreading awareness of the systematic nature of the problem, which is now universally admitted. But a fact is a fact, no matter who points it out. And the fact is that every possible political approach to development has been tried over the past twenty-five years (1950-1975) and that at the end of that time . . . a whole human generation . . . we are farther away from the goal than when we started. [64]

However vague and general Segundo appears in this passage, it is safe to assume that in his view "Marxism" — "the Marxist ideology" — is the only ideological tool of analysis that has been able to adequately expose the nature and causes of Latin American social problems, and account for the "failure" of Latin America to prosper.

But Segundo seems to lament the fact that "Marxism" became dislocated from its "most authentic form," in that any "creative thought and reflection were sacrificed on the altar of activism," so that "Marxism" ended up being utilized in its "most simplistic and oversimplifying version."[65] Segundo does not explain what he means by such a suggestive statement, so that one is compelled to infer that he is very critical of the various revolutionary movements and guerrilla groups operating throughout Latin America. Having seen something of what those groups espouse as revolutionary theory and practice, and having understood Segundo's concern with values, this hypothesis makes sense. Segundo is dismayed by the reductionist reification that has distorted much of Marx's thought since the Russian revolution, with its Leninist and Stalinist interpretations. By activism, Segundo means an ideology and practice that is not grounded in values as he means the word, but rather activism as translated into mere instrumental tactics. Segundo offers two basic, interrelated reasons for this criticism of revolutionary activism: one is that it has provoked severe repression on the part of the military and government authorities, and two, that this situation of violence, insurrection and counter-insurrection[66] will soon result in the complete destruction of the "social ecology" of Latin American society.

What concerns Segundo is the destructive effects within the society produced by prolonged guerrilla warfare, which in his view go far beyond the killing of people, but which nonetheless threatens to destroy the very core and fabric of social life, which is what he means be "social ecology."

> In guerrilla war . . . those prepared to do this destruction (killing people) will keep on using the social relations of a normal context with those who are to be destroyed. Such relations as family, friendship, and hospitality would be inhibited vis-á-vis a known and declared enemy, for example. But they are necessarily operative vis-á-vis an unknown or secret enemy. The latter does violence to those relationships at their very core: i.e., trust. The incognito enemy wittingly compromises and involves those who establish or maintain basic social relationships with him or her or with the causes the latter has espoused. And because people did maintain such relationships with the enemy, they may later be outraged, imprisoned, tortured, or killed. [67]

A prolonged guerrilla war inevitably draws in all citizens, targeting them for suspicion by both guerrilla and military forces (as is presently the case in Peru), so that the "basic rules of human and social co-existence" deteriorate.[68] The result is, in Segundo's view, that the efforts of those political parties who seek to change society "through legal means" are destroyed, thus foreclosing on the future possibilities of young Latin Americans to engage in a politics through which they might change the situation in Latin America, or at least reform it. [69]

In fact, Segundo seems to imply that the actions of the various revolutionary movements and guerrilla groups in Latin America are partly responsible for the increased repressive measures instituted by the government and military authorities because "the Left", the "subversives," or "the subversive side"[70] believed that the increased repression of the authorities would win over the general populace to their side. Of course, the very opposite happened with the result that "the middle classes called for and supported the repression and even the destruction of democratic government *without consciously realizing that they were abandoning the liberal, democratic ideology.*"[71] Segundo goes into no more detail or analysis than can be found is these quotations in his criticism of "the Left," so there is no possibility to pursue his argument. The point is, that Segundo lumps the various revolutionary movements and their differing ideologies together so that they are indistinguishable from one another. This could lead to an assumption, for example, that a guerrilla organization like Sendero Luminoso is representative of other revolutionary movements in Latin America, which it is not. Segundo obliterates these distinctions perhaps because to him they are unimportant. It may be as well easier for him to formulate an ideological alternative to those revolutionary, guerrilla movements, if their differences are minimized.

Segundo implies that the revolutionary movements in Latin America are excessively preoccupied with "ideological" questions to the exclusion of ethics and values,[72] which he seems to blame on particular interpretations or misinterpretations of Marx: "the ideology implemented by Marxist socialism has to some extent belied the hopes invested in it by the Marxist faith."[73] Since the issue of values in terms of a "predialectical" faith, which Segundo claims is inherent in Marx's thought as has already been discussed, there is no point to pick it up again. Segundo's main concern is to re-align a proper faith with an appropriate ideology, as a means whereby the destruction of Latin American society and culture may be counteracted. "At this point we find that an inappropriate ideology degrades faith and that a faith which fails to recognize all its components leads to a counter-productive ideology."[74] What is needed to rescue Latin America from social and cultural destruction is the rejuvenation of its culture through the creation of human values-structure along with the appropriate means for the "transmission" of those values into the wider culture. So we face the problem of shaping an effective cultural *tradition*. We must make a certain basic value-structure almost automatic. On that quasi-automatic structure we can then build the needed political ideologies with a certain degree of ease insofar as the use of energy is concerned. [75]

For a more humane Latin American society, Segundo proposes a revised Christian faith wherein people would "*first* accept certain human values and *then* recognize their sacred or absolute sense."[76] It should be remembered that in Segundo's view, "anthropological faith" in basic human values must always precede "religious faith," since the latter is simply the "prolongation" of the former.[77] Thus, Segundo proposes a revised Christian faith and practice whose ethical centre is a human values or meaning-structure, that is firmly rooted in history, and thoroughly mediated and conditioned by the concrete needs of human beings. He is optimistic that such a revised Christianity is possible to achieve in Latin America, since the Christian religion is already there intact, occupying a central position in the mainstream of Latin American culture:

> It would seem that a religious faith such as the Christian one would occupy a central point on our spectrum. It combines optimum possibilities for cultural transmission with a rich store of profound experiences and reflections on ethics and the meaning of life. That store has been accumulated by human beings over the course of many centuries. [78]

For Segundo, the main focus of a transformed Christianity would be in line with Paul's command to "hold to what is good" (I Thess. 5:20). Segundo assumes that Christianity could be the most effective and immediate means whereby human values could become the basis of social change for two chiefly pragmatic reasons: first, because those values are confirmed primarily by the historical Jesus and Paul, and second, because Christianity is already the prevalent religion in Latin America.

> In our Latin American culture, adherence to a non-Christian religious faith would substantially alter the energy equation which underlies the following considerations. Assuming that religious faith is of equal complexity, we know that adherence to it would entail a considerably greater expenditure of energy insofar as it was not transmitted in and through one's own culture. . . . The believer would have to start from scratch in building this new meaning-world. Scriptures, rites and practices would have to be explored and learned well enough to ensure a gratifying result. So I focus on the Christian faith here because it is related, however confusedly and ambiguously, with the actual cultural traditions of our Latin American countries.[79]

As far as Marxism is concerned, it "combines a system of meaning and values (a faith) with a more or less scientific system designed to build a society that accords with those values (an ideology)."[80] Segundo's main concern in relation to Marxism is that it does not degenerate into pure, mechanistic "ideology," but that it is brought into a proper interrelationship with faith, as I already explained. In other words, for Marxism to be accepted in Latin America as an effective vehicle for social change, for

Marxism not to appear as a "foreign" system of thought,[81] it must find a way of being culturally "transmitted" into Latin American society. This last point perhaps explains Segundo's efforts discussed earlier, to appropriate Marx into Christian faith, since it is by way of Christianity that Marxism may find a legitimate conduit into Latin American culture. Segundo, however, faces another problem on this point: the uncompromising opposition of the Vatican to all forms of Marxism. As far as the Vatican is concerned, there is no question that Marxism and Christianity are irrevocably opposed, and that Marxism is perceived furthermore as an enemy of the Christian faith. For Segundo, some of the basic insights of Marx's thought (irrespective of how he interprets them) have the potential to strengthen Christianity, rendering it historically a more relevant and effective force for making the world a better place. The entire question of the positive value of Marxian analysis, not to mention its central role in liberation theology's social analysis, is one of the most problematic and burning points of contention between liberation theology and the Vatican. Since Segundo has publicly addressed the Vatican's condemnation of Marxism and its critique of liberation theology, I will now turn to this issue.

NOTES

1. André Gunder Frank, *Latin America: Underdevelopment or Revolution: Essays on the Development of Underdevelopment and the Immediate Enemy* (New York and London: Monthly Review Press, 1969), p. 402.

2. Juan Luis Segundo, "Jesus of Nazareth Yesterday and Today", *The Historical Jesus of the Synoptics*, Vol. II, p. 13

3. Ibid., p. 17.

4. Juan Luis Segundo, *Faith and Ideologies*, p. 261.

5. Juan Luis Segundo, *The Liberation of Theology*, pp. 126-127.

6. Juan Luis Segundo, *Faith and Ideologies*, p. 290.

7. Juan Luis Segundo, *The Liberation of Theology*, p. 127. Segundo recognizes the fact that Catholicism in Latin America is the prevalent ideology, since the majority of Latin American people consider themselves to be Catholic Christians. If Catholicism as the existent prevalent ideology can be transformed into an effective ideological vehicle for social change, then perhaps it might be able to dislodge the dominant ideology of National Security, and at the same time marginalize the appeal of the revolutionary guerrilla movements. This seems to me to reflect the line of Segundo's thinking.

8. Noam Chomsky and Edward S. Herman point out that National Security ideology ("National Security Doctrine") has much in common with Nazism, and in fact has been very much influenced by it. They write that the development of the ideology of National Security "reveals startling similarities with patterns of thought and behaviour under European fascism, especially under Nazism. Fascist ideology has flowed into Latin America directly and indirectly. Large numbers of Nazi refugees came to Latin American during and after World War II, and important ingredients of fascist ideology have been indirectly routed into that area through the U.S. military and intelligence establishment." Noam Chomsky and Edward S. Herman, *The Political Economy of Human Rights*, Vol. I, *The Washington Connection and Third World Fascism* (Montreal: Black Rose Books, 1979), p. 252. Thus some of the main elements of Nazism and European fascism have become modified and adapted to the local requirements of many of the military and even civilian governments throughout Latin America, resulting in the ideology of National Security.

9. José Comblin, *The Church and the National Security State* (Maryknoll, N.Y.: Orbis Books, 1979), p. 54.

10. Ibid., p. 54. Chomsky and Herman present a similar definition of National Security ideology, whose main features in their view are: "1. that the state is absolute and the individual is nothing; 2. that every state is involved in permanent warfare, its present form being Communism versus the Free World; and 3. that control over "subversion" is possible only through domination by the natural leadership in the struggle against subversion, namely the armed forces" (Noam Chomsky and Edward S. Herman, *The Political Economy of Human Rights*, p. 253). One of the important differences between National Security ideology and Nazism, is that the former is not interested in ruining or annihilating specific minority groups, as was the case the Nazis' attempt to liquidate the Jews. Rather, the

127

enemy and target of National Security ideology is the majority population. "The special place of army and police merely assures that the military elite will share in the spoliation [of the majority] along with the traditional elite group" (Ibid).

11. John Gunther, *Inside South America* (New York, Evanston and London: Harper & Row, Publishers, 1966, 1967), pp. 220ff.

12. "Inter-Church Committee on Human Rights in Latin America" (ICCHRLA) Winter, 1983/1984, p. 78.

13. Ibid., p. 81.

14. Ibid., p. 81.

15. ICCHRLA, Winter, 1982/1983, p. 87.

16. Ibid., p. 87.

17. Ibid., p. 88.

18. Ibid., pp. 82-83.

19. "NACLA Report on the Americas," January/February, 1984, p. 44.

20. José Comblin, *The Church and the National Security State*, p. 65.

21. Ibid., p. 71.

22. Ibid., p. 72.

23. Ibid., p. 74.

24. Ibid., p. 75.

25. Ibid., p. 77.

26. Ibid., p. 82.

27. Ibid., pp. 82-83.

28. Ibid., p. 83.

29. Ibid., p. 83.

30. Ibid., p. 89.

31. Ibid., p. 89.

32. Jay Mallin (ed.), *Terror and Urban Guerrillas: A Study of Tactics and Documents* (Coral Gables, Florida: University of Miami Press, 1971), p. 77.

33. Ibid., p. 103.

34. Ibid., p. 72.

35. Ibid., p. 79.

36. Ibid., p. 114.

37. Juan Luis Segundo, *The Liberation of Theology*, p. 187.

38. Ibid., p. 101.

39. Régis Debray, *Revolution in the Revolution? Armed Struggle and Political Struggle in Latin America*, translated from the author's French and Spanish by Bobbye Ortiz (New York: Grove Press, Inc., 1967), p. 58.

40. Ibid., p. 102.

41. Ibid., p. 106.

42. Ibid., p. 107.

43. Ibid., pp. 105-106.

44. Ibid., p. 106.

45. *Venceremos! The Speeches and Writings of Ernesto Ché Guevara*, edited, annotated, and with an introduction by John Gerassi (London: Weidenfeld and Nicolson, 1968), p. 369.

46. Ibid., p. 112.

47. Ibid., p. 267.

48. Ibid., p. 389.

49. Ibid., p. 391.

50. Ibid., p. 393.

51. Ibid., p. 398.

52. Ibid., p. 398.

53. See Segundo's extremely brief, but no less intriguing comparison of Christ and Ché Guevara as reference points for a faith in a set of values and a way of life based on those values, which could be satisfying and productive (*The Liberation of Theology*, p. 105). What this passage reveals is that the "image" of Christ or Ché Guevara is of secondary importance to the human-oriented values they represent, i.e., the stress on human well-being that both gave their lives to. Segundo's implication here is that it does not matter if one is a Christian or a Marxist; the important point for Segundo is the values or meaning-structure which lay at the core of what Christ and Ché Guevara represent, which do not seem dissimilar from one another.

54. ICCHRLA, Vol. 1 and 2, p. 31.

55. "The Nation," December, 1984.

56. "NACLA Report on the Americas," May/June, 1983, p. 38.

57. Ibid., p. 38.

58. ICCHRLA, Summer, 1984, p. 2.

59. Ibid., Vol. 1 and 2, 1986, p. 31.

60. "The Nation," December, 1984.

61. ICCHRLA, Vol. 1 and 2, 1986, p. 31.

62. Juan Luis Segundo, *Faith and Ideologies*, p. 278.

63. Ibid., p. 279.

64. Ibid., p. 281.

65. Ibid., p. 285.

66. For a fuller discussion of the circular nature of violence in Latin America, but from the critical perspective advocating non-violence, see Dom Helder Camara, *The Spiral of Violence*, translated by Della Conling (Denville, N.J.: Dimension Books, 1971).

67. Juan Luis Segundo, *Faith and Ideologies*, p. 286.

68. Ibid., p. 287.

69. Ibid., p. 289.

70. Ibid., p. 290.

71. Ibid., p. 290.

72. This preoccupation with ethics and revolution has been taken up by some Marxists. Herbert Marcuse, whose essay, "Ethics and Revolution" (in *Ethics and Society: Original Essays on Contemporary Moral Problems*, ed. Richard T. De George, Garden City, N.Y.: Anchor Books, Doubleday and Company, Inc., 1966) reflects similar concerns with Segundo on this question, and which Marcuse develops more extensively. Marcuse opens his discussion with a question which formulates the problem in terms Segundo might well adopt himself. "Can a revolution be justified as right, as good, perhaps even as necessary, and justified not merely in political terms (as expedient for certain interests) but in ethical terms, that is to say, justified with respect to the human condition as such, to the potential of man in a given historical situation?" (p. 133).

73. Juan Luis Segundo, *Faith and Ideologies*, p. 318.

74. Ibid., p. 320.

75. Ibid., p. 321.

76. Ibid., p. 336.

77. Ibid., p. 336.

78. Ibid., p. 336.

79. Juan Luis Segundo, *Faith and Ideologies*, p. 335. Here, Segundo equates religious faith with religion as a cultural force. He implies that Christianity is best suited to function as an ideology for social change within the Latin American context because it is so deeply embedded in the culture. He acknowledges "that authentic types of religious faith can exist outside Christianity, but my concern here is to position the *Christian* faith on our spectrum, if only for practical reasons" (p. 335). This statement reflects a somewhat pragmatic approach to Christianity, and any religion which underlines Segundo's view that religion is both a cultural *and* ideological phenomenon.

80. Ibid., p. 329.

81. Ibid., p. 333.

Chapter VI

THEOLOGIES IN CONFLICT

In August 1984, and in March 1986, the Sacred Congregation for the Doctrine of the Faith issued two statements of great importance for Latin American liberation theology. The first document, entitled "Instruction on Certain Aspects of the 'Theology of Liberation'," was signed by Cardinal Joseph Ratzinger, prefect of the Congregation; the second document, "Instruction on Christian Freedom and Liberation," was personally approved by Pope John Paul II. The second document, (from here on referred to as the "second Instruction,") proclaims itself and its predecessor (the first Instruction) to be companion pieces, "organically" related and "to be read in the light of each other" (n.2). This statement is somewhat puzzling at first, since both documents could appear to express different attitudes toward liberation theology, at least upon an initial reading. The first document bears a harshly critical attitude toward liberation theology, so much so that Segundo wrote a book-length response to it in defense of liberation theology, and before the second Instruction appeared. The second Instruction, however, manifests a much more carefully worded, abstract, and generally supportive tone, but not on the actual question of liberation theology, as on the *theme* of Christian freedom and liberation, which is not exactly synonymous with liberation theology. In any event, the second Instruction clearly states in the Introduction that the warnings of the first document are "ever more timely and relevant" (n. 1). We may conclude that the second Instruction openly supports and endorses the contents of the previous document.

The difference between the two documents, in my view, may be expressed in this way: the first document directly and pointedly criticizes and rejects "certain forms" of some liberation "theologies," which are never specified, nor are their representatives identified, nor are these manifestations of "certain aspects" of liberation theology distinguished from one another. In fact, what this document does is to attack certain general features of liberation theology, particularly where Marxist concepts and categories are concerned, i.e., the concept of class struggle. The second Instruction, however, is a more subtle and sophisticated document in that while it too flatly rejects Marxist analysis and categories, for example, it never condemns liberation theology *as such*. What it does, is to affirm and embrace the *language* of freedom and liberation, and advocate justice for workers and the poor. In this sense, the second Instruction confirms the basic thrust of the social teachings of the Church, which traditionally uphold the principles of justice and dignity for all humanity.

However, this discourse of liberation that is used in the second Instruction should not be seen in any way as being necessarily an endorsement of liberation theology by the Vatican or the Pope. Even though the second Instruction follows upon the previous instruction in time, and bears a positive tone in relation to the themes of freedom and liberation, it is perhaps wise to resist the temptation to perceive the Second Instruction as in any substantial or indirect way undermining the previous document and its views on liberation theology. Actually, each document addresses a different subject. Moreover, as I will demonstrate below, the second Instruction, while directly staying away from liberation theology as a subject of discussion, does support and reiterate what are some of the most crucial points of theological and political incompatibility between the Vatican and the theology of liberation — points which are directly confronted by the first document. There is one final argument I wish to present now, and to which I will return later, and which is of especial relevance for Juan Luis Segundo: it is primarily the Vatican's sustained and total condemnation of Marx's thought which constitutes the unbreachable barrier between the Vatican and the theology of liberation. The attention that Segundo gives to Marx, along with his illustration of the impact of Marx on liberation theology, raises the possibility that *without the influence of Marx's analysis of history and society, liberation theology in its present form might not exist.*

In a lecture delivered at Regis College, Toronto, Segundo stated that liberation theology was never intended to be a "branch" of theology, which distinguishes itself from other branches of theology by its central preoccupation with liberation. Rather, the aim of liberation theology from its very beginning was "to re-make, to the extent of our possibilities, the whole of theology."[1] "Re-making" the whole of theology implies the construction of a theology with an opposite methodology to the existent theology, which Segundo calls "academic theology"[2] and Gutierrez refers to as "classical" theology. Liberation theology, in the form developed by Segundo, is a theology whose method is directly opposite to academic theology, and the 'official' theological approach such as is represented by the Vatican, which is discussed below. The key methodological feature of liberation theology, which begins with concrete humanity in its full historical and social contextuality, is clearly the result of the influence of the thought of Karl Marx. Juan Luis Segundo is a Latin American liberation theologian who has drawn from Marx's method and theory of history and society to the point of trying to appropriate some of Marx's most basic insights into his own theology, as I have stressed. Segundo has developed and made clearly explicit the nature and depth of Marx's general influence on liberation theology, and as such, has expressed the central point of irreconcilable conflict between the Vatican and the theology of liberation. In my view, the first Instruction and the subsequent document are both aware of this conflict. This is the reason why both documents so strongly condemn Marxist thought in general and Marxist influences on theology — liberation theology — in particular. Most Vatican documents that pertain to liberation theology or social justice in terms of liberation and freedom in any way reject all connection with Marxism. Otherwise, liberation and freedom and the goals of social justice for humanity appear to be completely supported by the Vatican. The statements of Pope John Paul II to the Brazilian bishops who assembled in Rome in 1986 are relevant to this part of the discussion. It should be noted that this address took place immediately prior to the release of the second Instruction, in March 1986.

> Little more than a year ago the instruction *Libertatis Nuntius*, [first document] which with my approval was published by the Congregation for the Doctrine of the Faith, confirmed that a theological reflection on liberation can and must exist which is based on solid doctrinal elements pertaining to the most authentic magisterium of the church as well as the treasure of the word of God. The church considers it its duty to proceed with this reflection, to update it and to deepen it more and more. . . . The same Congregation for the Doctrine of the Faith is about to publish a new document which focuses the principal aspects of liberation theology, understood in the terms which I have just mentioned. When purified of elements which can adulterate it, with grave consequences for the faith, this theology of liberation is not only orthodox, but also necessary.[3]

It is perfectly reasonable to assume that the "elements" which should be expurgated from liberation theology are connected with Marx.

In terms of the question of Marx's theory, it is not difficult to anticipate that the views of the Vatican and Segundo on this subject are almost in complete opposition to each other. The Vatican regards Marxism as totally antithetical to Christianity. It is part of my purpose here to explore the Vatican's position and the reasons for it. Another point to be demonstrated here is that the first Instruction and the subsequent document comprise a blend of explicitly *theological* and implicitly *political* statements. As such, these statements must be critically approached from the perspective that they do not, and furthermore cannot engage in a mode of discourse that is solely and specifically theological, or religious. However, both documents do base their argumentation upon closed theological and religious categories with a correspondingly strictly religious language, which together effect the impression of a morally and spiritually superior vantage point from which to criticize liberation theology and negate Marx. Both documents assume the existence of two distinct planes of reality that can be described as the sacred and the profane, the supernatural and natural, or the secular and religious. As such, the documents reflect an epistemological dualism whose architectonic structure places the religious realm as a separate dimension of reality over against the secular, or temporal dimension of human experience and action. Liberation theology is based upon an alternative epistemology which negates this distinction of planes as an invalid construct, by focusing upon the religious *value* or *meaning* of human history and action. According to Gustavo Gutierrez, who directly confronts this question of the "distinction of planes," "to participate in the process of liberation is already, in a certain sense, a salvific work."[4] He is opposed to a theological method which maintains the dualism of the religious and secular "as a burnt-out model with nothing to say to the advances in theological thinking." [5]

The insistence in the Vatican documents in question, upon the validity of a specifically religious or theological realm over against a temporal, secular dimension of reality is one of the key points of theological and political divergence between the Vatican and liberation theology. It cannot be overemphasized that the differences between the Vatican documents and the theology of liberation are both theological and political, in spite of the fact that the Vatican would in all likelihood refuse to acknowledge the inescapable political dimension of its own pronouncements. Liberation theology, on the other hand, explicitly acknowledges its own political nature, and indeed assumes the existence of a political dimension to theology in general. This view is completely unacceptable to the Vatican, which relegates politics to the secular world. My purpose in this chapter is to outline some of the most important and basic points of disagreement between the Vatican and liberation theology, especially with relation to Marxism, since the first Instruction specifically objects to the influence of Marx on liberation theology. Since this document addresses itself directly to liberation theology, it will be my central focus of discussion, especially since Segundo responded to it. However, for the reasons mentioned above, I will also include the second Instruction in my remarks about the previous document, since the second Instruction in my view, reinforces the negative critique of the theology of liberation, although indirectly.

A concrete illustration of the differences between the Vatican statements and liberation theology lies in the approach to the doctrine of sin. In both Instructions, sin is defined first and above all as an interior moral condition of each individual human being: according to the first document,

> The source of injustice is in the hearts of men. Therefore it is only by making an appeal to the moral potential of the person and to the constant need for interior conversion that social change will be brought about which will truly be in the service of man. [6]

The second Instruction echoes this view, while clarifying the relationship between interior, personal sin, and social justice:

> Moral integrity is a necessary condition for the health of society. It is therefore necessary to work simultaneously for the conversion of hearts and for the improvement of structures. For the sin which is at the root of unjust situations is, in a true and immediate sense, a voluntary act which has its source in the freedom of individuals. Only in a derived and secondary sense is it applicable to structures, and only in this sense can one speak of 'social sin'. [7]

This emphasis on sin as an interior moral category appears to be a point of irreconcilable opposition between the Vatican and liberation theology. The documents discuss sin as a purely religious phenomenon, which is overcome through the sacrifice of Christ and the redemption of the world. Redemption of sinful humanity is also contingent upon the inner contrition of human beings themselves, and the grace of God. Thus, sin and redemption are understood in terms of theological categories, such that the radical liberation from sin lies in the redemption of the individual through contrition and grace. Social injustice is then a derivative consequence of interior sin, and thus of secondary importance to the sin within each person. Thus sin is confined to the religious or theological sphere, with its corresponding language and set of symbols. This view of sin is contingent upon the division of spheres.

The Vatican's view of sin is quite different from the liberationist approach, precisely as a result of their differing epistemological premises involving the question of spheres of reality. To illustrate these contrasting views of sin, I turn to Gustavo Gutierrez's definition of sin, since the theological work of Gutierrez is widely recognized and accepted as representative of Latin American liberation theology, and "entirely orthodox," at least, in the view of Karl Rahner.[8]   Moreover, despite any "personal differences" among the theologians of liberation, "there is a clear, fundamental agreement on the parameters coordinates (sic) established by the work of Gustavo Gutierrez which gave its name to that theological current."[9] It is entirely legitimate to refer to Gutierrez at various points in this chapter, on the assumption that his work is a solid reflection of the basic premises and general theological method of liberation theology. Segundo himself often draws upon Gutierrez when explaining a point, at times acknowledging that Gutierrez's statements are often the best expression of a point of view he shares.

Gutierrez's emphasis on the social and structural nature of sin is widely reflected throughout much of the writings known as liberation theology. He writes:

> In the liberation approach sin is not considered as an individual, private, or merely interior reality—asserted just enough to necessitate a 'spiritual' redemption which does not challenge the order in which we live. Sin is regarded as a social, historical fact, the absence of brotherhood and love in relationships among men, the breach of friendship with God and with other men, and, therefore, an interior, personal fracture. . . . Sin is evident in oppressive structures, in the exploitation of man by man, in the domination and slavery of peoples, races, and social classes. Sin appears, therefore, as the fundamental alienation, the root of a situation of injustice and exploitation. . . . Sin demands a radical liberation, which in turn necessarily implies a political liberation.[10]

Gutierrez does not deny the existence of the interior dimension of sin, but he also stresses the social, collective nature of sin, which is equally important and radical as the sinfulness within individuals. In this view, sin is both collective and personal, and thus "redemption" from sin must occur on both levels, through the active, collective and individual efforts of human beings; the conversion of the human heart as well as the transformation of social structures are both the necessary conditions for the abolition of injustice. A "radical liberation from the slavery of sin,"[11] implies and demands liberation on the level of politics. It is in the political arena that the struggle against injustice must take place; politics is the *locus* of the liberation process. To understand what is meant by politics generally in liberation theology, I again quote Gutierrez, for whom the political realm encompasses contemporary human experience and also conditions praxis:

> It is always in the political fabric—and never outside of it—that a person emerges as a free and responsible being, as a person in relationship with other people, as someone who takes on a historical task. [12]

Gutierrez's concept of both sin and politics denies the existence of an autonomous religious or theological realm of reality and human experience. Gutierrez is interested in determining the religious meaning or value of human experience whose proper realm is historical and cultural. He does not accept a view of reality which is grounded in a "distinction of planes." In other words, Gutierrez's theology reflects a radically different epistemological approach to the relationship between Transcendence and Immanence than the Vatican documents. Gutierrez would disagree with the first Instruction that "the ultimate and decisive criterion for truth can only be a criterion which is itself theological."[13] This statement places theology, with its categories and concepts of truth as prior to human action, so that orthodoxy precedes action. If theological categories provide the "ultimate criterion" for "truth," then theology is understood as rooted in a separate, self-contained epistemological structure with its own specific mode of discourse and pantheon of symbols. Gutierrez directly refutes the existence of a primary and separate theological realm when he writes:

> Theology is reflection, a critical attitude. Theology follows; it is the second step. . . .
> The pastoral activity of the Church does not flow as a conclusion from theological
> premises. Theology does not produce pastoral activity; rather it reflects upon it. [14]

In this passage, Gutierrez identifies the *locus theologicus* within the sphere of social interaction, which includes the political and historical, the context of human existence. In Gutierrez's theological method, there is no properly, self-contained religious or theological sphere apart from the world of social interaction and politics. This theological position is shared by Charles Davis, who agrees that religious language and concepts do not constitute a separate realm of meaning in the modern world; "it is at least arguable that in our present historical situation if there is any privileged locus for religious experience it is . . . social interaction."[15] Transcendence (the "Unlimited") is "beyond any direct grasp or experience" of human beings, and as such, there can be no "conceptual," "imaginative," or linguistic expression specific to Transcendence itself.[16] Religious language, concepts and symbols derive from the larger cultural sphere, and thus religious knowledge is inevitably and inescapably mediated by human culture. It is erroneous "to suppose . . . that religion constitutes a distinct world, defined as sacred over against . . . the secular."[17] If religion is insisted upon as relating to an autonomous, separate sphere of reality, it is in danger of falling into "idolatry by identifying the Transcendent with its finite symbols,"[18] a concern shared by Segundo, as we have seen. "The effect upon religion, which has been seduced into trying to maintain itself as a distinct cultural sphere, is to make it canonize obsolete cultural elements as sacred."[19] Thus religious language and its symbols of the Transcendent are historically, socially and politically embedded such that they must always be understood in relation to a particular form or stage in human history and culture. Theology and its concepts do not reflect or transmit the Transcendent directly to human beings. Rather it is human consciousness, historically mediated and conditioned, which reflects its apprehension of what cannot be known directly, through religious symbols and language:

> It would be truer to say that religious experience is the product of religious doctrines, dependent upon the mediation of religious doctrines, than to say that religious doctrines are the product or sedimentation of experience. [20]

Davis reiterates that there is no separate religious realm, which leads to the conclusion that "all religion has a political dimension in so far as it always occurs in a social and political context,"[21] and that indeed, this has always been the case throughout the history of Christianity. "But if there is one type of religion which, as it is found in the West . . . and is undoubtedly Christian, it is the political."[22] Davis is in full agreement with liberation theology when he underlines his argument with the reminder that Jesus was executed "because of his impact upon the social order."[23] According to Segundo, "Even the *non-Christian* historical witnesses to the time insist on one point, which seems beyond doubt: Jesus of Nazareth died, after having been condemned by the Roman authorities, as a *political agitator*."[24]

The stress placed on the political significance of Jesus' death by Davis and Segundo is in no way intended to deny the religious meaning of the Crucifixion and resurrection as a validly held, faith-based belief. The death of Jesus is not given an "exclusively political interpretation," in the way that the first Instruction suggests.[25] When the religious meaning of human history and activity is recognized, when the "presence of Transcendence" (by virtue of the Incarnation) in the social world is acknowledged, "it opens the social horizon beyond the limits of any existing order to further possibilities, while acting as the animating but discriminating principle of what already exists."[26] Davis here articulates a basic theological principle of liberation theology, which assumes the unitary nature of the historical and the sacred, the emancipatory and salvific dimensions of reality, which interpenetrate one another in a fashion that must be understood as dynamic and dialectical, but not identical.

This theological perspective is grounded in the conviction that God is encountered in history and in the neighbour, and thus in the area of social interaction and politics, in keeping with the definition of politics proposed by Gutierrez. Segundo applies this political perspective to the Gospels:

> The radicalness of Jesus' approach lies precisely in demanding a historical (or secular) sensitivity toward one's neighbour's need. It is only that openness or sensitivity from the heart . . . that can serve as the hermeneutical presupposition for a correct reading of the Word of God. [27]

This understanding of the relationship between Transcendence and history attempts to overcome the type of epistemological dualism reflected in the Vatican documents, which is the basis for the assertion in the first Instruction that liberation theology "reduces" the Gospel to an earthly gospel.[28] It is ironic that the same document accuses liberation theology of lacking a "careful epistemology critique." [29]

We can see more clearly that one of the fundamental, key theological differences between the Vatican documents and liberation theology is precisely located in this question of a specific, distinct theological or religious realm of reality which stands over and above the temporal, historical and social dimension which is the immediate, material context of the human condition. Liberation theology is methodologically opposite to the theology of the Vatican documents in that its starting point lies within the historical, social and political context of human experience, a fact which is by now widely known, and which I have emphasized. It follows that, due to its theological method, liberation theology cannot logically accept a theology which is based upon the "distinction of planes," wherein strictly theological categories and concepts constitute the ultimate criteria of religious knowledge and truth. Thus, the differences between the theological methods and presuppositions reflected in the Vatican documents and liberation theology are deep, and, I would venture to say, irreconcilable. Segundo himself seems to be aware of the implications of the opposing views of the Vatican statements and liberation theology when he writes: "I understand that my theology (that is, my interpretation of the Christian faith) is false if the theology of [the first Instruction] is true—or it is the only true one."[30] He also identifies the basic antagonism of this document toward liberation theology as stemming precisely from the former's insistence upon a distinct, religious sphere of reality that actually opposes the secular.

> The realm of the invisible, because it belongs to the root of reality, to the realm of causes, is opposed to the realm of the visible where consequences flourish . . . the entire matter emphasizes an undeniable linguistic fact: there exists one language for speaking of *religious* realities (sin, grace, etc.) and another for secular, earthly or temporal realities. [31]

Thus, Segundo concludes that, in terms of the first Instruction, the "'really real' is the invisible world, while the world about us is mere shadow and simulacrum. Thus this 'theology' is build (sic) on a kind of textbook Platonism." [32]

Segundo is obviously aware that the scope of the first Instruction's critique of liberation theology does not restrict itself to pointing out certain theological errors or deviations, even though the document leaves this impression:

> We will only be discussing developments of that current of thought which, under the name 'theology of liberation', proposes a novel interpretation of both the content of faith and of Christian existence which seriously departs from the faith of the church and, in fact, actually constitutes a practical negation. [33]

Furthermore, the difference in theological method or orientation of both Vatican documents and liberation theology points toward a political difference between the two theological approaches that centres around the question of what authority legitimately transmits Christian faith and the revelation of God. Both Vatican documents repeatedly assert the final authority of the magisterium in all questions of faith. In a particularly explicit passage from the second Instruction, the "fullness of the Christian faith" can only be understood "through listening to the word of God, fidelity to the teaching of the magisterium, to the hierarchical order of the church and to the sacramental life."[34] The first Instruction asserts that the specific message of revelation can only be "authentically interpreted by the magisterium of the Church."[35] And again, in order to support and preserve the exclusive role of the magisterium in interpreting revelation and Christian faith, it logically follows that theological perspective of the Vatican documents presupposes a distinct and separate religious sphere or reality. Otherwise, the specific function of the magisterium and its authority would be open to question.

If this presupposition of the separation of planes is taken as given, then it is reasonable that some mechanism or body must exist whereby religious orthodoxy is regulated and ensured – thus, the necessity of the magisterium as the arbiter and interpreter of Christian faith and revelation. According to Segundo, in disputes between theologians and the magisterium, it often appears as if the latter argues from the position of faith, rather than ideology, which Segundo denies as actually being the case. "Without denying institutional differences, the magisterium also has its theology. By definition, no one can explain faith and define its limits without understanding it, that is, without a definite theology."[36] Finally, a theology which denies the validity of a religious sphere of reality existing in contradistinction to the secular, social sphere, which is the position of liberation theology, inevitably challenges the self-professed authority of the magisterium, whether it intends so or not. A theology which denies the existence of a separate religious sphere does not necessarily require an authoritative body to interpret the Christian faith and divine revelation. In my view, the first Instruction manifests an awareness of the challenge of liberation theology to the exclusive authority of the magisterium when this document refers to the "novel interpretation of both the content of faith and of Christian exist-ence" proposed by that "current of thought" which is "theology of liberation."[37] The reference to the "practical negation" of the "faith of the church" in the same section can also be interpreted in a similar light, wherein "practical negation" includes the authoritative role of the magister-ium. Segundo is also aware of the political meaning of the magisterium's assertion of its privileged role in correctly defining what should be an "authentic theology of liberation."[38] "Chapter III proposes positive definitions of liberation theology with the aim of showing that the magister-ium of the Church . . . has already developed it correctly and sufficiently." [39]

The fully blown political nature of the conflict between the Vatican documents and liberation theology is most apparent in the outright and total repudiation of Marxism[40] contained in the documents. However, the argument against Marxism is somewhat fragmented through scattered remarks which appear in various places in both documents. The clearest and most concise way to present the statements against Marxism, is to systematize them under four general themes. Basically, the documents reject the thought of Marx on the grounds that: 1. Marxism constitutes an exclusive and total ideological system and world view; 2. at the core of Marxist thought is a dependence upon atheism; 3. there is a central focus on the concept of class struggle in Marxism; 4. Marxism asserts that the human being is the sole, autonomous subject of history. Before considering each of these themes in turn, it should be noted that the Vatican documents never define Marxism in any analytical way. The documents simply make negative statements about it. They do not quote directly from Marx's work, nor from any work about Marx's theory. The Vatican documents reject Marx (and Marxism) completely and unequivocally in the absence of any sustained or developed critical argument. Such a presentation of Marxism, especially as it is treated in the first Instruction, "seems to be filled with a resentment that leads to a caricature, and this discredits its critique "as far as Segundo is concerned.[41] Since the nature of the comments on Marxism contained in the documents precludes any extensive response in terms of a systematic, critical discussion, I will explain the Vatican point of view under the headings mentioned above, along with some relevant critical statements drawn from Segundo and Gutierrez.

The first Instruction baldly describes the thought of Marx as an indivisible "global vision of reality" in which "no separation of the parts of this epistemologically unique complex is possible. If one tries to take only one part, say, the analysis, one ends up having to accept the entire ideology."[42] Furthermore, Marxism is described as a system that "is a perversion of the Christian message as God entrusted it to his church."[43] "Materialism" is understood to encompass that which relates to the temporal, the profane, and the earthly, excluding that which is spiritual and relates to the other-worldly. In this way, the document reinforces the dichotomy between the spiritual and the material realms (the religious and the secular) of reality. The question is, however, on what basis do both Vatican documents make the claim that Marxism is an ideological system so total and all encompassing that it is completely impossible to incorporate certain of its categories and concepts into different analytical theories?

> Does Marxism — or better, do all Marxisms — have a distinct epistemological status that makes impossible what is possible . . . in other analytical methods: to accept certain processes, separating them from the rest of the system and even integrating them into an ideology, a global view of the universe? [44]

Segundo can properly ask this question, since he himself has seriously engaged with Marx's thought in order to incorporate into his own theology what he deems are those "proper and positive" elements of Marx. Segundo is justified in doing this, since efforts to incorporate aspects from other systems of thought is not unknown to Catholic theological tradition, a fact openly acknowledged toward the end of the second Instruction: "The Church, which is a communion which unites diversity and unity through its presence in the whole world, takes from every culture the positive elements which she finds there."[45]   This process of "inculturation" is described by Bernard Lonergan as the "despoiling of the Egyptians": "There is the modern secularist world with all its riches and all its potentialities. There is the possibility of despoiling the Egyptians."[46]   Segundo claims that in practice, the church has on occasion even borrowed some categories from Marx's thought:

> The Supreme Pontiff himself makes excellent use of Marxist analysis, such as the category of *alienation*, to describe the worker who gives up the fruits of his or her labor in exchange for a salary in capitalist (or socialist) systems. [47]

Segundo has some important criticisms of the first Instruction's description of Marxism as an ideology. He points out that the document condemns Marxism as an ideology, without ever defining what ideology is. Segundo concludes that the implicit understanding of ideology in this document is both pejorative and general, and goes beyond the usual critical view of ideology as false social consciousness,[48] which would refer to a particular system of thought. Segundo claims that ideology is used in the document to designate any system of thought that is not religious. The condemnable and general meaning ascribed to ideology derives from the epistemological premises of the document that have been discussed throughout this chapter:

> In the document the word [ideology] appears always, or almost always, in relation to religious *faith*. It seems to say that faith becomes ideological when it has lost its character as faith to become a merely human thought. In other words, we are once again up against the problem of two languages, the religious and the secular. What for a secular language has a merely neutral meaning acquires in religious language a pejorative connotation. What is merely human for the former is *too* human for the latter. The use of the term thus becomes a bit esoteric, a privatized language, but not an unintelligible one. It means something very particular and so has synthesized the other two understandings of the word. 'Ideology' thus acquires a *general* and *negative* meaning. [49]

Thus "the document insists upon a particular theology where the religious and the secular are opposed."[50] It reflects an epistemological structure the implications of which are not only theological, but also political, in that the insistence upon a sacred/profane split reinforces the authority of the magisterium.

The first Instruction also rejects Marxism on the grounds that it is an "atheistic" ideology:

Let us recall the fact that atheism and the denial of the human person, his liberty and his rights, are at the core of Marxist theory. This theory, then, contains errors which directly threaten the truths of the faith regarding the eternal destiny of individual persons. [51]

Segundo's response to this part of the text is to say that it is "strange" because it locates atheism as the "core" of Marxist theory. As I pointed out earlier, atheism was not a central concern for Marx because he did not consider it to be important. For him the issue of belief or non-belief in God was a symptom of alienation, which would be overcome when human beings fully realized and embraced their own autonomous, historical subjectivity. Segundo himself admits that many Marxist thinkers would agree that the question of the existence of God is incidental to Marx's thought. [52]

There is a further aspect of "strangeness" in the first Instruction's uncompromising negation of Marxism, and that is the way in which the document establishes a causal link between atheism and "the denial of the human person, his liberty and his rights." First of all, there is no necessary or inherent connection between atheism and the "denial" of the rights of human beings. Even more significant, however, is the fact that the document seems completely unaware of the statements about atheism made at Vatican II. There it was explicitly recognized that Christians bear some measure of responsibility for the existence of atheism, which is not a "spontaneous development" but which has a variety of causes, which includes "a critical reaction against religious beliefs, and in some places against the Christian religion in particular. Hence believers can have more than a little to do with the birth of atheism" (*Gaudium et Spes*, n. 19). Furthermore, the Council did not share the view that atheism is antithetical to human justice, but in fact recognized the opposite: "While rejecting atheism root and branch, the Church sincerely professes that all men, believers and unbelievers alike, ought to work for the rightful betterment of this world in which all alike live" (*Gaudium et Spes*, n. 21).

It should be noted that the attitude toward atheism in the first Instruction is far different than that expressed in *Gaudium et Spes*. In fact, Segundo is disturbed by the possibility that the real intent of the document is to mount an attack not only on Marxism and liberation theology, but on Vatican II itself:

A final observation on the whole of the *Instruction*: Let no one be deceived into thinking that only Latin American theology is involved here. If the analysis I have made is correct, the two parts (of the document) . . . are united by one point that affects the entire Church: *the negative evaluation of Vatican II and of the postconciliar period.* [53]

Although it would be far beyond the scope of my analysis to debate this last point in detail, it is nonetheless important to mention it because according to Segundo liberation theology is actually a particular development and application of Vatican II. However, I will raise this theme in more detail, when I present a general assessment of Segundo's later theological work which reflects the continuing influence of Vatican II on his thought.

The first Instruction rejects "the theory of class struggle as the fundamental law of history"[54] as another central category of Marxism. The document objects that class struggle inevitably promotes violence,[55] disunity among Christians because of its partisan nature[56] and leads to the distortion of the meaning of the eucharist as "the eucharist of the class."[57] "At the same time it is disputed that the participation of Christians who belong to opposing classes at the same eucharistic table still makes any sense." [58]

Perhaps the most pertinent response to the kind of objections to class struggle such as are contained in this document is to be found in the work of Gustavo Gutierrez. He reminds his readers that Marx did not invent or discover class struggle, but rather attempted to analyze its causes and indicate the means of overcome the class structure of society.

> The class struggle is inherent in the classist organization of society. The objective which Marx proposes is to abolish that which gives origin to the very existence of social classes. But the causes of the class struggle cannot be overcome without first becoming aware of the struggle and its demands in the process of building a new society. [59]

Gutierrez could not agree with the first Instruction that Marxism "advocates" class struggle because class struggle "is a fact" as far as Marx is concerned. By acknowledging the existence of class society and class struggle which is its inevitable consequence, Gutierrez claims that people actually wish to "reject a situation in which there are oppressed and oppressors."[60] Gutierrez recognizes the difficulties and challenges to Christians and the Church of the "revolutionary turmoil" and "violence" present in the world. Since Vatican II "broke open a new path on which there is no turning back: openness to the world,"[61] then the Church cannot refuse to confront the factual reality of class society and class struggle. A simple rejection of the presence of class struggle in the world merely avoids the issue, and undermines the post-conciliar direction of the church to be of service to the world. Segundo criticizes the position of the document on class conflict as "facile"[62] because it does not recognize that "neutrality" is impossible within an unjust social order based on class. The practice of "universal love" does not in itself negate class society or the existence of class enemies, nor does the call to universal love exempt Christians from choosing sides in situations of class conflict, as far as Segundo is concerned.[63]

Gutierrez also notes that Marxism is not an inflexible body of principles which must be rigidly imposed upon society. He again cites José Carlos Mariategui, who describes Marxism as "a method for the historical interpretation of society"[64] which is adaptable to the specific modalities of a particular milieu. Like Segundo, Gutierrez accepts the usefulness of some aspects of Marx's social theory in aiding Latin Americans in "the search for indigenous social paths."[65] Gutierrez is also aware that liberation involves more than "overcoming economic, social and political dependence."[66] Along with Ché Guevara, whom he cites, Gutierrez also acknowledges the necessity of the creation of a *new man* as part of the liberation process.

In terms of the first Instruction's concern about the negative implications of class struggle for the meaning of the eucharist, it is Gutierrez again who can perhaps best articulate liberation theology's interpretation of the sacrament. Gutierrez maintains that communion with God, as symbolized in the eucharist, "presupposes the abolition of all injustice and exploitation."[67] Gutierrez analyses the meaning of the eucharist in terms of a three-fold definition of *koinonia*:

First it signifies the common ownership of the goods necessary for earthly existence. . . . Second, *koinonia* designates the union of the faithful with Christ through the Eucharist. . . . And third, *koinonia* means the union of Christians with the Father . . . with the Son . . . and with the Spirit. [68]

The first level of meaning links the eucharist with the love and charity towards the neighbour, which is commanded by God (Heb. 13:16; Acts 2:44; 4:32; Matt. 25:40). Furthermore, reconciliation with the neighbour is a necessary precondition for participation in the eucharist (Matt. 5:23 - 24) especially since the "essential elements" of the eucharist are "communitarian" and oriented toward "the constitution of human brotherhood."[69] The eucharist, then is more than a religious rite of worship; it also has social and political dimensions which are understood as constitutive elements of its religious meaning. Gutierrez claims that without this social and political aspect,

> Without a real commitment against exploitation and alienation and for a society of
> solidarity and justice, the Eucharistic celebration is an empty action, lacking any genuine
> endorsement by those who participate in it. [70]

The eucharistic rite is empty of meaning if it is understood as restricted to the religious sphere, cut off from its human, cultural context. If this happens, the sacraments absolutize their own outward, symbolic forms, falling into idolatry.

The final aspect of the objections of Marxism raised by the first Instruction concerns the question of human subjectivity. Segundo sees that this question is treated in the context of the document's exegesis on the Psalms, which constitute "an implicit, yet clear criticism" of liberation theology. The document focuses upon the personal, subjective nature of the anguish expressed in the Psalms, an anguish which is largely interior and spiritual, having to do with "the hostility of one's enemies, injustice, failure and death."[71] Segundo admits that liberation theology has little theological interest in the Psalms, primarily because they do not adequately address the contemporary problems of Latin American society.[72] "In the Psalms, the human soul . . . is placed before the greatness and transcendence of God."[73] The first Instruction views the Psalms as an affirmation of the power and complete subjectivity of God in regulating and solving human affairs: "God, and not man, has the power to change the situations of suffering."[74] Segundo does not accept this view of the relation between God and history, in which God is understood as the only subject. Rather, the historical process and social change are for Segundo the result of the active efforts of both human subjects and God, as co-subjects, or co-workers.[75] The exegesis of the Psalms contained in the document is perceived by Segundo as a direct "assault" on liberation theology:

> In effect, separating this text [on the Psalms] from the chapter's other paragraphs (which
> form its natural context) we would be faced with the most blatant assault on liberation
> theology's idea of God and of human activity in history. Or, to say better, one would
> have to speak of the *non*-activity of people in history because all concrete change
> concerning human suffering is taken from the human field of action and attributed *only*
> to God. [76]

Segundo's reading of the first Instruction in this respect is well-founded: the question of history, and of the relationship between God and humanity constitutes another fundamental, and irreconcilable point of conflict between the Vatican and liberation theology. Liberation theology is too much influenced by Marx to deny the importance of human initiative and action in the project for human liberation.

It will be recalled that Marx specifically rejects the concept of creation in the *Economic and Philosophical Manuscripts* along with the consequent belief in God, which were for Marx ideological chimeras that obscured the fact that human beings are potentially autonomous subjects in the shaping of their individual and collective lives. Marx's view on the question of subjectivity in history has certainly influenced liberation theology to a large – but not total – degree. Humanity is not viewed as a passive object of divine will no more than God is understood as the only means through which to alleviate human suffering. Injustice and oppression can only be abolished through a liberation process that is thoroughly human and historical, which involves the active efforts of human beings. Segundo rightly sees that if the Vatican position on the question of human subjectivity is accepted as "absolute truth, liberation theology would collapse." [77]

Neither of the Vatican documents outrightly condemns or rejects liberation theology in an explicit fashion, although they do completely negate Marxism as "incompatible with Christian faith and the ethical requirements which flow from it."[78] In my view, and I suspect in Segundo's, this rejection of Marx is practically tantamount to an implicit rejection of liberation theology. The first Instruction expresses the wish to caution against "the deviations and risks of deviation, damaging to the faith and Christian living, that are brought about by certain forms of liberation theology[79] which use, in an insufficiently critical manner, concepts borrowed from various currents of Marxist thought." [80] When carefully considered, this statement locates a contradiction within the document itself in terms of its previous statements on Marxism. How can liberation theology be accused of borrowing concepts from "various currents of Marxist thought" if Marxism is a global, indivisible ideology that must either be accepted totally or not at all? According to the Vatican documents, Marxism is an atheistic, thoroughly materialist, anti-religious ideology which is incompatible with the Christian faith on all counts. Furthermore, "certain forms" of liberation theology are accused of reducing the gospel message to earthly, secular and political meaning which is emptied of religious and theological content. The first Instruction certainly implies that the reductionist nature of liberation theology is due to the influence of Marxism. And thus the suspicion begins to assert itself that perhaps the Vatican documents also intend, indirectly, to repudiate liberation theology as the logical consequence of the latter's connections – whatever they in *fact* may be – with Marxism. Segundo is convinced that the first Instruction would condemn liberation theology irrespective of Marxism, which implies that Marxism provides a convenient vehicle whereby the Vatican may indirectly confront liberation theology.

> Even if Marxism did not exist — and today many of the most famous theologians in Latin America have nothing more than a polite relationship with Marxism — liberation theology would be condemned as a humanistic, earthly, and secular reduction of the Gospel of salvation. [81]

Certainly much of the critique of Marxism contained in the Vatican documents amounts to little more than unfounded assertions with no scholarly or analytical foundation. Given the epistemological structure underlying these documents, there is no reason why they should undertake such a project, since the scholarly and the analytical, as well as all systems of thought that are not strictly theological, belong to the secular, temporal realm of reality. The discourse of the Vatican documents is self-consciously theological and religious, yet implicitly but conceivably, consciously political. In any event, because of the assumption of the division of realms contained in both Vatican documents, wherein the religious sphere exists as its own distinct dimension of truth and universality, it follows that the secular, historical world and all that belongs to it may be rightfully judged by the church and her magisterium[82] which sees itself as " 'an expert in human-ity'."[83]

From what has been presented so far, it is apparent that the theology of the Vatican documents examined here and the theology of liberation face each other as two very different interpretations of the Christian message.[84] Their differences are not superficial and incidental, but are rather ingredient to the opposing theological perspectives and methodologies that each represents. It can only be concluded that these theological positions are irreconcilable, and hardly capable of prolonged mutual toleration and co-existence. The profound differences between these two oppositional theologies pose crucial questions for the future of both the Latin American theology of liberation and the status of the Vatican's authority in interpreting the Christian faith. Whatever are the implications resulting from the divergencies between these theologies, there is as yet no final resolution to the objections each has toward the other.

NOTES

1. Juan Luis Segundo, S.J., "The Shift Within Latin American Theology," p. 6.

2. Segundo often refers to "academic theology," but does not identify it with a particular school of theology or group of theologians. For Segundo, academic theology refers to a "theological discipline divided into many branches and dominated by scholarly experts" (*The Community Called Church*, 1973, p. vii). Here Segundo is probably referring to theology as taught in North American and Western European universities, and described by José Comblin in a manner Segundo would agree with: "The classical idea of theology was that it was a system of ideas, propositions, and statements, which was a true representation of God's revelation, a good translation of God's word: It supposed that in God there are a collection of logically connected ideas, that God communicated this system to human beings by means of the Bible, in which Divine Providence adopted the extremely abstract thought of God to the weak understanding of primitive peoples, and that theology comes back to the abstract divine ideas. Understood this way, theology is a system of ideas, universal and equally valuable in all times and places" (*The Church and the National Security State*, p. 48). Many Latin American liberation theologians, including Segundo, view this theology as ahistorical and counterproductive to the liberation process in Latin America. Thus "academic theology," that has dominated theological thinking in Latin American since the conquest, must be replaced by a different kind of theology that is rooted in the concrete circumstances and experiences of human beings in Latin America, as far as many liberation theologians are concerned.

3. John Paul II to Brazilian Bishops: Giant Brazil at a Crossroads, *Origins NC Documentary Series*, April 3, 1986, Vol. 15, No. 42, n. 6.

4. Gustavo Gutierrez, *A Theology of Liberation*, p. 72.

5. Ibid., p. 72.

6. "Instruction of Certain Aspects of the 'Theology of Liberation'," *Origins, NC Documentary Service*, September 13, 1984, Vol. 14, No. 13, XI, p. 8.

7. "Instruction of Certain Aspects," V. 75.

8. Segundo quotes Rahner's letter to the Cardinal Archbishop of Lima: "I am convinced of the orthodoxy of the theological work of Gustavo Gutierrez. The Theology of Liberation that he represents is entirely orthodox." Juan Luis Segundo, *Theology and the Church: A Response to Cardinal Ratzinger and a Warning to the Whole Church*, translated by John W. Diercksmeier (Minneapolis: Seabury Winston Press, 1985), p. 17.

9. Ibid., p. 18.

10. Gustavo Gutierrez, *A Theology of Liberation*, pp. 175-176.

11. "Instruction of Certain Aspects of the 'Theology of Liberation'," Introduction.

12. Gustavo Gutierrez, *A Theology of Liberation*, p. 47.

13. "Instruction of Certain Aspects of the 'Theology of Liberation'," VII, p. 10.

14. Gustavo Gutierrez, *A Theology of Liberation*, p. 11.

15. Charles Davis, "From Inwardness to Social Action: A Shift in the Locus of Religious Experience," *New Blackfriars*, March, 1986, p. 115.

16. Ibid., p. 117.

17. Ibid., p. 117.

18. Ibid., p. 118.

19. Ibid., p. 118.

20. Ibid., p. 120.

21. Ibid., p. 122.

22. Ibid., p. 122.

23. Ibid., p. 123.

24. Juan Luis Segundo, *The Historical Jesus of the Synoptics*, p. 72.

25. "Instruction on Certain Aspects of the 'Theology of Liberation', p. X, p. 12.

26. Charles Davis, "From Inwardness to Social Action," p. 123.

27. Juan Luis Segundo, *Theology and the Church*, p. 32.

28. "Instruction of Certain Aspects of the 'Theology of Liberation'," VI, p. 5.

29. Ibid., VII, p. 4.

30. Juan Luis Segundo, *Theology and the Church*, p. 14.

31. Ibid., p. 28.

32. Ibid., p. 28.

33. "Instruction on Certain Aspects . . .", VI, 9.

34. "Instruction on Christian Freedom and Liberation," *Origins, NC Documentary Service*, April 17, 1986. Vol. 15, No. 44, IV, p. 69.

35. "Instruction on Certain Aspects . . .", II, p. 3.

36. Juan Luis Segundo, *Theology and the Church*, p. 17.

37. "Instruction on Certain Aspects . . .", VI, p. 9.

38. Ibid., VI, p. 7.

39. Juan Luis Segundo, *Theology and the Church*, p. 40.

40. It is not clear what exactly the documents mean by "Marxism" because the term is never defined. It appears that "Marxism" includes the entire thought of Karl Marx, as well as other ideologies and systems of thought that claim to derive from Marx, and are hence forms of "Marxism."

41. Juan Luis Segundo, *Theology and the Church*, p. 118.

42. "Instruction on Certain Aspects . . ." VII, p. 6.

43. Ibid., IX, p. 1.

44. Juan Luis Segundo, *Theology and the Church*, p. 97. See also Roger Haight, S.J., *An Alternative Vision* (New York: Paulist Press, 1985), pp. 262-263, who also questions the assumption of the first Instruction, that Marxism must be taken as a total system of thought, or not at all: "That the systems of thought that are generated in history need not be taken and used exclusively as objective complete wholes can be demonstrated by innumerable cases in the history of ideas simply because the historicity of consciousness makes this the norm rather than the exception . . . One does not have to dwell on the achievement of Aquinas to show that one can use categories of even a tight system of thought such as Aristotle's without embracing the whole doctrine if it is taken existentially as a medium for expressing a prior and deeper faith and a commitment to analyze reality as it is revealed through actual data."

45. "Instruction on Christian Freedom and Liberation," V, p. 96.

46. *Collection: Papers by Bernard Lonergan*, S.J., edited by F. E. Crowe, S.J. (Montreal: Palm Publishers, 1967), p. 248.

47. Juan Luis Segundo, *Theology and the Church*, p. 96.

48. Ibid., pp. 37-38.

49. Ibid., p. 38.

50. Ibid., p. 46.

51. "Instruction on Certain Aspects . . ." VII, p. 9.

52. Juan Luis Segundo, *Theology and the Church*, p. 99.

53. Ibid., p. 155.

54. "Instruction of Certain Aspects . . ."IX, p. 2.

55. Ibid., VIII, pp. 6, 7.

56. Ibid., IX, p. 8; X, p. 16; XI, p. 5.

57. Ibid., X, p. 16.

58. Ibid., IX, p. 8.

59. Gustavo Gutierrez, *A Theology of Liberation*, p. 284, n. 51.

153

60. Ibid., p. 274.

61. Ibid., p. 273.

62. Juan Luis Segundo, *Theology and the Church*, p. 117.

63. Ibid., p. 117.

64. Gustavo Gutierrez, *A Theology of Liberation*, p. 90.

65. Ibid., p. 90.

66. Ibid., p. 91.

67. Ibid., p. 263.

68. Ibid., p. 264.

69. Ibid., p. 263.

70. Ibid., p. 265.

71. "Instruction on Certain Aspects . . ." IV, p. 5.

72. Juan Luis Segundo, *Theology and the Church*, p. 51.

73. Ibid., p. 51.

74. "Instruction on Certain Aspects . . ." IV., p. 5.

75. Juan Luis Segundo, *The Liberation of Theology*, p. 148. I must state once more that Segundo does not push, or develop this idea of human beings and God as co-subjects in the process of historical change.

76. Juan Luis Segundo, *Theology and the Church*, p. 52.

77. Ibid., p. 52.

78. "Instruction on Certain Aspects . . ." Introduction.

79. The references to "certain forms of liberation theology" as the focus of concern in the Ratzinger document are unconvincing. These "forms" of liberation theology are never specified, and this fact taken together with the statements on Marxism, and the other criticisms of liberation theology mentioned above, lend credence to Segundo's conclusion that the Ratzinger document constitutes an attack on the theology of liberation *per se*.

80. "Instruction on Certain Aspects . . ." Introduction.

81. Juan Luis Segundo, *Theology and the Church*, p. 91.

82. "Instruction of Christian Freedom and Liberation," VI, p. 65.

83. Ibid., V, p. 72.

84. Juan Luis Segundo, *Theology and the Church*, pp. 24-25

Chapter VII

CONCLUSION:
THE NEGATION OF THEOLOGY?

It is not easy to say when exactly the theology of liberation, as a distinctive and different theology from what the liberation theologians call 'classical' or 'academic' theology actually came into being in Latin America. It is still disputed if "there is one, and only one, theology of liberation," as is maintained by Leonardo Boff[1] or if indeed there are a variety of "theologies of liberation," which is, for example, the position of the "Instruction on Certain Aspects of the 'Theology of Liberation.' " I am in complete agreement with Boff's statement, because the distinctive essential nature of liberation theology is defined by its method. The object of liberation theology is to construct a coherent social analysis, whose intention is to explain, and in the process of explanation also address, the widespread social, economic and political injustices which exist throughout Latin America. As a method of social analysis, liberation theology has a universal dimension insofar as its methodology can be applied to any concrete, historical situation, and not be restricted to Latin America. Therefore, it is not valid to claim that there are a multiplicity of varying theologies of liberation. The actual content of the arguments of different liberation theologians may vary on specific points, but this does not mean that liberation theology *as such* does not hold a single methodology. It does. Those commentators, critics and even supporters of liberation theology who insist that there are different theologies of liberation in fact reduce liberation theology to a local, specific branch of theology which calls into question its authentic universal significance. In this way, whether it is consciously intended or not, liberation theology is divested of its critical force and potential, long-range challenge to Christian theology, with its consequent implications rendered obscure.

Juan Luis Segundo's later work is an important development of the methodology of the theology of liberation. An analysis of his critical method, which is what this book is about, reveals some of those implications of liberation theology, as well as pointing out the nature of its challenge to the whole of Christian theology. In what follows, I will identify some of the logical implications of Segundo's (explicitly) methodological works for a fully (or nearly fully) developed theology of liberation. I do not intend to argue that Segundo's work can be or should be rigidly divided into a pre- or post-liberation theology phase. To make such a division within Segundo's writing would be too abstract and artificial, and would deny the fact of the evolution of his thought. It is true that in earlier volumes Segundo has been preoccupied with themes similar to those presented here and that certain concerns and ideas discussed here have been present in Segundo's work for quite some time. However, there is little point to summarize Segundo's thought from his earliest publications to the present, or to try to trace the development of those themes that he deals with in greater depth in his recent work and which are the topic of the present study. This kind of treatment of Segundo has already taken place,[2] and it would be repetitious to engage in the same task.

Having said the above, it can nonetheless be reasonably argued that the theology of Segundo took a more radical critical turn with the publication of *The Liberation of Theology*. In this and some later books, Segundo directly and systematically confronts the central questions of methodology, which is the key, defining characteristic of the theology of liberation. These later works demonstrate what Enrique Dussel refers to as the "theology of concrete, critical, subversive, real thinking."[3] They also show how liberation theology radicalizes the political realm of human existence, so that politics nearly becomes an ontological category. The definition put forward of politics by Gutierrez is fully endorsed by Segundo, yet bears repeating, because the view of politics it supports is highly controversial within theology. "It [politics] is the sphere for the exercise of a critical freedom which is won through history. It is the universal determinant and the collective arena for human fulfilment. . . . Nothing lies outside the political sphere understood in this way."[4] It is through an analysis of Segundo's methodological approach to theology that most fully reveals his theology as liberatory.

The Influence of Vatican II

Enrique Dussel, in his detailed studies of the history of the church in Latin America and the historical development of liberation theology, states that the theology of liberation was discussed explicitly and in detail for the first time at meetings of Latin American theologians in Argentina and Colombia in 1970.[5] These meetings followed the Second General

Conference of the Latin American Episcopal Council (CELAM II) that took place in Medellin, Colombia, in 1968 where the theme of liberation as an historical and political project was discussed, with the result that "liberation" as a concept became permanently lodged within Latin American theology. Behind the Medellin conference, of course, were the progressive theological statements of Vatican II, and at Medellin, the bishops attempted to give "concrete form and application to Vatican II."[6]

In its conscious attempt to apply and extend some of the basic implications of Vatican II, the Medellin conference was the connective link between a call to social justice and a "clear commitment to liberation."[7] Segundo affirms Dussel's perspective on the relationship between Vatican II and the Medellin conference when he writes:

> It can be said that the Catholic Church in Latin America was the first Catholic community to set out resolutely on the new pathway opened up by Vatican II. The new pathway was based on the assumption that faith has as its function the task of guiding the human mind towards more fully human solutions in history; that the Church does not possess those solutions in advance but does possess elements that have been revealed by God; that these revealed elements do not preserve the Church from ideologies; that instead the Church must take advantage of those elements to go out in search of (ideological) solutions to the problems posed by the historical process; and that such solutions will always remain provisional. The Medellin conference was the first result of the new pathway opened by Vatican II, embodying the enthusiasm of the early post-conciliar days. [8]

There can be no doubt that Segundo understands his own development of liberation theology as a continuation of the basic directions outlined at the second Vatican Council. Segundo often refers to Vatican II as a way of justifying many of his theological claims as, for example, his refusal to acknowledge as valid the separation of the religious from all other spheres of human experience: "Thus it was that the Catholic Church officially abandoned the theology of the two planes and opened the way for a theology that was quite different: i.e., liberation theology."[9] He concludes explicitly that, "My point here is that the statements of Vatican II are clear enough to ensure that the basic theological foundations of liberation theology may not be declared heterodox." [10]

Not only does Segundo view himself as a post-conciliar theologian, but he also understands liberation theology as the logical consequence of any serious attempt to realize Vatican II through a concrete, historical praxis specific to the conditions of Latin America. However, there is one important modification to this statement that must be pointed out. For

Segundo, as well as for other liberation theologians of Latin America, the importance of Vatican II is largely contained within the document *Gaudium et Spes*, and to a much lesser extent, *Lumen Gentium*. But it is clearly *Gaudium et Spes* that has had the deepest impact on Segundo's (and others') development of liberation theology, and he refers to it again and again whenever he discusses the relationship between Vatican II and liberation theology. In his view, *Gaudium et Spes* is "undoubtedly" representative of the "high point of Vatican II." [11]

It is not difficult to see why this particular document from Vatican II has had such a profound influence on Segundo. In the first place, *Gaudium et Spes* addresses itself,

> Not only to the sons of the Church and to all who invoke the name of Christ, but to the whole of humanity. . . . Therefore, the Council focuses its attention on the world of men, the whole human family along with the sum of those realities in the midst of which that family lives. It gazes upon the world which is the theatre of man's history . . .[12]

Gaudium et Spes stresses the role of the Church in the world as one of service to humanity, acknowledging the legitimacy of the material needs of humanity and the quest for social justice:

> . . . the conviction grows . . . that it devolves on humanity to establish a political, social and economic order which will to an even better extent serve man and help individuals as well as groups to affirm and develop the dignity proper to them. . . . As a result very many persons are quite aggressively demanding those benefits of which with vivid awareness they judge themselves to be deprived either through injustice or unequal distribution. . . . People hounded by hunger call upon those better off. . . . Still, beneath all these demands lies a deeper and more widespread longing. Persons and societies thirst for a full and free life worthy of man — one in which they can subject to their own welfare all that the modern world can offer them so abundantly. [13]

These excerpts from *Gaudium et Spes* illustrate sufficiently well the appeal that Vatican II continues to exert for liberation theology and explains why Segundo refers back to this particular document so often. Perhaps Segundo has pushed the implications of even this specific conciliar document in a more radical and political direction than the authors of the document might have intended; he himself at one point (prior to the publication of *The Liberation of Theology*) admits that *Gaudium et Spes* is not free of ambiguity that is generated by its own two internal "tendencies."

> One tendency sees the world and its history as being disconnected in itself from redemption, which operates supernaturally within the Church and unites human values

to their divine source through religion. The other tendency sees only one vocation, one history, and one end result, even though the unity of the religious and the nonreligious in Christ constitutes a datum of faith . . . even though it does not provide readymade solutions to the problem of history; and even though we do not know to what extent God wills to transmit it effectively, in an explicit manner, to the concrete human beings with whom we are engaged in dialogue. The texts of the Council which are the most clear theologically accord with the second line of thought, but the recurrence of other expressions that do not accord with it shows us that a problem persists here. [14]

Obviously, if the statements of Vatican II do not lend themselves to a singular, monolithic interpretation, then Segundo and other liberation theologians must be interpreting them in the light of their own preoccupations, which are rooted in the specific circumstances affecting Latin America. Thus the importance of Vatican II for Segundo's theology of liberation is very much based upon a selective reading of this conciliar document, at least in so far as he describes the role of Vatican II and its importance for the emergence of liberation theology. Not *all* conciliar texts are cited in justification of liberation theology. The claim that liberation theology must be viewed as an application of Vatican II, or the claim for the theological validity of liberation because it is in accord with "the profound change in spirit that Vatican II produced"[15] is by now somewhat problematic, given the direction of the Catholic Church since Vatican II, which seems to many to be away from the council.[16]

Whatever the inspiration and direction drawn by liberation theology from Vatican II, it must be said that the later methodological writing of Segundo, most notably as contained in *The Liberation of Theology* and *Faith and Ideologies*, goes far beyond Vatican II precisely in the area of attempting to render the Catholic faith and the Catholic Church relevant to the contemporary world. In these volumes, Segundo explores the implications of his own thought through an explication and formulation of theological method. In his five volume series A Theology for the *Artisans of a New Humanity*, he was more concerned with illuminating the social dimension and meaning of theology, and with "situating" Christianity on "the level of the Christian's real-life questions."[17] Segundo describes "this new type of theology" as "reductive" in so far as it only addresses itself to "certain fundamental mysteries of revelation"[18]; it is a theology that "essentially starts with, and takes account of, the world in which our contemporaries live and work."[19] The goal of these seminars was limited to provide a forum whereby "mature persons" looking for an "adult theology" could come together in order to explore "new pathways" in faith which is "related to their temporal commitments."[20] The five volumes of this series attempt to relate certain statements of Vatican II directly to contemporary issues, while also using the language of liberation, making statements like "the individual can only be liberated within his total human condition, within his social context," and that "man's liberation . . . is concretized in ideological transformation and political action."[21] In these books Segundo makes it clear that human history is the context of human liberation, and that within an historical commitment to the emancipatory project, "we encounter the authentic face of God." [22]

Many more examples could be cited from *A Theology for the Artisans of a New Humanity* which would further bear out the consistency of Segundo's effort to render Christianity historically efficacious, and to situate the meaning of faith in relation to people's lived experience. However, to continue this line of argument would be to do little more than summarize this series, which would not allow for a discussion of some the more important developments in Segundo's thought. Neither do the Artisans volumes demonstrate the kind of method which comes later in his work. Segundo's more theoretical and methodological works show how far he has politicized liberation theology, a process which is the inevitable end result of a theology so completely understood as historically conditioned, relative and ideological.

Violence

One of the most effective ways to illustrate the impact of Segundo's method on Christian concepts is to raise the issue of violence, and Segundo's treatment of this question, especially in terms of the Christian imperative to love of the neighbour. Love of the neighbour is the crux of Christian ethics, and Segundo's theological method subjects Jesus' commandment to universal love to a particular interpretation that could be considered unacceptable to Christianity.[23] The implications of Segundo's methodology which so completely contextualizes theology within the historical, concrete, and ideological dimensions of human social reality, are clearly delineated and illustrated in his discussion of violence and love.

Segundo explains his interpretations of Jesus' commandment to mutual love in terms of the relationship between faith and ideology:

> the concrete kind of love proclaimed by Jesus constitutes an ideology – that is, a concrete system conditioned by history. It represents a way to attain the most love possible in a given concrete situation which, as such, will never be repeated in exactly the same terms. [24]

In other words, Jesus' commandment to mutual love is more relative than universal, in Segundo's view, so that Christians are "left free to operate imaginatively and creatively, to figure out what would be the most effective and comprehensible sort of mutual love at a given moment in history."[25] Thus, the commandment to love the neighbour is contingent upon concrete, historical particularity, with the result that to love the neighbour does not mean that all humanity is to be considered as neighbour:

> Jesus does not end up his parable (of the Good Samaritan) saying that every human being *is* our neighbour. His point is that we can make any given human being our neighbour if we take advantage of the countless opportunities offered us in life. [26]

Segundo argues against the universality of love of the neighbour on the grounds of what he calls "the economy of energy in the process of love,"[27] meaning that it is impossible for human beings to love too many people at the same time, a rule which he also applies to Jesus. In Segundo's view, the importance of the love of the neighbour is located in efficacy, and in order to love effectively, human beings must "keep a whole host of people at arm's length so that we can effectively love a certain group of people."[28] He explains this "economy of energy in the process of love" briefly in terms of the psychology of individuals, in which a kind of internal "mechanism" is operative that allows one to love some, but not to love others. This "mechanism" which excludes the majority of people from the category of the neighbour who must be loved, "is not precisely hatred, it is *violence* — at least some initial degree of violence."[29] The key to understanding Segundo's concept of the relationship between love and violence lies in his emphasis on that which is effective and concrete in human praxis. Thus, he can only conclude that a universal command to mutual love can mean nothing unless it is realized in the context of the concrete and the particular. Otherwise, "the neighbour" is reduced to an abstract category, and real, living human beings disappear behind this abstraction. Thus the nature of love in Christianity, as Segundo interprets it, must be both functional and relative.

Segundo understands the behaviour of Jesus toward John the Baptist and the Syro-Phoenician woman (Mark 7:27) exactly in terms of the economy of energy involved in love, as outlined above. Jesus, "being truly man, had to conceive and orient his existence in history by taking due account of this inexorable law"[30] such that despite his "admiration" for John the Baptist, he was compelled to abandon John to his fate,[31] apparently unconcerned with the latter's suffering and imprisonment, since Jesus did nothing to help him.

In other words, because of "the real-life co-ordinates of the economy of energy"[32] operating in Jesus (as in any other human being) Jesus could not preach his message of the Kingdom and be of service to others and at the same time involve himself in efforts to save John the Baptist.

As for the universality of mutual love, Segundo argues that not even Jesus adhered to this concept of love during his historical mission, which he further illustrates through Jesus' encounter with the Syro-Phoenician woman. Segundo interprets Jesus' answer to her request to cure her daughter as a direct expression of his personal attitude reflecting "the relationship between Jesus and Pagans."[33] Segundo reminds his readers that Jesus instructed his disciples to restrict their ministry to Israel (Matt. 10:5-6) and concludes that the general, social attitudes of Palestine at that time which insisted upon the "segregation" of Jews and Pagans, attitudes which constitute an inherent violence against others, "was rooted in the mind and emotional life of Jesus himself."[34] Segundo does not attempt to provide an apologetic of any kind to account for Jesus's prejudice, but rather accepts Jesus' behaviour in this regard as entirely understandable because it is entirely human, going so far as to see the positive implications in Jesus' "violence" toward both John the Baptist and the Syro-Phoenician woman:

> It would be much more logical to assume that Jesus' concrete and effective love for his neighbours, for those of his own country, had to operate with the same mechanisms used by all human beings. He had to put some people at arm's length in order to let other people get close to him as real human beings. And putting them at arm's length meant accepting the common prejudices against aliens in order to maintain them in that status. . . . And all prejudice is latent or expressed violence in relation to something or someone on the outside. Without any such violence, however, love dies; human beings are left at the mercy of an even worse violence. [35]

Following upon this kind of argumentation, it is logical for Segundo to conclude that "*violence is an intrinsic dimension of any and all concrete love in history.*" [36]

Segundo underlines his approach to the issue of violence as having a proper place in Christianity, by appealing to Scripture in an exegetical interpretation of the commandment "Thou shalt not kill." Segundo argues that the commandment against killing is not intended as a universal, absolute moral rule, since there are several passages in the Hebrew Bible which demand killing in certain circumstances, which in turn "presupposes that killing is legitimate."[37] Thus, the Biblical command against killing "was not universal in any absolute sense," but is "equivalent to saying that one could not kill *without justifiable reason*. So once again we are forced to confront the question: What criteria enable us to know when violence that takes away another's life is justified?"[38] Segundo answers this question with a logical consistency that is the result of his own methodological assumptions and approach: the criteria by which to judge whether violence is justifiable or not are determined by historically specific situations and ideologies, since ideologies are what bridge the void "between faith and concrete historical realities."[39] Thus, in a revolutionary situation, the corresponding ideology would justify violence. For Segundo, not only are violence and killing justified under certain circumstances, but violence may also be understood at times as an intrinsic element of love. Faith, then, is no guarantee against relativism, and thus there are no absolute, unchanging moral codes or standards, not even the Christian ethic of love of neighbour. "The point, in other words, is not that without faith we live in the midst of relativism. It is that even with the Christian faith we live in the very same situation." [40]

Segundo's understanding of the problem of violence and its relationship to the divine command to mutual love is rooted in a sense of the irrefutable fact of the historical, the particular and the contingent nature of human existence. For Segundo, there can be no ahistorical fixed truths, no absolute moral standards in which to ground human praxis or search for some universal meaning, whether one is Christian or not. In the works of Segundo, liberation theology completely breaks down the distinctions between the religious and secular spheres of reality, to the point that even concerning Jesus, Segundo adopts a thoroughly historical and humanized view. Segundo's treatment of Jesus and his mission puts as much distance as possible between the historical Jesus and Christological claims with the result that Segundo refers to his recent study of Jesus as an "antichrist-ology," which reflects "an effort to talk about Jesus in such a way that it may open people up to seeing him as a witness to a more humane and liberated human life."[41] In fact, in *The Historical Jesus of the Synoptics*, Segundo develops and elaborates upon the picture of Jesus he presented in *The Liberation of Theology* and *Faith and Ideologies*, wherein Jesus appears more as a paradigmatic, prophetic human figure than as any kind of Incarnated God. In Segundo's view, Jesus does not, and cannot, manifest an abstract, pure revelation of God on a purely religious level. Such an approach to divine revelation reduces the Transcendent to "some sort of sacred magic," which is not faith as he understands it. For Segundo:

> God can only be revealed in connection with values that are humanly meaningful, and those values must be manifested historically on one or more of the planes where the human being stakes the meaning of its life and the possibilities for happiness. Strictly

164

speaking, then, we can say that there is no divine revelation that does not take its course through preferences and concrete realization on the plane of interpersonal relations, education, economics, politics, and societal life. The revelation of Jesus does not, could not, constitute an exception. [42]

Underlying this study of the historical Jesus, is the assumption of a necessary cleavage "between *history* and *christology*," which opts for the former as the proper vehicle for understanding Jesus and the meaning of his ministry. In this way, Segundo can claim that the means through which Jesus revealed the Father were embodied in ideologies, since Jesus could only convey the message of the proximity of the Kingdom with reference to the concrete conditions and problems of his own historical epoch, if he was to be intelligible to his hearers. And Jesus' message can only be interpreted and reinterpreted in successive historical periods through changing ideologies which are relevant to their historical situation and the process of human liberation. Thus Segundo refers to his discussion and interpretation of the historical Jesus as an "antichristology" because that is precisely what it is; Segundo is not so interested in the christological claims of the Christian tradition, since these claims reflect more about the religious needs of the people who believe them, than about the "prepaschal," real-life man, Jesus.

The historical portrait of Jesus—and future christologies as well—must be based on those facts or events which are more certain and must proceed from that nucleus. And logically what seems more certain . . . is what was attributed to Jesus *without reference* to his passion, death, and resurrection. [43]

However, it would be erroneous to leave the impression that Segundo denies the validity of the resurrection as a transcendent datum of faith. Although the resurrection cannot be subjected to the same criteria of historical verification as is possible with the execution of Jesus, and even though Jesus' post-resurrection appearances were not witnessed by a single "impartial" observer,[44] nonetheless, Segundo acknowledges (in an appendix), that the resurrection may be seen as "the irruption of a new world of meaning that is offered to human existence."[45] In his study of the historical Jesus, and the political meaning and implications of his ministry, Segundo applies his methodology already worked out in *The Liberation of Theology* and *Faith and Ideologies*, which necessarily means that to be consistent with his own approach, Segundo must begin his study of Jesus and the gospels from the point of concrete, historical particularity. Thus the pre-paschal, historical and human Jesus assumes far more importance and meaning for Segundo, than the postpaschal, resurrected Christ, who is for Segundo largely the product of the interpretation and faith of Christian tradition, which itself constitutes a particular ideology, or succession of ideologies over two thousand years of human history. The result of Segundo's nearly exclusive focus on the historical Jesus finally obliterates the distinction between the religious and the secular, which is a further consequence of his methodology and which actually marginalizes the religious dimension of Jesus' presence in history to a place of secondary, almost incidental importance. The religious meaning of Jesus' mission follows the deeper significance of Jesus as the bearer of a system of values whose central focus is human welfare in the material, concrete sense. Thus the locus of divine revelation lies entirely within the realm of the thoroughly human and historical. History, as the locus of the liberation process, is the primary reference point of Segundo's theology; it is not man, and not Jesus, although man is the historical subject and object.

At this point, one may not avoid asking, is Segundo a theologian or is he more of a critical social theorist?[46] His methodology, which begins with human beings in their concrete, historical context and their efforts to effect their own liberation, his dialectical conception of the relationship between human beings and the material world in which they live, and his insistence upon the open-ended nature of the historical process in which there is no absolute, universal or fixed truth anywhere present, seems to mark Segundo as being closer to a critical social theorist. Dennis McCann refers to Segundo as the most "tough-minded" of all the liberation theologians, in that so far, he develops the basic methodological tendencies of liberation theology to their farthest conclusion. McCann identifies the essential problematic of liberation theology in terms of the paradox of the relationship between the Transcendent and the constantly changing "relativities of history."[47] This paradox generates a tension which gives liberation theology its dynamic character but which also threatens to bring about its own dissolution.[48] McCann agrees that Segundo completely politicizes theology, and he is well aware that this fact is entirely due to the "subversive method" of liberation theology which Segundo has developed to "its logical conclusion."[49] With relation to Segundo, it is entirely reasonable to apply the question which McCann poses for liberation theology itself: "Is liberation theology still recognizable as theology?"[50] It seems to me that very often, Segundo is writing critical social theory in the language of theological symbolism and metaphor.

McCann's questions are relevant for my critical assessment of the implications of Segundo's methodology. These questions recall the kind of objections to liberation theology raised by the "Instruction on Certain

Aspects of the 'Theology of Liberation'", although not necessarily with the same negative attitude. It could be argued, for example, that the accusations that liberation theology "reduces" — or perhaps, more accurately, transforms — the gospel to an "earthly gospel,"[51] and the concern about the complete politicization of the meaning of Jesus' death, along with the emphasis upon the historical Jesus rather than the "Jesus of faith" [52] are not totally unfounded, despite the underlying political bias. The question can also be put in another way: if a theology assumes there is no such thing as a separate, distinct religious realm of reality, if there is no possibility for a separate religious and theological epistemology, language, or symbol system and set of categories, if the separation between the supernatural and natural world is obliterated, does this theology in fact result in its own self-negation? If the theological enterprise is reduced to mere second stage "reflection," as is maintained by Segundo and Gutierrez, then the only relevance and justification for theology at all is its ability to point out the religious significance or meaning of reality.[53] In terms of liberation theology, it is the political process of liberation only which receives ultimate meaning and value in human history, such that it could be argued that liberation as a process and goal, becomes itself absolutized. This is inevitable and should not be surprising in a theology which understands the *locus* of divine revelation as entirely within the bounds of history, and which views God's action in history as serving the liberation of human beings.

The problem with this view of history, which must be mentioned again is of course the whole question of the historical subject. If the inner dynamic of history is the liberation process itself, if human praxis through the medium of politics is understood as fundamental and indispensable to the realization of the emancipatory goal, then it logically follows that human beings are the subjects of history, and not God. Segundo is finally unconvincing when he refers to humanity and God as "co-workers" in history because his own methodology implies the presence of one, and only one historical subject, which is the human being. In my view, Segundo has been too deeply touched by Marx to mean anything else. The tension between theological truth claims and the claims of a critical social theory as outlined by Segundo cannot be satisfactorily resolved by resorting to a concept of a dialectical relationship of co-subjectivity between the human and the Absolute. Marx effectively put this question to rest in his critique of Hegel, and Segundo likewise rejects Hegelian philosophy. One of the main points of disagreement, it will be recalled, that Segundo expressed toward Hegel is precisely related to the question of historical subjectivity. Segundo does not insist on the concept of co-subjectivity; but in that he raises it at all, then Lukács' critique of Hegel applies directly to Segundo in this instance. Like Hegel, Segundo flies straight into the "arms of mythology."[54] However, I must emphasize that Segundo does not insist on this point of humanity and God acting together as co-subjects within history. In any event, Segundo's method disallows any other approach to the question of the historical subject other than the conclusion that human beings actively bring about the process of liberation by their own efforts. Again, it was the question of subjectivity that formed the basis of Segundo's critique of European, mainly Protestant political theology.[55] As I argued in the previous chapter, this question is also another point of serious division between Segundo and the Vatican. However, rather than repeating what I have already argued throughout these pages, I will state my central point as concisely as possible: liberation theology, by virtue of its "subversive" methodology, especially as elaborated by Segundo, indeed bears the seeds of its own negation as theology *per se*.

In concluding this argument, I turn again to Alfredo Fierro whose remarks concerning the implications of political theology are both helpful and applicable to an analysis of Segundo's concept of the relationship between transcendence and immanence:

> Of course any discovery of the socio-economic correlates to theological ideas and beliefs will considerably reduce the sense and import of transcendence. . . . But it is precisely the rejection of transcendence, of a certain kind of cosmological and ontological transcendence at least, that constitute one of the features of current political theology.[56]

And further:

> Political theology knows nothing about the action of God in the world; political theology simply believes in such action. It has knowledge only about the activity of Christian symbols and representations in the world; that is all it can talk about with any degree of knowledgeable certainty. [57]

Given his own methodological perspective, Segundo would have to concur that Fierro's view applies to liberation theology. I think the latter quote from Fierro explains why Segundo so consistently emphasizes the historical and political meaning of the gospels, and why he is interested in the historical Jesus, and not in christological claims. Christologies (for Segundo) only reveal the nature of the individuals and communities of faithful who hold them; they reveal nothing about the nature of Transcendence, which is why Segundo insists that the "significance of Jesus of Nazareth" can only be grasped through an analysis of those few historical facts that are known about him, because whatever Jesus did and said took place in an historical context, with its own specific "motivations and interests."[58]   For Segundo, Jesus the man cannot be separated from history, and like any other human being, was a part of and even product of his time, even though he posed a threat and challenge to those around him.   But since his context "is not our context,"[59] the little we know about Jesus must be interpreted and reinterpreted in and through each historical situation according to the demands and conditions of that particular context, through the methodological application of the "hermeneutic circle."   This dialectical process produces historically-based Christian ideologies which function as the medium of the gospel message.   This approach to Jesus and his significance for people today would be impossible if Jesus is understood via dogmatic christologies that focus upon the postpaschal Christ.

I hesitate to offer any final, definitive conclusion about Segundo's theology as the negation of theology, since he is still living and writing. What can only be analyzed and discussed is what he has already written, but certainly it can be said that Segundo brings theology very close to something that could be called the end of theology.   And this may be said despite whatever religious beliefs he himself may hold.   As Segundo has said, theology and faith are not synonymous.   Segundo severs the historical human Jesus from the risen Christ, and if Jesus represents the "Incarnation" of anything, it is primarily a system of values which are thoroughly human and human-oriented.   The irony may well be that in attempting to formulate a theology that is public and relevant to the social, political world of today, and which seeks to bring about solutions to profound human problems, Segundo has unintentionally driven religious faith back into the realm of the privatized and the interior.   In the socio-historical process of liberation, religious faith may have very little relevance after all.

NOTES

1. Leonardo Boff and Clodovis Boff, *Salvation and Liberation*, translated from the Portuguese by Robert R. Barr (Maryknoll, N.Y.: Orbis Books, 1984), p. 24.

2. For a summary of Segundo's thought until *The Liberation of Theology*, see, for example, Alfred T. Hennelly, *Theologies in Conflict: The Challenge of Juan Luis Segundo* (Maryknoll, N.Y.: Orbis Books, 1979).

3. Enrique Dussel, *A History of the Church in Latin America: Colonialism to Liberation (1492-1979)*, translated by Alan Neely (Grand Rapids, Michigan: William B. Eerdmans Publishing Co., 1981), p. 247.

4. Gustavo Gutierrez, *A Theology of Liberation*, p. 47.

5. Enrique Dussel, *A History of the Church in Latin America*, p. 246.

6. Ibid., p. 113.

7. Ibid., p. 143.

8. Juan Luis Segundo, *The Liberation of Theology*, p. 126.

9. Ibid., p. 141.

10. Ibid., p. 142.

11. Juan Luis Segundo, *Grace and the Human Condition*, Vol. II, *A Theology for the Artisans*, translated by John Drury (Maryknoll, N.Y.: Orbis Books), p. 133.

12. *Gaudium et Spes*, n. 2 (Abbott edition).

13. Ibid., n. 9.

14. Juan Luis Segundo, *Grace and the Human Condition*, pp. 133-134.

15. Enrique Dussel, *A History of the Church in Latin America*, p. 141.

16. See, for example, Hans Küng, "Why I Remain a Catholic", *Consensus in Theology?*, ed. Leonard Swidler, (Philadelphia: The Westminster Press, n.d.), p. 159: "Many are wondering if the wheel of history is to be turned back in our Catholic Church to the time before John XXIII and the Second Vatican Council. Are the new open-mindedness, readiness for dialogue, humanist and Christian spirit again to yield to the triumphalism disavowed by the Council?"

17. Juan Luis Segundo, *The Community Called Church*, Vol. I, p. ix.

18. Ibid., p. ix.

19. Ibid., p. ix.

20. Ibid., p. xi.

21. Juan Luis Segundo, *Grace and the Human Condition*, p. 39.

22. Juan Luis Segundo, *Our Idea of God*, Vol. III, *A Theology for the Artisans*, p. 17.

23. See, for example, Dennis P. McCann, *Christian Realism and Liberation Theology*, pp. 225 - 226, for a critique of Segundo's approach to violence and Christianity.

24. Juan Luis Segundo, *The Liberation of Theology*, p. 155.

25. Ibid., p. 155.

26. Ibid., p. 159.

27. Ibid., p. 159.

28. Ibid., p. 159.

29. Ibid., p. 159.

30. Ibid., p. 162.

31. Ibid., p. 162.

32. Ibid., p. 163.

33. Ibid., p. 163.

34. Ibid., p. 163.

35. Ibid., pp. 163-164.

36. Ibid., p. 161.

37. Ibid., p. 165.

38. Ibid., p. 166. Jürgen Moltmann takes the same situational approach toward violence: "The problem of violence and nonviolence is an illusory problem. There is only the question of the justified and unjustified use of force and the question of whether the means are proportionate to the ends." *Religion, Revolution and the Future*, translated by Douglas Meeks (New York: Scribner, 1969), p. 142.

39. Ibid., p. 166.

40. Ibid., p. 167.

41. Juan Luis Segundo, *The Historical Jesus of the Synoptics*, p. 16.

42. Ibid., p. 85. Segundo's insistence on separating the historical person, Jesus of Nazareth, from the interpretation of Jesus through the language of Christian religious faith and his significance for the early Christian communities, for example, may seem over-rigid, and perhaps exegetically suspect. (See, for example, Edward Schillebeeckx, *Jesus: An Experiment in Christology*, trans. Hubert Hoskins, (New York: The Seabury Press, 1979), pp. 44-45.) However, Segundo's interpretation of Jesus is significant insofar as it illustrates a concrete and direct application of his methodology, particularly as developed in *Faith and Ideologies*, which is intended as the interpretive framework for reading *The Historical Jesus of the Synoptics*. When his methodology is applied to Jesus, what results is an emphasis on the political dimension, or meaning, of his ministry, and the humanitarian nature of the

values he as a person embodies, as far as Segundo is concerned. Whether Segundo's interpretation of the gospels is exegetically sound or not, is beside the point. The relevant issue is to show where Segundo's methodology takes him in relation to Christian theology.

43. Ibid., p. 47.

44. Ibid., p. 171.

45. Ibid., p. 177.

46. I want to be perfectly clear that my question is not only how Segundo understands himself. Rather, my interest is to try to assess the nature of Segundo's thought through a critical analysis of his writing. Thus it is valid to pose the question concerning the actual subject of Segundo's writings, i.e. whether it is theology, or unfolds into a critical theoretical approach to history and society.

47. Dennis P. McCann, *Christian Realism and Liberation Theology*, p. 228.

48. Ibid., p. 157.

49. Ibid., p. 231.

50. Ibid., p. 231.

51. "Instructions on Certain Aspects . . ."VI, p. 5.

52. Ibid., X, p. 8.

53. However, in pointing out the religious meaning of history, theology must always act in an ongoing, *critical* manner in relation to the existent social and political order, so that no established order can become absolutized. Theology, in that it does not evaluate human achievements by strictly human criteria, is thus perhaps able to exert a continuous critique of all historical and social products and the human actions which generate them. Theology is then a *critical*, second-stage reflection on human praxis.

54. Georg Lukács, *History and Class Consciousness*, p. 146. The rest of this quotation is relevant to Segundo on the question of the historical subject: "Having failed to discover the identical subject-object in history it [Hegel's philosophy] was forced to go out beyond history and, there, to establish the empire of reason which has discovered itself. From that vantage point it became possible to understand history as a mere stage and its evolution in terms of 'the ruse of reason'. History is not able to form the living body of the total system: it becomes a part, an aspect of the totality that culminated in the 'absolute spirit' . . ."

55. See Juan Luis Segundo, *The Liberation of Theology*, pp. 139-149, in which Segundo is critical of the mainly Protestant approach to the question of Transcendence and history, focusing on theologians such as Jürgen Moltmann, Rubem Alves and Richard Schaull. The nature of Segundo's critique can be summarized in the following quotation: "Now German 'political theology' is markedly dependent on the Lutheran theology of justification. So it should not surprise us that it systematically tries to eliminate from theologico-political language any term that might suggest a causal relationship between historical activity and the construction of the eschatological Kingdom. And this is true even when it is talking

about revolution. Except in rare exceptions, the historical reality produced by human effort is described as "anticipation" (Moltmann), "Analogy" (Weth), "rough draft" (Metz) and so forth," (*The Liberation of Theology*, p.144).

56. Alfredo Fierro, *The Militant Gospel*, p. 382.

57. Ibid., p. 411-12.

58. Juan Luis Segundo, *The Historical Jesus of the Synoptics*, p. 27.

59. Ibid., p. 27.

BIBLIOGRAPHY

Abbott, Walter (Ed.). *The Documents of Vatican II.* Msgr. Joseph Gallagher, translation editor. New York: Corpus Books, 1966.

Alexander, Robert J. *Today's Latin America.* Garden City, N.Y.: Anchor Books, Doubleday Company, Inc., 1968.

Alves, Reubem. *A Theology of Human Hope.* New York: Corpus Books, 1971.

Arato, Andrew, and Gehardt, Eike (Eds.). *The Essential Frankfurt School Reader.* New York: Continuum, 1982.

Arato, Andrew. "Immanent Critique and Authoritarian Socialism," Canadian Journal of Political and Social Theory,*Ideology/Power*, Hiver/Printemps, 1983, Vol. VII, Numbers 1-2, pp. 142-162.

Assman, Hugo. *Practical Theology of Liberation.* Translated by Paul Burns. London: Search Press, 1975.

_____. *Theology for a Nomad Church.* Translated by Paul Burns. Maryknoll, N.Y.: Orbis Books, 1975.

Bateson, Gregory. *Steps to an Ecology of Mind.* New York: Ballantine Books, 1972.

Baum, Gregory. *Religion and Alienation: A Theological Reading of Sociology.* New York: Paulist Press, 1975.

Berger, Peter. *The Sacred Canopy: Elements of a Sociological Theory of Religion.* Garden City, N. Y.: Doubleday Company, Inc., 1967.

_____. *Pyramids of Sacrifice: Political Ethics and Social Change.* Garden City, N. Y.: Anchor Press, Doubleday, 1974.

Berlin, Isaiah. *Karl Marx: His Life and Environment.* A Galaxy Book. New York: Oxford University Press, 1963.

Bernstein, Richard J. *Praxis and Action: Contemporary Philosophies of Human Activity.* Philadelphia: University of Pennsylvania Press, 1971.

Berryman, Phillip. *The Religious Roots of Rebellion: Christians in Central American Revolutions.* Maryknoll, N.Y.: Orbis Books, 1984.

Between Honesty and Hope. Documents from and about the Church in Latin America. Issued at Lima by the Peruvian Bishops' Commission for Social Action. Translated by John Drury. Maryknoll, N. Y.: Orbis Books, 1970.

Boff, Clodovis. *Theology and Praxis: Epistemological Foundations.* Translated by Robert R. Barr. Maryknoll, N.Y.: Orbis Books, 1987.

_____. *Jesus Christ Liberator: A Critical Christology for Our Time.* Translated by Patrick Hughes. Maryknoll, N. Y.: Orbis Books, 1978.

_____. *Liberating Grace.* Translated by John Drury. Maryknoll, N.Y.: Orbis Books, 1979.

Boff, Leonardo and Boff, Clodovis. *Salvation and Liberation.* Translated from the Portuguese by Robert R. Barr. Maryknoll, N. Y.: Orbis Books, 1984.

Bonino, José Miguez. *Doing Theology in a Revolutionary Situation.* Philadelphia: Fortress Press, 1975.

_____. *Christians and Marxists: The Mutual Challenge to Revolution.* London, Toronto: Hodder and Stoughton, 1976.

Bruneau, Thomas. *The Political Transformation of the Brazilian Catholic Church.* Cambridge University Press, 1974.

Camara, Helder. *The Spiral of Violence.* Translated by Della Couling. Denville, N. J.: Dimension Books, 1971.

_____. *Revolution Through Peace.* Translated by Amparo McLean. New York: Harper and Row, 1972.

Cassirer, Ernst. *Language and Myth.* Translated by Susan K. Langer. New York: Dover Publications Inc., 1953.

Chomsky, Noam, and Herman, Edward S. *The Washington Connection and Third World Facism, The Political Economy of Human Rights.* Vol. I. Montreal: Black Rose Books, 1979.

Comblin, José. *The Church and the National Security State.* Maryknoll, N.Y.: Orbis Books, 1979.

"Concilium Board Expresses Solidarity With Liberation Theologians." *Origins, NC Documentary Service*, July 26, 1984, Vol. 14, No. 9, pp. 134-135.

Cort, John C. "Christians and the Class Struggle." *Commonweal*, July 1, 1986, pp. 400-404.

Cullman, Oscar. *Jesus and the Revolutionaries.* Translated by Gareth Putnam. New York: Harper and Row, 1970.

Dahlin, Therrin C., and Gillum, Gary P. *The Catholic Left in Latin America: A Comprehensive Bibliography*, 1981.

Dahrendorf, Rolf. *Class and Class Conflict in Industrial Society.* Stanford: Stanford University Press, 1959.

Davis, Charles. *Theology and Political Society.* Cambridge: Cambridge University Press, 1978.

_____. "From Inwardness to Social Action: A Shift in the Locus of Religious Experience." *New Blackfriars*, March 1986, pp. 114-125.

Debray, Régis. *Revolution in the Revolution?: Armed Struggle and Political Struggle in Latin America.* Translated by Bobbye Ortiz. New York: Grove Press, Inc., 1967.

Dehainaut, Raymond K. *Faith and Ideology in Latin American Perspective.* Centro Intercultural de Documentation, Cuernevaca, n.d.

Dewart, Leslie. *Christianity and Revolution: The Lesson of Cuba.* New York: Herder and Herder, 1963.

Dixon, Marlene, and Jonas, Susanne (Eds.). *Revolution and Intervention in Central America.* Contemporary Marxism: Journal of the Institute for the Study of Labour and Economic Crisis, No. 3, Summer, 1981.

176

Dussel, Enrique. *History and the Theology of Liberation: A Latin American Perspective.* Translated by John Drury. Maryknoll, N. Y.: Orbis Books, 1976.

_____. *A History of the Church in Latin America: Colonialism to Liberation (1492-1979).* Translated by Alan Neely. Grand Rapids, Michigan: William B. Eerdmans Publishing Company, 1981.

Eagleson, John, and Scharper, Philip (Eds.). *Puebla and Beyond: Documentation and Commentary.* Maryknoll, N.Y.: Orbis Books, 1979.

Eagleson, John (Ed.). *Christians and Socialism.* Translated by John Drury. Maryknoll, N.Y.: Orbis Books, 1975.

Ellul, Jacques. *Violence: Reflections From a Christian Perspective.* Translated by Cecilia Gual King. New York: Seabury Press, 1969.

Fanon, Franz. *The Wretched of the Earth.* Translated by Constance Farrington. New York: Grove Press, Inc., 1968.

Fierro, Alfredo. *The Militant Gospel.* Translated by John Drury. Maryknoll, N. Y.: Orbis Books, 1977.

Frank, Andre Gunder. *Capitalism and Underdevelopment in Latin America: Historical Studies of Chile and Brazil.* New York: Monthly Review Press, 1967.

_____. *Latin America: Underdevelopment or Revolution: Essays on the Development of Underdevelopment and the Immediate Enemy.* New York: Monthly Review Pres, 1969.

Freire, Paulo. *Pedagogy of the Oppressed.* Translated by Myra Bergman Ramos. A Continuum Book. New York: The Seabury Press, 1968.

Fromm, Erich (Ed.). *Socialist Humanism: An International Symposium.* Garden City, N.Y.: Anchor Books, 1966.

Garaudy, Roger. *From Anathema to Dialogue.* Translated by Luke O'Neill. New York: Herder and Herder, 1966.

Geertz, Clifford. "Ideology as a Cultural System." In *The Interpretation of Cultures.* New York: Basic Books, Inc., Publishers, 1973, pp. 193-233.

Gerassi, John (Ed.). *Revolutionary Priest: The Complete Writings and Messages of Camilo Torres*. London: Jonathan Cape, 1971.

_____. *Venceremos! The Speeches and Writings of Ernesto Ché Guevara*. London: Weidenfeld and Nicolson, 1968.

Geuss, Raymond. *The Idea of Critical Theory: Habermas and the Frankfurt School*. Cambridge: Cambridge University Press, 1981.

Gheerbrant, Alain. *The Rebel Church in Latin America*. Translated by Rosemary Sheed. Harmondsworth: Penguin Books, 1974.

Giddens, Anthony. "Four Theses on Ideology." Canadian Journal of Political and Social Theory, *Ideology/Power*, Hiver/Printemps, 1983, Vol. VII, Nos. 1-2, pp. 18-21.

Gouldner, Alvin. *The Dialectic of Ideology and Technology: The Orgins, Grammar and Future of Ideology*. New York: Seabury Press, 1976.

Gunther, John. *Inside South America*. New York: Harper and Row, 1966, 1967.

Gutierrez, Gustavo. *A Theology of Liberation*. Translated by Sister Caridad Inda and John Eagleson. Maryknoll, N.Y.: Orbis Books, 1979.

_____. "Liberation Praxis and Christian Faith." In R. Gibellini (Ed.),*Frontiers of Theology in Latin America*. Maryknoll, N.Y.: Orbis Books, 1979, pp. 1-33.

_____. *The Power of the Poor in History: Selected Writings*. Translated by Robert R. Barr. Maryknoll, N.Y.: Orbis Books, 1983.

_____. *We Drink From Our Own Wells: The Spiritual Journey of a People*. Translated by Matthew J. O'Connell. Maryknoll, N.Y.: Orbis Books, 1984.

Haight, Roger. *An Alternative Vision*. New York: Paulist Press, 1985.

Hennelly, Alfred T. *Theologies in Conflict: The Challenge of Juan Luis Segundo*. Maryknoll, N.Y.: Orbis Books, 1979.

Horkheimer, Max. *Critical Theory: Selected Essays*. New York: Herder and Herder, 1972.

178

_____. *Critique of Instrumental Reason.* Translated by Matthew J. O'Connell and others. New York: The Seabury Press, 1974.

"Inter-Church Committee on Human Rights in Latin America" (ICCHRLA), Winter, 1983/1984; Winter, 1982/1983; Summer, 1984, Vols. 1 and 2, 1986.

Jay, Martin. *The Dialectical Imagination: A History of the Frankfurt School and the Institute of Social Research, 1923-1950.* Boston: Little, Brown and Company, 1973.

Keane, John. "Democracy and the Theory of Ideology." Canadian Journal of Political and Social Theory,*Ideology/Power*, Hiver/Printemps, 1983, Vol. VII, Nos. 1-2, pp. 5-17.

Lakeland, Paul. *Freedom in Christ: An Introduction to Political Theology.* New York: Fordham University Press, 1986.

Lamb, Matthew. *Solidarity With Victims: Toward a Theology of Social Transfor-mation.* New York: Crossroad Press, 1982.

Landsberger, Henry A. *The Church and Social Change in Latin America.* Notre Dame: ND Press, 1970.

Lash, Nicholas. *A Matter of Hope.* London: Darton, Longman Todd, 1981.

Laurentian, René. *Liberation, Development and Salvation.* Maryknoll, N.Y.: Orbis Books, 1972.

Lefort, Claude. "On the Genesis of Ideology in Modern Societies." Canadian Journal of Political and Social Theory,*Ideology/Power*, Hiver/Printemps, 1983, Vol. VII, Nos. 1-2, pp. 43-83.

Lehmann, Paul. *Ethics in a Christian Context.* New York: Harper and Row, 1963.

Lenin, Vladmir Il'ich. "What is to be Done?" In*Selected Works*, Vo. I. Moscow: Progress Publishers, 1970.

Levine, Daniel (Ed.). *Churches and Politics in Latin America.* Sage Publications, 1979.

_____. *Religion and Politics in Latin America: The Catholic Church in Venezuela and Colombia.* Princeton, 1981.

Lernoux, Penny. *Cry of the People: Unites States Involvement in the Rise of Fascism, Torture, and Murder and the Persecution of the Catholic Church in Latin America.* Garden City, New York: Doubleday and Company, Inc., 1980.

Lukács, Georg. *History and Class Consciousness: Studies in Marxist Dialectics.* Translated by Rodney Livingstone. London: Merlin Press, 1971.

Maduro, Otto. *Religion and Social Conflicts.* Translated by Robert R. Barr. Maryknoll, N.Y.: Orbis Books, 1982.

Mahan, Brian, and Richesin, L. Dale (Eds.). *The Challenge of Liberation Theology: A First World Response.* Maryknoll, N.Y.: Orbis Books, 1981.

Mallin, Jay (Ed.). *Terror and Urban Guerrillas: A Study of Tactics and Documents.* Coral Gables, Florida: University of Miami Press, 1971.

Mannheim, Karl. *Ideology and Utopia: An Introduction to the Sociology of Knowledge.* Translated by L. Wirth and E. Shils. New York: Harcourt Brace Johanovitch, 1936.

Marcuse, Herbert. *Reason and Revolution: Hegel and the Rise of Social Theory.* Boston: Beacon Press, 1960.

_____. "Ethics and Revolution." In Richard T. de George (ed.),*Ethics and Society: Original Essays on Contemporary Moral Problems.* Garden City, N.Y.: Anchor Books, Doubleday and Company, 1966, pp. 133-147.

_____. *Negations: Essays in Critical Theory.* Translations by Jeremy J. Shapiro. Boston: Beacon Press, 1969.

Markus, György. "Concepts of Ideology in Marx." Canadian Journal of Political and Social Theory,*Ideology/Power*, Hiver/Printemps, 1983, Vol. VII, Nos. 1-2, pp. 84-103.

Marx, Karl, and Engels, Frederick. *Selected Works*. Moscow: Progress Publishers, 1970.

_____. *Karl Marx and Friedrich Engels on Religion*. New York: Schocken Books, 1964. Reprinted from the 1957 edition published by The Foreign Languages Publishing House, Moscow.

Marx, Karl. *Capital, Vol.* I. Edited by Frederick Engels,*The Process of Capitalist Production*. Translated from the third German edition by Samuel Moore and Edward Aveling. New York: International Publishers, 1967.

McAfee Brown, Robert. *Theology in a New Key*. Philadelphia: Westminster Press, 1978.

McCann, Dennis P. *Christian Realism and Liberation Theology: Practical Theologies in Creative Conflict*. Maryknoll, N.Y.: Orbis Books, 1981.

McFadden, T. (Ed.). *Liberation, Revolution and Freedom*. New York: Seabury Press, 1975.

Melville, Thomas, and Melville, Marjorie. *Guatemala -- Another Vietnam?* Harmondsworth: Penguin Books, 1971.

Metz, Johannes. *Theology of the World*. Translated by William Glen-Doepel. New York: Seabury Press, 1969.

_____. *Faith in History and Society*. Translated by David Smith. New York: Seabury Press, 1980.

_____. *The Emergent Church: The Future of Christianity in a Postbourgeois World*. Translated by Peter Mann. New York: Crossroad, 1981.

Moltmann, Jürgen. *Theology of Hope: On the Grounds and the Implications of a Christian Eschatology*. New York: Harper and Rox, 1967.

_____. *Religion, Revolution and the Future*. Translated by M. Douglas Meeks. New York: Scribner, 1969.

NACLA Report on the Americas. May/June, 1983; January/February, 1984; September/October, 1985.

Nystrom, J. Warren, and Haverstock, Nathan A. *The Alliance for Progress: Key to Latin America's Development*. Princeton, New Jersey: D. Van Nostrand Company, Inc., 1966.

Oestreicher, Paul (Ed.). *The Christian Marxist Dialogue: An International Symposium*. London: Collier-Macmillan Limited, 1969.

Ogden, Schubert M. *Faith and Freedom: Toward a Theology of Liberation*. Nashville: Abingdon Press, 1979.

Plamenatz, John Petrov. *Ideology*. London: MacMillan, 1971.

Pope John Paul II. (Letter to the Nicaraguan Bishops). "Popular Churches: A Papal Warning." *Origins, NC Documentary Service*, August 26, 1982, Vol. 12, No. 11, pp. 166-169.

_____. (Letter to the African Bishops). "Class Struggle and Identification With the Poor." *Origins, NC Documentary Service*, September 6, 1984, Vol. 14, No. 12, pp. 177-179.

_____. (Letter to the Brazilian Bishops). "Giant Brazil at a Crossroads." *Origins, NC Documentary Service*, April 3, 1986. Vol. 15, No. 42, pp. 682-685.

_____. Encyclical*Dominum et Vivificantem*. "The Holy Spirit in the Church and the World." Origins, NC Documentary Service, June 12, 1986, Vol. 16, No. 4.

Raney, Ernest W. "Under the Peruvian Volcano." *Commonweal*, February 14, 1986, pp. 78-82.

Schillebeeckx, Edward. *Jesus: An Experiment in Christology*. Translated by Hubert Hoskins. New York: The Seabury Press, 1979.

Segundo, Juan Luis. *The Community Called Church*, Vol. I. *A Theology for the Artisans of a New Humanity*. Translated by John Drury. Maryknoll, N.Y.: Orbis Books, 1973.

_____. *Grace and the Human Condition*, Vol. II. *A Theology for the Artisans of a New Humanity*. Translated by John Drury. Maryknoll, N.Y.: Orbis Books, 1973.

182

_____. *Our Idea of God*, Vol. III. *A Theology for the Artisans of a New Humanity.* Translated by John Drury. Maryknoll, N.Y.: Orbis Books, 1973.

_____. *The Sacraments Today*, Vol. IV. *A Theology for the Artisans of a New Humanity.* Translated by John Drury. Maryknoll, N.Y.: Orbis Books, 1974.

_____. *Evolution and Guilt*, Vol V. *A Theology for the Artisans of a New Humanity.* Translated by John Drury. Maryknoll, N.Y.: Orbis Books, 1974.

_____. *The Liberation of Theology.* Translated by John Drury. Maryknoll, N.Y.: Orbis Books, 1976.

_____. "Statement by Juan Luis Segundo." In Sergio Torres and John Eagleson (eds.),*Theology in the Americas*, pp. 280-283. Maryknoll, N.Y.: Orbis Books, 1976.

_____. "Capitalism Versus Socialism: Crux Theologica." In Rosino Gibellini (ed.),*Frontiers of Theology.* Translated by John Drury. Maryknoll, N.Y.: Orbis Books, 1979, pp. 240-259.

_____. "Faith and Ideologies in Biblical Revelation." In Norman K. Gottwald (ed.),*The Bible and Liberation: Political and Social Hermeneutics*, pp. 482-496. Maryknoll, N.Y.: Orbis Books, 1983.

_____. "The Shift Within Latin American Theology." Public Lecture. Regis College, Toronto, March 22, 1983, Regis College Press, 1983.

_____. *Faith and Ideologies*, Vol I. *Jesus of Nazareth Yesterday and Today.* Translated by John Drury. Maryknoll, N.Y.: Orbis Books, 1984.

_____. *The Historical Jesus of the Synoptics*, Vol. II. *Jesus of Nazareth Yesterday and Today.* Translated by John Drury. Maryknoll, N.Y.: Orbis Books, 1985.

_____. *The Humanist Christology of Paul*, Vol. III. *Jesus of Nazareth Yesterday and Today.* Edited and translated by John Drury. Maryknoll, N.Y.: Orbis Books, 1986.

_____. *Theology and the Church: A Response to Cardinal Ratzinger and a Warning to the` Whole Church.* Translated by John W.

Diercksmeier. Minneapolis: Winston Press, 1985; London: Geoffrey Chapman.

Sher, Gerson S. *Praxis: Marxist Criticism and Dissent in Socialist Yugoslavia*. Bloomington: Indiana University Press, 1977.

Shils, Edward A. "The Concept and Function of Ideology." In*International Encyclopedia of the Social Sciences*, pp. 66-75, 1968.

Sobrino, Jon. *Christology at the Crossroads: A Latin American Approach*. Translated by John Drury. Maryknoll, N.Y.: Orbis Books, 1978.

Sölle, Dorothy. *Political Theology*. Translated by John Shalley. Philadelphia: Fortress Press, 1974.

Swidler, Leonard (Ed.). *Consensus in Theology?*   Philadelphia: The Westminster Press, n.d.

The Congregation of the Doctrine of the Faith. "Instruction on Certain Aspects of the 'Theology of Liberation'." *Origins, NC Documentary Service*, September 13, 1984, Vol. 14, No. 13, pp. 193-204.

_____. "Instruction on Christian Freedom and Liberation." *Origins, NC Documentary Service*, April 17, 1986, Vol. 15, No. 44, pp. 713-728.

Theissen, Gerd. *On Having a Critical Faith*. London: SCM Press Ltd., 1979.

Thompson, John B. "Ideology and the Critique of Domination (1)." Canadian Journal of Political and Social Theory,*Ideology/Power*, Hiver/Printemps, 1983, Vol. VII, Nos. 1-2, pp. 163-183.

_____. (Ed.). *Paul Ricoeur: Hermeneutics and the Human Sciences: Essays on language, action and interpretation*. Translated by John B. Thompson. Cambridge: Cambridge University Press, 1981.

_____. *Studies in the Theory of Ideology*. Cambridge: Polity Press, 1984.

Tillich, Paul. *Dynamics of Faith*. New York: Harper Torchbooks, Harper and Row, 1958.

Tracy, Paul. *Blessed Rage for Order: The New Pluralism in Theology*. New York: The Seabury Press, 1975.

184

Tucker, Robert C. (Ed.). *The Marx-Engels Reader.* Second Edition. New York: W.W. Norton and Company, Inc.

Turner, Frederick C. *Catholicism and Political Development in Latin America.* Chapel Hill: University of North Carolina Press, 1971.

Vallier, Ivan. *Catholicism, Social Control and Modernization in Latin America.* Englewood Cliffs, New Jersey: Prentice Hall, 1970.

Walzer, Michael. *Just and Unjust Wars.* New York: Basic Books, Inc., 1977.

West, Charles C. *Ethics, Revolution, and Violence.* Published by the Council on Religion and International Affairs, New York, 1969.

West, Cornel. "Wither Liberation Theology?" In*Commonweal*, January 27, 1984, pp. 53-57.

Wiener, Philip P., and Fisher, John (Eds.). *Violence and Aggression in the History of Ideas.* New Brunswick, New Jersey: Rutgers University Press, 1974.

DATE DUE

HIGHSMITH   # 45220